CHRISTIAN FAITH AND THE
INTERPRETATION OF HISTORY

Christian Faith and the Interpretation of History

A Study of St. Augustine's Philosophy of History

by

G. L. KEYES

University of Nebraska Press · Lincoln

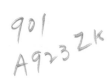

To Mary

Foreword

I assume that any man's philosophy of history lies in a particular application, to historical studies, of the general premises which explicitly or implicitly govern his intellectual response to all experience. What is his "theory of knowledge"? How is this applied in his study of history? What picture emerges when history is studied in this way?

At thirty St. Augustine was a skeptic, with no confidence in the evidence of sensation and reason, and unimpressed by other possible sources of truth. Without knowledge, one must resort to faith, and the essence of faith is the taking of a calculated risk. Faith is strong in proportion to one's confidence, on whatever grounds, that the risk is justified. One lives by appearances. Every generalization and judgment is ultimately founded upon our recognition, in the world of our experience, of similarities which may be illusory or misleading; and every hypothesis which is based upon these supposed similarities must be held liable to revision or rejection in the light of new and contradictory evidence. As far as the findings of sensation and reason were concerned, St. Augustine remained a skeptic all his life, obliged to live by "faith" since "knowledge" seemed unattainable.

By the time he was thirty-two, he was seeking an escape from this state of intellectual grace. He craved the comfort of certainty, of a knowledge such as he could not find within the bailiwick of sensation and reason. Like Descartes he found this in part in the "direct knowledge" of self-existence. This did not tell him much about the nature of things. But it worked wonders for his morale by persuading him that truth is not after all completely unattainable, and by reminding him of other thoughts—of God and his plan, of eternal and universal Platonic Forms—which could never have been inferred by reason from sensation which cannot perceive the universal or eternal, the origin of things, or the end of the universal process. He is inclined to think that these thoughts come to us by divine

vii

revelation. But divine revelation is seldom direct. For the most part it comes to us by what amounts to hearsay, on the authority of alleged prophets, or of the Church, which claims to be able to communicate to the many the wisdom revealed by God to the few. This means that most men can accept "revealed truths" only on faith, like the propositions born of reason by sensation. St. Augustine is admirably skeptical with regard to secular hypotheses held on faith, and keeps them under constant review. But he rejects skepticism for the hypotheses which he thinks spring ultimately from divine revelation, and which constitute his Christian faith. The authority of the Church, and the validity of the propositions which it certifies to be of divine origin, are not to be tested against experience. They may have come to one by hearsay, but they are not to be taken as tentative. If experience does not seem to bear them out, experience must be reinterpreted to bring it into line.

Over the centuries gifted and subtle scholars, culminating in Gilson, have developed "Augustinianism" by systematizing St. Augustine's very excursive thought and interpreting it in the light of their several versions of Christian orthodoxy. What follows is more in the nature of an essay than a dissertation; so far as it is not a deliberately personal reaction, it should reflect the rather different bias of a friendly but skeptical classicist. My standpoint is generally similar to that of the late C. N. Cochrane (*Christianity and Classical Culture*, Oxford, 1940), with whom I was privileged as a graduate student to read *The City of God*, although I think that in drawing his conclusions he may have let himself be unduly influenced by St. Augustine's posthumous status as Doctor to so many Schools. My own conclusion is that whatever one may think of St. Augustine's religious faith as an expression of Christianity, it was, and can still be, disastrous for the study of history considered as anything more than material for the elaboration of an edifying "Noble Lie."

I gratefully acknowledge the help and advice of the late Professor C. B. Sissons, Professor H. G. Robertson, and Professor D. O. Robson of Victoria College, and of Professor G. Bagnani of University College, Toronto; the generosity of the Canada Council in awarding me a Senior Research Fellowship to pursue this subject; the consideration of the Board of Regents of Victoria University in granting me leave of absence; the hospitality and facilities of the British Museum; and a grant in aid from the University of Toronto for stenographic assistance.

G. L. KEYES

Victoria College, Toronto

Contents

CHRISTIAN FAITH AND THE
INTERPRETATION OF HISTORY

CHAPTER ONE

St. Augustine in Context

St. Augustine would be the first to disclaim originality in his interpretation of the world of experience. His intention is to serve as a mouthpiece of Catholic Christianity. But he is no "mere Christian." Nor is the Christianity of the fourth century the "mere Christianity" of apostolic times, but the complicated product of 350 years of evolution, showing the effect of religious, intellectual, and social circumstances with which it has had to come to terms in order to survive in a highly competitive religious market. Christ and Caesar are no longer at loggerheads, but have entered into an uneasy partnership destined to lead to the res publica christiana so variously conceived in later times. "Unworldly" and "worldly" no longer distinguish Christian from non-Christian, for men of each sort are to be found in either camp. Christianity and non-Christianity have come to share an impressive common denominator. There is much to be said for the proposition that post-Nicene Christianity, far from being in conflict with classical culture, is in fact its culminating achievement. Some will insist that the unshared christological dogmas are the essence of Christianity, and the aforesaid common denominator largely accident. But whatever one's position on this issue, there can be no doubt that St. Augustine must be recognized as the chief spokesman not just of the Christian community but of the general climate of opinion of his age. If he is in some sense the first great medieval figure, he is also the last or almost the last great representative of Greco-Roman civilization. The "classical attitude" is not to be identified exclusively with the point of view of the more emancipated element in fifth- and fourth-century Athens—nor with the humanism of Cicero, nor the mysticism of the Neo-Platonists. It is these and more—a constantly changing intellectual reaction to 1,500 years of historical change. What was the pattern of evolution which led to the "classical attitude" to which St. Augustine gives expression? What circumstances in his own life may have given peculiar color and emphases to his thought? How does he weave together this general and this particular?

The following simile, fabricated for the occasion, not true for every individual, and not to be taken for an analogy, may suggest the pattern of Greco-Roman development.

In infancy Everyman depends upon the authority, wisdom, and power of his parents and under their guidance learns certain basic traditional skills. As a youth he ranges farther afield. Teachers supplement, perhaps sometimes contradict, the authority of parents. In school he faces a series of problems tailored to his developing capacities and generally is able to solve them. Teachers and even parents encourage him to "think for himself," and he becomes increasingly able and willing to generalize upon his own experience. But authority transmitting tradition both remote and recent is still very much in the saddle. High adolescence comes after years of success in the controlled and artificially friendly setting of home and school. Everyman not unnaturally extrapolates success; he says in effect, "With mine own right arm have I gotten myself the victory." He assumes that every problem, personal, social, or professional, which life may present will fall before his sharp steely brain. He displays boundless self-confidence and an arrogance at once amiable and pathetic. He is heavily skeptical of traditional views supported only as it seems by authority. But the spring soon goes from the year. In the world outside school he will encounter problems which have not been cut down to his size. He may never be led by "overweaning self-confidence" into dramatic disaster. But his tragedy will lie in the discovery sooner or later, mildly depressing or cruelly frustrating, that he simply cannot live up to his own expectations for himself, or solve every problem simply by taking thought, however carefully.

In maturity Everyman still sees visions and undertakes great projects, but he learns to live with a juster sense of his own powers. Still skeptical of traditional lore propagated by authority, he now grows increasingly doubtful of his own ability to control his life by the exercise of reason. Such double-barreled skepticism occasionally leads to intellectual debility. Happy or unhappy, decisive or indecisive, Everyman must live by assumptions which, on critical assessment, may now seem to him no more than plausible. But he lives and carries on his daily business *as if* life and work made sense and were worth while. He gambles upon uncertainties, and in this sense "lives by faith." His state may depress adolescent observers, but it has its comforts and satisfactions. When one need no longer pretend *to know* that authority is always right, one can listen to it with good humor as a source of interesting suggestions. Dogmas once rejected may now be reappraised, as suggestive hypotheses. It may go against the grain to reappraise the dogmas of an authority against which one has staged a bloody rebellion; but the same ideas may be acceptable enough on the lips of a new authority unassociated with past conflict and disillusionment. Thus the lapsed Catholic may come to Geneva, the lapsed Anglican to Rome. Propositions drawn from authority or personal observation will be accepted by the mature Everyman in a critical spirit, kept while experience and observation seem to bear them out, modified or abandoned if and when observation and experience seem to go against them.

Everyman slips imperceptibly into age. He settles down with the assumptions which he has agreed with himself to make; he tests them against his experience and explores their implications. If no proposition seems demonstrably true, none seems demonstrably false. At times he seems the complete scientist willing to revise or jettison any or every opinion as experience may dictate, at other times the gullible slave of any superstitious notion not absolutely implausible. He grows increasingly willing to deny or pervert evidence which taken straight could endanger assumptions which have become comfortable. Preserving the jargon of his maturity, he may still claim to live by faith, not knowledge. But in certain key issues faith seems to have become something more, rather than less, than the knowledge which is reasoned conviction. He is likely to attribute his favorite propositions not to sensation and reason, which he remembers to distrust, but to some supposedly supra-rational source like divine revelation. As dissolution approaches, the will *to know* grows stronger and he clings tenaciously to the "comfortable words" on which his peace of mind depends. Skepticism and faith finally give way to senile certitude.

I think that the Greco-Roman civilization made a pilgrimage somewhat similar to that described above. It was born in a *volker-wanderung* of Greek-speaking tribes, drifting from east-central

Europe into the coastlands and islands of the Aegean Sea, and there confronting, mingling with, and eventually swamping the survivors of an ancient culture (Minoan-Mycenaean) which had flourished in those regions for over two millennia. In the dark age which followed (from 1100 to about 800 B.C.), the technical skills and the religious and other practices of the defeated were not so much lost as debased or driven underground. The Homeric epics preserve the genealogical, religious, and cultural traditions of the newcomers, traditions which dominated the infancy of a new civilization which would come in time increasingly to exploit the inheritance from its other parent as well. The new masters lacked specialized knowledge of the world and thought themselves surrounded by a host of unseen Powers which might intervene in their lives at any or every moment. But victory brought much self-confidence. The present was compared not with a more sophisticated future but with a primitive past. Life was exhilarating and the gods were held to be well disposed and approachable, though (judged by their apparent activity) as whimsical, unpredictable, and amoral as their human worshipers. Death was feared not so much for itself as for bringing an end to life that was generally good. Homer's reference to *moira* ("fate") which stands in an undefined relationship to the gods may imply a certain vague feeling for natural cause and effect, due perhaps in part to incipient specialization. His occasionally flippant accounts of the gods, and Hesiod's systematic classification of their relationships, suggest a decrease in awe before the supernatural as men came to feel more at home and surer of themselves in the world. But authority was still paramount; the gods were still enthroned.

The youthful stage saw slow but steady advances in political and economic life. Relative security brought overpopulation, and this posed a variety of problems the more easily solved because experiments could be made in the small laboratory of the city-state. What sort of government would be best suited to each successive stage of growth? What could be done to meet the basic fact that there was not enough land to go around? In these difficult circumstances caution was the keynote. Shrewd peasants were not ready to overlook possible sources of help in traditional bardic wisdom, ancient rites, or the oracles of the gods. They felt the need of discipline, and believed that natural and not merely social sanctions pursue the murderer and the adulterer. The wise man pursues modest objectives; he prepares himself for disappointment; he knows that the gods and luck give nothing without hard work on his own part. Great success is dangerous, either because the gods are jealous or because success can lead to dangerous self-confidence. Social problems were gradually solved. Monarchy, aristocracy, dictatorship, and democracy or commercial oligarchy followed one another, as each in turn was made obsolete by events; and this evolution was accomplished with relative ease by a people whose genius was as clearly political as the genius of the peoples of India has always been religious. Land shortage was countered by colonization, in which men could keep their familiar way of life at the price of moving to a new land, and by industrialization and commerce, which enabled other men to stay in the familiar land at the price of adopting the new specializing life which Plato was to think the very essence of civilized living. Political and economic advances were probably more obvious in retrospect than at the time. If tradition was honored and hopefully exploited, hard work and modest successes were nourishing a spirit of cautious self-reliance. But not all the men of the age were hard-headed peasants. There were laggards —simple-lifers, failures, women, whose role in the family was diminished by industrial specialization—who found relief for their frustrations in Dionysian orgies and Orphic mysticism. The pre-Socratic philosophers, on the other hand, were ahead of their age in the matter of self-confidence. Sprung from a wealthy merchant class, they were concerned with physical substance, unlike those other philosophical pioneers the contemporary Indian sages, and our own scholastics, whose intellectual operations reflect a priestly milieu. The outlook of the pre-Socratics was secular and they dealt in scientific hypotheses, not religious dogma. They foreshadowed an emancipated age which would have unbounded confidence in human reason.

High adolescence was brought on by unexpected victory over the Persians, the culmination of several centuries of hard-won political and economic success. Reason was king, and man the measure of all things. Not everyone was changed overnight, or completely. The tragedians presented the case for old-fashioned caution to receptive audiences in Athens itself, the chief seat of the "New Learning." Herodotus, the "father of history," nicely blended new-fangled rationalism with old-fashioned conservatism. Chief exemplars of the new spirit were the sophists, self-professed efficiency experts, impatient with the traditional and eager to rebuild society on rational lines. They were most impressive as destructive critics of ill-founded traditional hypotheses; they showed to least advantage on the constructive side, claiming to teach any man efficiency for a price, willing to pontificate on subjects too many and too deep, identifying their own intellectual agility with superior wisdom. Perhaps the rational humanism of the age appeared at its best in those fifth- and fourth-century physicians of the school of Cos who contributed to the so-called Hippocratic Canon of medical texts. Their conclusions were meticulously based on observation, not ancient authority. They confined themselves to a limited range of ailments, and were careful to observe the effect of diet upon various stages of pleurisy, enteric fevers, and the like. They attempted only what they knew that they could do. Their opinions on the effect of geography upon national character were a little too dogmatic: their observation of Europeans and Asiatics ignored the effect of political factors on "national character," and was on too short-term a basis. But their scientific spirit appears in the comment of the author of the treatise *On the Sacred Disease* (epilepsy, commonly thought to be a form of divine seizure), that while he cannot actually offer a natural explanation for the seizures he is sure that there is one. Thucydides the historian displayed the strength and weakness of his age. He paid meticulous attention to detail and has left an account of the Peloponnesian War which in other terms would have done credit to a Coan physician describing the progress of a case of pleurisy. But he showed sophistic glibness in his willingness to generalize upon his study of one war's effect upon society. He dismissed earlier history, which might have given him a basis for comparison, as unimportant, and hardly concealed his contempt for his great predecessor Herodotus, who attempted to interest as well as to edify his readers. Within his chosen field, his confidence in his judgment was so great that he thought it necessary to retail only such evidence as supported his own conclusions.

On another plane Athenian democracy, with its unbounded confidence in the common man and majority rule, gave a practical expression to the humanism of the age. The sophists diu place a value upon expertise, and saw rational *potentialities* in the common man. But in Athenian politics the potential was confused with the actual. Leaders did not lead; apart from offering advice, which might or might not be taken by the common man, they were expected to confine themselves to carrying out the majority decisions of common men whose rational potentialities were still awaiting development. Huge "people's courts" enforced laws tempered by what passed with the common man for equity. Looking outward, the Athenians had emerged from the Persian Wars with naval strength proportionate to their self-assurance. But when they tried to draw the states of continental Greece into a strong defensive system under their leadership, they aroused the resistance of neighbors less stimulated by the war and ready to proceed at a slower pace. Athens' claim to be "the school of Hellas" can have been no easier to accept because it was true. In the "First Peloponnesian War" (459–445 B.C.) the healthy if less interesting tissue managed for the time being to throw off the attacks of the cancerous cell. Subsequently power blocs began to crystallize: the Peloponnesian League of land powers was revitalized under Spartan leadership, while Athens strengthened her hold over maritime subjects who had once been free allies. Mutual fear led the factions into the Great Peloponnesian War (431–404 B.C.), which ended the Greek age of euphoria as decisively as ours was terminated by the wars of religion in the sixteenth century. The war brought atrocities, civil strife, and disillusionment with democracy, and was followed by a long period of international conflict which ended only with the establishment of the Roman Empire. The Peloponnesian War proclaimed the fact that fifth-century man had grossly exaggerated his ability to manage his affairs by the exercise of reason.

Socrates was a central figure of the period of disillusionment. Like the Sophists he was skeptical of traditional values and hoped to put human behavior on a more rational basis. But he was wryly amused by the scope of their efforts and their pretensions to teach for a fee the secret of success. He confined himself to ethical questions, where he had himself and others to observe, and he and his friends discussed the meaning of such terms as piety, bravery, and justice. His method was to appeal to a supposed expert for a definition. His own ideas were insinuated in the form of questions and objections to be dealt with by this "authority." With time and patience, the latter—ideally—would digest Socrates' indirect contribution to the discussion and end by "giving birth" to a new formulation owing something to each intellectual parent. Socrates modestly disclaimed the role of "father" and preferred to call himself "midwife." In fact, experts were likely to break off discussion at the point when it became clear that their original pronouncements were not going to be accepted out of hand. Spectators were likely to see only the destructive side, the discrediting of acknowledged authority and traditional ideas. For years, before and during the Peloponnesian War, Socrates carried on in this way without let or hindrance. But shortly after the end of the war he was condemned to death with some show of reason for "corrupting the young men," by destroying their feeling for traditional values without providing them with a substitute, rational or otherwise. The disillusioned post-war Athenians were not only condemning Socrates—whom they had tolerated for decades; they were repudiating their own trust in the untrammeled exercise of reason, a trust which after the Persian Wars had exhilarated them and made them great, but now seemed to have led them to ruin.

Maturity was setting in, but the disillusionment caused by the Pelopponesian War was far from total. Plato still conceded himself a chance of creating a rational society in Syracuse. Sparta, Thebes, Phocis, and Syracuse tried, if unsuccessfully, to transform themselves into Great Powers and Managing Directors of Greek affairs. The old-fashioned but unexhausted kingdom of Macedon succeeded here where others had failed, when her king became chairman of a Hellenic League after 338 B.C. Meanwhile the rational humanism of the fifth century was being further subtly subverted. In Plato's thought there was a drift away from the world of sensation—the environment which *civilization* seeks to understand and control—toward a subjective intelligible world of universal and eternal concepts. Knowledge of this latter world was not to be obtained by reason alone, although reason could prepare the mind for such knowledge. Reason can generalize; but the generalizations of reason can only *be seen* to apply to specific instances past and present. Knowledge that they are universal and eternal, that they form a coherent system, and that phenomena are real only in the sense that they embody these ideas, must come from some other quarter than reason working upon observation. Plato suggested that this knowledge comes from *reminiscence*, a remembering of truth planted in the soul before birth, and that these memories might be evoked by the sort of study of scientific generalizations of which reason is capable. Theories of its nature might change, but from this time forward the notion was abroad that there is some form of knowledge as superior to reason as reason itself to mere traditional authority. Aristotle was perhaps less confident than Plato that the wise man could put society to rights; there is no Syracuse in his life—his tutorship of Alexander hardly fits the case. He set himself to show the relationship of the intelligible to the sensible, and believed that reality lay in their conjunction. He attempted a classification of human knowledge whatever its bases. He is of course maligned by those who think that he was concerned only with deduction—the interpretation of particular instances by the application of general laws—without realizing that those general laws were suggested by a prior process of induction. Society profited by his researches, but Aristotle's own preoccupation was with the classification rather than the practical application of scientific knowledge.

With the breakup of Alexander's empire and the subsequent articulation of a number of first-, second-, and third-class powers, a pragmatic age began in which both authority and reason were eyed with much skepticism, and politicians took short views. The Hellenistic "Concert of Powers" was joined in the third century B.C. by the Roman Republic. The Italian stock to which the Romans belonged was akin to the Greek, but had not faced the stimulus of as hard a country, or predecessors as advanced. For this reason cultural development had been slower. But from the eighth century many Italians, and among them the Romans, had come under the influence of the Greek colonists of the southern Italian coastlands, and while like every other people on earth they gave plentiful evidence of originality, they were to develop what in time might fairly be called (*pace* latter-day little-Romans) a provincial version of Greek culture. This development did not spring from the fact that they lacked imagination or were intellectually inferior, but from the fact that they were wise enough to see the advantage of learning from a kindred people who for historical reasons which owed nothing to innate superiority were more advanced than they in the arts of civilization. The Romans during the fifth, fourth, and early third centuries B.C. had drawn the Italian states into a system of defensive alliances, and by the end of the third century had become one of the great Mediterranean powers in virtue of their victories over Semitic

Carthage. This was an age of great empirical progress: of scientific research, of new methods, of mass production, of concern for public welfare. States like the Seleucid and Ptolemaic monarchies, far larger than the city-states of the preceding period, were founded and efficiently administered. But the very real progress made in detail was jeopardized by failure to achieve a stable international order. The long series of wars frustrated the larger ambitions of one power after another and ended with the military supremacy of the Roman Republic, economically cruder than Seleucid Syria and Ptolemaic Egypt, but rich in the manpower of Italy and blessed with a governing aristocracy not too proud to learn from experience.

Traditional Greek religion was now in decline if not decay. Personal and official piety was not extinct, but the credit of Delphi at least had been tarnished by its miscalculation of prospects in the Persian Wars, and now Plato, who rejected "immoral" myths, and the Stoics, who converted "true stories" into allegories, broke the *élan* of traditional religion. The broader geographical horizons of the Hellenistic age, and the overshadowing of the old city-states by larger political units, were bound to weaken the vitality of cults traditionally preoccupied with the life and prosperity of the city-states. Euhemerus advanced a theory that the gods were culture heroes. Roman religion may have preserved vitality a little longer than the Greek in virtue of a cultural time lag—but Euhemerus' was the first Greek book to be translated into Latin.

Meanwhile reason, long since turned by the Sophists against authority, came at last to investigate its own credentials. Practical disillusionment was provided with philosophical underpinnings. Pyrrho and Timon of Phlius may have been Aristotle's intellectual inferiors, but they gave classical expression to the skepticism which peculiarly characterized this age of maturity. They held that sensation is fallible; that all thought is based ultimately on sense impressions and is therefore as fallible as its source. Dogmatists like Plato with claims to suprarational *gnosis* drawn from some source superior to sensation and reason are collectively discredited by their mutual disagreements. Truth is unknowable, or at least unrecognizable. The wise man will suspend judgment. This point of view captured Plato's Academy in the person of Arcesilaus, its president in the third century, who went a step farther and denied the very possibility of knowledge. The arguments of the Skeptics may not have been coercive, but their pessimism regarding man's power to understand and control the universe was real enough, and they crystallized the age's inclination to doubt. Henceforth men had to live with a conscious distrust not only of tradition but of their own ability to supplement or replace this by the exercise of reason.

With authority and reason each in retreat, men groped for plausible hypotheses to help them face life. Stoics and Epicureans gave up the old search for the nature of the physical universe. Their respective theories of physics did no more than provide a perfunctory quasi-scientific "justification" for their ethical propositions. Having given up the quest for scientific knowledge of the world, they were also ready to abandon any hope of controlling it. Their ethical teachings were, in effect, recipes for serenity and peace of mind in a world beyond either understanding or control. The attraction of Stoic *apatheia* may have been enhanced by the heroic desperation with which it was pursued. Epicurean *ataraxia* was less challenging: the pleasures of this world were acknowledged to be worth something. On the political plane, those who had not given up hope of making something of the world could put their faith in those new savior gods, the Hellenistic princes, recognizing their practical power to provide prosperity and security of sorts in the material field. There was also a curious "worship" of Tyche, personification of the unpredictable element—an acknowledgment of the limits of understanding, combined with a gambler's trust in luck.

Carneades, president of the Academy in the first half of the second century B.C., sought an escape from the debility of skepticism, and in his doctrine of probability he laid the intellectual groundwork for the coming "Age of Faith." The probable is not to be identified by its apparent approximation to some truth of which we have inklings. But appearances uncontradicted by other appearances and propositions which are consonant with what else we are ready to accept are to be taken *as if* true—and described as probable. What is probable today may not be probable in the light of tomorrow's evidence. But today we get on by pretending that it is true. One might almost say that an adaptation of the "Noble Lie" was the part of the Platonic heritage particularly emphasized by Carneades. One pretends that things *are* what they seem. But the pretense may involve no more self-deception than when a scientist agrees to accept for working purposes a hypothesis which he knows he cannot prove.

Principles and laws are held on a tentative basis, subject to modification or abandonment if they come to seem inconsistent with experience and with what else we accept. Here is a basis for pure science, and also for gross superstition: if nothing can be proven, nothing can be disproven. These views, accepted by Cicero and transmitted by him with so much else of Hellenistic thought, may be said to have played in the inner life of Greco-Roman civilization a role comparable to that of the Augustan settlement in its outward life. Carneades put the thought of his civilization on a track which it would never entirely desert. Probably he would have been no more pleased with the age of religious faith which followed than Augustus would have been with the absolute monarchy which evolved out of his political settlement.

Meanwhile a *modus vivendi* in politics was sought. The republican constitution under which they had won their empire was dear to the Romans, but its machinery was ill adapted to governing an empire. Annually elected officials were expected to govern distant provinces and to wage wars as a sort of extension and addendum to their municipal duties. The constitution was a miracle of checks and balances in which any strong initiative whether from right, left, or center could be blocked, and no decisive action likely to be taken without the need to defy either law or hallowed custom. The system could not be excused on the ground that it worked. The frontiers were not properly defended, and during its first century the Roman "world state" was plagued with piracy, slave risings, contentions with allies, and civil war. The Italian peasants were failing from the land, and a great unemployed or semi-employed mob was growing in the capital. The provinces were undergoverned and at the same time economically exploited by Roman financiers, tax-farmers, and governors. What can be said for a government which provides neither security nor prosperity? The executive element was nearly paralyzed. But a century of unhappy experiment preceded the discovery, or evolution, of an acceptable alternative. The Gracchi and Drusus offered a tribuneship, elected annually and supported by "the people," as a legal alternative. But the popular assembly which would have represented "the people," choosing and supporting these possible "prime ministers of the proletariat," was ignorant and, because of its grinding poverty, corrupt. The other alternative was the warlord, seizing power or coercing the government with the backing of veterans who believed with some show of reason that the aristocratic Establishment had no concern for their welfare. Marius (104–100 B.C.), Sulla (88, 82–79 B.C.), Pompey (60–52 B.C.), and Caesar (49–44 B.C.) cut red tape with their swords, broke the political impasse and, in the cases of Sulla and Caesar, accomplished more in a few years than the Establishment in fifty. But they affronted public opinion, which still sentimentalized the republican constitution, and with the exception of Sulla alienated the republican nobility, whose political expertise was still required for any efficient, permanent regime. An executive was needed at once strong enough to do what had to be done (a great deal), acceptable to public opinion, and able to win the cooperation of the nobles, at least until a new professional governing class could emerge or be created.

This century of transition saw traditional Roman religion in trouble, but at the same time a heightened interest in religious revelation in a world where reason itself had ceased to command confidence. Most men could not face life with tentative "scientific" hypotheses alone. Local and family cults were weakened or eliminated by dislocation of population. Official religion had come to be, and to seem, an instrument in the hands of the ruling class. The gods of philosophers—personification of energy—and the Varronian pantheus had no blood in their veins and no popular appeal. The new cults from the east were not necessarily more elevated in tone than the native ones, but they were at least untarnished by past disillusionments. Cybele Magna Mater had arrived as early as 204 B.C. to support morale during the last phase of the Second Punic War. Various Syrian cults had appeared in Italy with slaves and prisoners of war in the first half of the second century B.C. The worship of Isis and of Osiris-Serapis was spread throughout the Mediterranean ports by Alexandrian sailors and probably reached Rome itself by Sulla's time. Mithraism was brought to Italy in 62 B.C. by Pompey's veterans. Christianity would not appear for several generations yet. These several movements, with many modifications and much syncretism, would address themselves to the spiritual needs of an aging civilization.

The period of age in the Greco-Roman civilization displayed various temperamental and intellectual characteristics which were intensified with time. Basic here was a mood of pessimism and self-doubt. This was not of course constant or universal. The emperors for instance conceded themselves some chance still of implementing the "great society." But there was preoccupation with the idea of *evil.* Sometimes this was conceived as an independent principle battling with the good on more or less equal terms. Mithraism inherited Persian dualism and saw the world as the battlefield of God and the Devil. Gnosticism improved upon this by claiming that God had abandoned this world, and the Manichees believed that the material world was wholly evil and that our only hope lay in escaping from it. Christians could not go so far, because of their belief in God as the Creator of all things visible and invisible. For them evil could be only the absence of good, an abuse of free will, a misinterpretation of God's handiwork.[1] The world and its material pleasures were not evil but second best; men should never become so preoccupied with the *creation* that they forgot the *Creator* whose lovingkindness was shown both in giving and in withholding material satisfactions. There was an increasing interest in the conquest not of the world but of self. If one could not control the world one might at least hope, with the Stoics, to control one's attitude toward it. Neo-Platonism, which arose in the later second century A.D., greatest of the "native" schools of thought of the period, was anti-scientific in outlook and sought not to conquer and exploit but to escape from this world. This pessimistic attitude toward the external and material world had established itself during the preceding period, and had been confirmed and intensified by the breakdown of the Hellenistic "concert of powers," by subsequent Roman misgovernment, by economic difficulties, and by philosophical skepticism. The mood of the age was read into the new religious movements from the east. Isis, Cybele, Mithra, and the Syrian deities, like their Greco-Roman counterparts, were traditionally concerned in their homelands with fertility, prosperity, and victory, and it could be argued from the Synoptic Gospels, at least, that Jesus was largely concerned with improving human relations in the external material world. But their transference westward shook these movements free of their racial, territorial, and (in time) materialistic moorings. In the imperial context, they became media for the age's mood.

Confidence in man's ability *to understand* this world by the exercise of reason continued to decline. The imperial age agreed with Carneades that since nothing could be known, men must seek a *modus vivendi* with the unknown. They must accept, on faith,

[1] Methodius of Olympus *Peri tou Autexousiou.*

tentative propositions which might arise from induction but were increasingly likely to be attributed to divine revelation. Even in the bogus science of astrology the view came to obtain that suprarational knowledge would come to the man who was willing to prepare himself for it by a life of moral austerity. Neo-Platonism came, in its time, to emphasize a suprarational approach to a suprarational Object, and displayed an increasing interest in divine revelation of all sorts, substituting mystical experience and esoteric *gnosis* for the more obviously tentative conclusions of induction.

Suprarational knowledge, far more effective now than scientific knowledge in winning faith, was often traced to ancient revelation. There was a new, or revived, willingness to consider the possibility of wisdom in precepts handed down from a happier past when men were closer to the nature of things. The cult of Cybele, with its wild "enthusiasm" and self-inflicted mutilations and blood-lettings, was an anthropological museum piece. Europeans were impressed by the incredible antiquity of the Egyptian cult of Isis. Mithraism struck the western imagination with ancient Persian rites involving honey, milk, and sacred fire, and with incomprehensible Persian words in its liturgy. In this company Christianity would have seemed parvenu had it not found an impressively ancient basis for itself in the Jewish scriptures: the Old Testament was "discovered" to be a Christian document, and more ancient than any competitor.[2] Great concern was shown for the text itself.[3] Although there is evidence for a historico-grammatical approach, especially in the Antiochene patriarchate, the usual exegesis was allegorical: the scriptures had several levels of meaning; if one looked deep enough and with a properly pious intention, one could discover premonitions of Christianity in every part of the Old Testament. Christ's incarnation, crucifixion, resurrection and ascension were constantly suggested in the historical no less than in the professedly prophetic books.[4] By this uphill road the Old Testament could everywhere be seen to support the articles of the Christian faith.[5]

[2] Justin Martyr *Dialogus cum Tryphone* 10–47; Theophilus of Antioch *Ad Autolycum* ii.

[3] Origen *Hexapla*.

[4] E.g., Aristo of Pella; Justin Martyr *I Apologia*; Tertullian *Adversus Marcionem* 3; St. John Chrysostom *Contra Iudaeos et Gentiles quod Christus est Deus*.

[5] St. Barnabas *Epistola*; Justin Martyr *Dialogus cum Tryphone* 48–108; St. Hilary of Poitiers *Commentarius in Matthaeum*; St. Ambrose, *passim*.

High regard for ancient wisdom was also shown in the secular sciences, where transmission of the heritage of the past became the great object. Research was undertaken in the library rather than the laboratory. A similar willingness to rely on the past was shown in the political sphere. The emperors tried, in Rome at least, to stress the continuity of their regime with "the brave days of old." The Senate and the magistrates were the symbols of a proud past. Under the emperors they continued to play an important part in the work of government. Augustus' powers, to Roman eyes at least, were largely contained within a republican context, and he and his successors could with much legal justification describe themselves as the appointees and agents of the Senate, which was seen as the legatee of the glorious old republic. There was a deliberate exploitation of the Roman temperamental responsiveness to tradition. Vergil, Horace, Livy, and, in his own way, Ovid did their part to glorify the heritage of the past, and if in some lights Augustus seemed a sort of secular messiah, his role was conceived to involve a turning back to a long-gone golden age. For the Romans, self-confidence in the present was bound up with pride in the Roman past. Augustus tried to rebuild or revive temples, priesthoods, and festivals, hoping also to revive through an association of ideas the old patriotism, morality, and frugality. Such emperors as Claudius were ready to exploit constitutional and religious antiquarianism for what it was worth. But as the emperors acquired an official and personal charisma of their own, the appeal to the republican past became less necessary.

If the universe was beyond purely human understanding, it was also beyond human control. There was a general assumption, not thought to be comfortable, that all things in the world of our experience are bound together in a causal nexus. The Greek concept of *moira* may have been a contributing factor, but the influence of astrology was probably much greater. Astrology could be taken to imply pure determinism, with universal authority and power vested in the heavenly bodies. Astrological theories followed the Mesopotamian conquerors into Syria during the first half of the first millennium B.C. and had a profound effect upon Syrian religion. Local gods (Yahweh is normally an exception) were identified with the ruling heavenly bodies and were thought to share in their qualities of universality and omnipotence, as had been the case a little earlier with the gods of Nineveh and Babylon. Zoroastrianism and its offshoot Mithraism were soon affected: Zervan Akarana was identified with Time Unlimited, an astrological concept, and thrice-daily prayers were offered to the god-of-the-day as determined by the astrologers. By the third century A.D. Mithra and Attis were identified with the Sun, and the pseudoscientific jargon of astrology could be used to enhance the show of intellectual respectability in their cults. The Christian God, like the Syrian Jewish Yahweh, was conceived to be universal and omnipotent, though He was never identified with the Sun. Determinism in Christianity and Islam should probably be credited to astrology through a Syrian medium. Universal determinism was regarded not as a comfortable hypothesis encouraging trust in order behind apparent chaos, but as a cruel scientific fact to be counteracted if possible. Thus Isis was described as the Queen of Fate, able to help her elect by modifying the otherwise inevitable. Christianity tried to reconcile divine determinism with human free will by distinguishing between an external world which followed the divine plan in every detail, and an inner one where man was more or less free to choose his subjective reaction to external circumstances. On a lower level there was a widespread if inconsistent concern with horoscopes and lucky days, as if man by foreseeing the inevitable could somehow improve upon it.

Asceticism, here as elsewhere, was an attempt to rise above a world which one could not control, to prove oneself indifferent to pleasures hard to get and impossible to keep. In addition, fasting and sexual continence were thought to enhance spiritual insights and powers. Neo-Platonists in search of salvation practiced "purifying virtues" to free their immaterial souls from physical sensuality, abstaining from flesh, wine, and sexual intercourse in preparation for a state of being where the senses would make no claim. The *pistis sophia* of the age prescribed penance for purification. Resurrection as conceived by the astrologers depended not only on esoteric knowledge but upon a progressive purification from all worldly affections, interests, and emotions. Even Mithra came to show an interest in celibacy. Among the Manichees the elect might carry their detachment to the point of self-starvation. Julian the Apostate contrived to present Cybelean emasculation as an outward symbol of an inner emancipation from things material. In Christianity the ascetic state is called "virginity," conceived as freedom from sexual and other worldly attachments. Fasting was recommended,[6] and frequent warnings issued against vanity in dress,[7] Epicurean materialism,[8] plays and festivals,[9] and the fine arts.[10] Rich men were to use their wealth not for worldly pleasure but for good works.[11] Marriage could not be written off as evil, because of Christ's unfortunate (?) presence at the marriage feast at Cana of Galilee, but it was described as an inferior "good," for those who would otherwise presumably "burn." A strong case was made for chastity,[12] and fornication was thought, by some, to be the worst of sins.[13] The Gnostic heretics were against sexual intercourse under any conditions.[14] Monasticism permitted physical withdrawal to a controlled environment in which this unnatural life could be lived with as few distractions and temptations as possible.[15]

"Welfare programs" had been commonplace in the towns of the Hellenistic age, and under the empire the government was quick to relieve distress. But the ascetic indifference to material things had some effect in this field, too, although Julian paid tribute to the effectiveness of Christian charity in helping the poor and the sick.[16] But the first objective here was not really to help the poor, who in any case were in the hands of a wise and loving God, but to bring the benefactor into rapport with God by doing His will and imitating His lovingkindness. Charity was thought to win forgiveness for post-baptismal sins.[17] The most charitable act of all was to offer oneself

[6] Hermas *Shepherd* Mand. 12; *Didaskolion Apostolorum.*

[7] Tertullian *De Habitu Muliebri, De Virginibus Velandis*; St. Cyprian *De Habitu Virginum.*

[8] Dionysius of Alexandria *De Natura*; *see* Eusebius *Praeparatio Evangelica* iv. 23–27.

[9] Tertullian *De Spectaculis*; St. John Chrysostom *In Kalendas, Contra Circenses Ludos et Theatra, De Diabolo.*

[10] Tertullian *De Idolatria.*

[11] Clement of Alexandria *Quis Dives Salvetur?*

[12] Clement of Rome *Epistola ad Virgines* (probably early third century); Hermas *Shepherd* Mand. 4; Methodius of Olympus *Symposium*; Tertullian *De Exhortatione Castitatis.*

[13] Tertullian *De Pudicitia.*

[14] *Acta Petri*; *Acta Thomae*; *Acta Pauli et Theclae*; a virgin commended for breaking off betrothal, on becoming a Christian.

[15] St. Athanasius *Vita Antonii*; Theodoret of Cyrus *Historia Religiosa seu Ascetica Vivendi Ratio.*

[16] Hermas *Shepherd* Simil. 2; Clement of Alexandria *Paedagogus* 2, 3.

[17] St. Cyprian *De Opere et Eleemosynis.*

as God's instrument for converting others to a better way of thinking.
If Christians were charitable to all men, Mithraists and Manichees
were full of good works for the benefit of their coreligionists at
least. But the Neo-Platonists put "civil virtues" last on their
list: they might "adorn life," but they did nothing to elevate the
soul.

Justice may be done in this world, but it is not seen to be done.
Perfect peace and perfect assurance of God's loving justice can come
only in some other life than this. St. Paul, St. Gregory of Nyssa, and
many other Christian spokesmen declared that without the Resurrection the Christian game is not worth the candle. Christians had a
strong eschatological interest,[18] and a hopeful belief that death would
prove to be the doorway to a better life.[19] Argument was offered to
make plausible the Christian doctrine of the resurrection of the
body.[20] Interest in personal survival was lively and general in the
imperial age. Propertius, Lucan, Seneca, and Aulus Gellius wrote of
ghosts and necromancy.[21] The *Hermetic Corpus* is a treasury of
resurrection *gnosis*. Personal survival was not always, or usually,
taken to imply physical resurrection. Vergil looked for man's escape
from "this muddy vesture of decay,"[22] and P. Nigidius Figulus, a
contemporary of Cicero, and the late fourth-century writer Cornelius
Labeo showed how men could raise their souls, but not their bodies,
to the sublunary sphere. The Syrian cults, the Gnostics, the
Manichees, the astrologers, and—weightiest of all—the Neo-
Platonists looked for survival of the soul cleansed from all physical
taint. But Isis, like Christ, promised corporeal immortality. Christianity was most graphic and made the most of its great historical
instance. Mithraism began with this belief, but probably progressed
to less carnal expectations as it acquired astrological elements.

Whether men still cherished hopes of happiness in this world, or
whether they were ready to write the world off and attach their
hopes to a better world beyond the grave, they had a sense that their

[18] Irenaeus *Adversus Haereses* 5.

[19] Tertullian or St. Cyprian *De Immortalitate*; Clement of Rome *II
Corinthians*.

[20] Marcion (?) *Martyrium Polycarpi* 1.2; 2.1; Aristeides of Athens *Apologia*
17–18; Athenagoras of Athens *Apologia* 1.10.

[21] Propertius iv.7, 11; Lucan *Pharsalia* vi; Seneca *Oedipus, Agamemnon*;
A. Gellius *Noctes Atticae*.

[22] Vergil *Aeneid* vi, *Georgics*.

goal was beyond their own unaided strength. There was a willingness to have faith in love behind apparent indifference—in savior
gods who could give if not worldly prosperity then peace of mind
and the hope of a glorious resurrection. The emperor himself was at
first, at least, accepted as a savior god, a superman who might
perhaps make world renunciation unnecessary after all. An ecumeni-
cal ruler might still succeed where those localized divinities the
Hellenistic princes had failed. One man was now supreme. The
auctoritas of Augustus arose in part from the fact that he had brought
to an end an age of warfare and seemed able to ensure stability for
the future, in part from wealth, patronage, awe-inspiring titles, and
sheer longevity. He and his imperial successors had the necessary
legal power to do what they thought needed to be done, and in their
evolving bureaucracy they had an instrument to make this legal
power really effective. The new order was soon justified empirically.
In the field of security, areas in Spain, Gaul, and the Alps which had
been "overlooked" in the course of annexations were now brought
into the fold; invasions were repelled; the frontier, especially in the
Balkans, was judiciously extended to secure a better defense; the
soldiers were given a contract which seemed to promise them
economic security. As far as the economy was concerned, the
emperors provided an atmosphere in which private enterprise could
and did thrive. Life and limb were safe, communications good,
taxes moderate, and currency sound. The Roman mob may not have
been rehabilitated, but it was at least given new protection against
fire, famine, and flood. Italy in the first century enjoyed an economic
boom; the east began to recover from a century of misgovernment
and exploitation; the west entered upon a long period of prosperous
development. Fair play was now the rule in the provinces, and the
regime was vastly popular here. The Romans themselves clung for
historical reasons to symbols and traces of the republic. But the
great majority of his subjects throughout the Roman world thought
of the emperor as a "present god." From the beginning emperor
worship was spontaneous in the eastern provinces and it was
encouraged in the western ones. Emperor worship both expressed
and confirmed confidence in the benevolent efficiency of this great
Patron of the *civitas terrena*. In metropolitan Italy the emperor's
genius or guardian angel was worshiped rather than the emperor himself, in a compromise calculated to soothe republican

susceptibilities. But good emperors were officially deified after their deaths. Gaius (A.D. 37–41) even tried to extend worship of the living emperor to Rome by having himself identified with Jupiter Latiaris, but this assertion of universal divine monarchy, in the chief seat of republican sentiment, was dropped by his successors.

The first century was one of general prosperity. In the second century the outlying provinces were perhaps even more thriving. Emperor worship reached its apex in the reign of Hadrian, the "giver of every good and perfect gift" to so many people. His divinity was not universally accepted, but even the Christians prayed *for* the Emperor as God's appointed instrument. But Italy was now in the grip of a chronic agricultural depression caused by overproduction, and there were many municipal bankruptcies in the older provinces. The new provinces of the west and north had developed beyond the point of serving as dumping grounds for the produce and manufactures of the older territories. The late second and the third centuries saw a general decline in productivity due to war, plague, and civil strife—while military and administrative expenditures rose. The state was faced with bankruptcy, and desperate and crushing measures were taken to secure the funds needed for defense. Before the middle of the third century the empire was under heavy attack from the Persians in the east and from an assortment of Germanic tribes in the north and west, and its end seemed near. The idea of the emperor as a savior god must now have seemed a wry joke. Emperors found themselves at the mercy of soldiers desperate not only for money but for competent leadership to meet the continual military crises, and all too willing to desert, murder, and replace an incumbent at the first sign of failure or of inattentiveness to their needs. The emperors were anxious to salvage some support from religion, and now they attempted to project an image of themselves rather less as "present gods" with full responsibility, and rather more as God's instruments or agents, "the Lord's anointed," an idea already familiar to the Christian and Mithraic constituencies. Decius and Valerian sought to build a religious "common front" to face the national emergency, and Aurelian (A.D. 270–275) presented himself less as *dominus et deus* than as the earthly shadow and vicegerent of the Unconquered Sun.

The third century was the heyday of other savior gods, who promised salvation not in this world—a seemingly hopeless proposition—but in another one. From the early days of the empire, and even earlier, these gods had been strongest among the poor, the worried, and the disillusioned—those who were below the level of the "affluent society" promoted by the emperors. They had gained strength as men had lost faith in the emperors' ability to control the physical environment. Their devotees told an increasingly receptive public that their respective gods, who might be one and the same under different names, loved man, *appearances to the contrary*. God's love was not to be thought a national or tribal phenomenon. The "saved" might be adopted, by grace, from any and every nation. Isis was a loving mother and the queen of men's fates. Apuleius described how she had chosen him "all unworthy," and she was blamed for being the friend of prostitutes, as was Jesus for associating with winebibbers, publicans, and sinners. Even Cybele, once the symbol of reproductive motherhood, came to symbolize maternal solicitude for a weary world. Mithra was the Universal Helper, providing all humanity with sunlight and his elect with spiritual illumination. The fatal weakness of Neo-Platonism as a popular movement lay in its lack of a divine Founder who could symbolize the cosmic love for which men longed, and provide a focus for the personal devotion which they wanted to express. In the first century Christianity made its appearance, and Cybele and Isis grew in popular esteem. In the second, the Egyptian cults continued to thrive. Christianity and Mithraism grew in numbers and enjoyed much toleration and favor respectively from the authorities. In the religious boom of the third century the Syrian cults enjoyed imperial patronage, and Christianity and Mithraism entered upon a period of rivalry in which the latter, with its doctrine of "divine right" and its propagation of muscular morality, could count upon official sympathy.

One of the most striking phenomena of this, as perhaps of every age, was syncretism, the growing together openly or covertly of religious and intellectual movements which at one time seemed sharply opposed and radically different. This mutual assimilation, in the varying degrees to which it was accomplished, was promoted by the discovery that for all their undoubted individuality these movements had much in common and could give each other timely support. Thus men might say with Apuleius and Labeo that the several gods were merely local conceptions of One God, or personifications of functions or qualities of the One. The identification of Roman gods with Greek had been an early exercise in this vein. Similarly the "Dea Syria" was a synthesis of local female deities. By the third century A.D. solar monotheism was beginning to attract to itself many onetime "independent" movements, and Attis, Mithra, Adonis, and others came to be identified with the Unconquered Sun, while Neo-Platonism provided a philosophical basis for the resulting mélange. If Christians rejected formal integration, they at least conformed to the pattern to the extent of being rigorous monotheists—on their own terms.

The rites of the several movements disclosed a considerable similarity. Christian baptism had counterparts in the *Taurobolium* and in the initiation ceremonies of Isis, Serapis, and Mithra. The Christian Eucharist suggested the Mithraic "Last Supper," "the table of our Lord Serapis," and the holy meal of Cybele served from a tamborine. Increasing degrees of enlightenment or spiritual power were attained in the seven Mithraic grades, the various Egyptian initiations, and Christian orders. This similarity in outward form, at least, was fully recognized by contemporary Christians, who accused their rivals, and were accused in turn, of perpetrating devilish imitations and hellish parodies. There were traces of a "common ministry" and of something like a common membership, with each movement catering to a different temperament, perhaps even to different moods in the same man. But Christianity probably profited by making an unusual, rigorously exclusive claim to its adherents' loyalty.

All religious movements saw that, in the interests of intellectual respectability, they must come to terms with secular thought. Almost from the beginning Christians showed an interest, usually unfriendly or defensive but sometimes friendly, in classical Greek philosophy.[23] Neo-Platonism came in time to provide intellectual underpinnings for the religious life of the later empire. The Neo-Platonists were the heirs of the Academy, the Stoics, and perhaps in some degree of Aristotle. But it cannot be shown that Plotinus, at any rate, was significantly influenced by Christianity or Judaism. But in due course the Neo-Platonists developed an interest in all

[23] Athenagoras of Athens notes Platonic similarities; Arnobius (*Adversus Nationes*) thinks much Christian doctrine in line with Platonism. But see Justin Martyr, Tertullian, *passim*.

religious traditions and revelations, including the Christian; the animosity between them and the Christians sprang from the Christian claim to have a monopoly of absolute truth. With Iamblichus in the third century the Neo-Platonic interest in revealed theology became more pronounced. In the fourth, Julian and Sallustius tried to present the non-Christian mystery religions as Neo-Platonic "parables" for the philosophically unsophisticated. Christian theologians were equally willing to use Neo-Platonic argument for their purpose, to give a greater show of intellectual plausibility to their Christian beliefs, but never to the point of consciously modifying Christian dogma *ex hypothesi* infallible. The main outlines of Christian theology had been set before Plotinus; but with time a close intellectual relationship, though hardly friendship, grew up between the two schools. They shared the same high ethical standard and the same abhorrence of sensuality. Each inherited Platonic subjective idealism. They had a common regard for revelation and for mystical experience. By the fourth century the Christian doctrine of the Trinity was being enriched by knowledge of the Neo-Platonic "Trinity." The One is the source of all being: sole reality, without attributes, life, or thought, as man conceives of these. All things emanate from the One, without diminishing it. *Nous* is the perfect image of the One: the archetype of all things (e.g., the Logos), containing all Forms and Ideas. Soul is permeated by *Nous* but is related to all phenomena. Unified, it is World Soul, belonging in essence to the intelligible world; but it is scattered in fact in the multitude of individual souls. These portions of Soul have become involved in lust and are seeking an "independence" which is illusory. They may become reunited, for they have not lost their freedom. Men who want to save their souls and return to the One must cultivate civil, purifying, and above all "divine" virtues. The last entail blissful ecstatic contemplation of the One.

A curious instance of syncretism was the alliance struck in the fourth century between Christianity, the most exclusive of the mystery religions, and the onetime imperial savior god. It was not quite clear—perhaps it never would be—which had captured the other and would be the senior partner. The hand of past emperors had been against Christianity because of its dual loyalty (God's claim having precedence over the state's), its indifferentism, and lately its sporadic pacifism. Now under Constantine the government decided to try what could be got from a close and friendly relationship with Christianity. Constantine's personal conversion was probably genuine; but he showed no intention of resigning his worldly mission and his imperial responsibilities—or his title *pontifex maximus*. From the worldly-imperial viewpoint the new policy had several possible justifications. Christians probably were a majority in the eastern provinces and a strong minority in the west; the Christian clergy were intelligent, educated, powerful with the laity, and potentially useful to the government for controlling or influencing the latter. The loyalty of the pagan community could perhaps be taken for granted. The Church found Constantine hard to contain after his conversion, like an eagle among chickens. He convened and put pressure upon the Council of Nicaea in A.D. 325, and enforced the "party line" which it established. Later, in his wisdom, he adopted Arianism and in A.D. 335 had this version of the faith confirmed by the Council of Tyre. He was very much the senior partner, for all his abdication of divine pretensions, and in some sense held a shield over Christian and pagan subjects alike. In A.D. 311 (?) and 324 edicts of religious *toleration* were issued or reaffirmed, and until Gratian's reign the emperors, though generally friendly to Christianity in one or other of its forms, preserved a policy of official neutrality. Constantius was an exception, and his policy strongly favored Arian at the expense of Athanasian Christianity. Julian stood for toleration, although his personal sympathies were not with Christianity. On questions of faith, the Christian emperors assumed a high quasi-pontifical mien. Thus in A.D. 355 at the Council of Milan Constantius said, "My decision must be taken as final. My Syrian bishops approve of my taking this stand. You will obey me; otherwise you will be banished." These emperors were not gods but they were God's agents, awful and unaccountable, honored with orb, scepter, mantle, diadem, and proskynesis. Hereditary claims to the succession were made and acknowledged. They still had hopes of mastering environment, and they intended that the Christian community should help rather than hinder. For half a century their hopes seemed justified by a modest measure of success. Government was far more stable than in the third century. There were some unspectacular signs of economic recovery. Imperial defense was fairly effective until Adrianople in A.D. 378. The association of Christianity with the emperor was *more or less* on the emperor's terms. He conferred favors on the church and enjoyed the support of the Christian constituency; but he continued to strengthen his own position, adding to his power by whatever means seemed expedient to him, and pursuing thoroughly worldly ends.

But various factors combined to humble the emperors of the later fourth and fifth centuries. The quality of administration had long been deteriorating, and extortion, bribery, and embezzlement had become the order of the day. The cost of defense was staggering. Labor, supplies, and transportation services were requisitioned at need, and regular taxation was well on the way to ruining what vestiges of prosperity remained, or had seemed to be returning, to the middle class. Collection was in the hands of local *decuriones*— once gentry, but now including in their numbers even substantial peasants—hated as oppressors by the humbler taxpayers, but themselves desperate, for they had to make up from their own pockets any deficit in their municipality's assessed tribute. Many of them went to the wall. Labor was under increasing control, and workers were frozen in hereditary occupations. Martial law prevailed in munitions and textile plants to ensure supplies for the armed forces, and munitions workers might be branded. A quasi-serfdom was legalized, assuring the "serf" of protection against officials and soldiers, his patron of a steady labor supply, and the government of the produce of these estates. This society was supported by peasant labor ground down by the demands of soldiers, imperial officials, and the local *decuriones*; and in Gaul and Africa, at least, peasants formed terrorist organizations to afford themselves protection or revenge.

But economic sacrifice did not buy security. The security of the western empire was never really restored after the Battle of Adrianople, on August 8, A.D. 378, when the Goths destroyed the army of Valens. This Roman defeat was sadly decisive. Theodosius waged a successful guerrilla warfare in the Balkans, but the Goths remained, a cancer in the body of the empire. After such a failure the quondam imperial savior god could hardly aspire to a "senior partnership." In A.D. 395 in the Battle of the River Frigidus—the year of St. Augustine's consecration as a bishop—Theodosius defeated Eugenius, who had been set up as puppet emperor in the west by Arbogast the Frank, and he reunited the empire for the last time, with an army largely composed of Goths, Alans, and Iberians.

When he died later in the same year the resources of the empire, which might if united, or at least cooperative, have sustained the defense of the empire, were finally and fatally divided. In the west his young son Honorius reigned under the guardianship of the faithful Vandal Stilicho. In A.D. 400 Alaric and the Visigoths threatened Italy. Stilicho withdrew detachments from the garrisons in Britain and on the Rhine and the upper Danube, and in A.D. 402 and 403 he beat off the invaders. When the Ostrogoths appeared two years later, fresh drafts were needed. Honorius retired to Ravenna, and Stilicho carried the day against the Ostrogoths. But the barbarians were now invading Britain; and Suevi, Vandals, Alans, Burgundians, and Franks broke into Gaul. Then the Visigoths returned to Italy. Stilicho's policy of stripping frontier defenses was deplored by some, his tolerant religious policy by others; and the one really effective imperial general was murdered with the connivance of Honorius. In A.D. 408 Alaric beseiged Rome and made peace on favorable terms with the authorities there. When Honorius in Ravenna refused to confirm the agreement, Alaric set up a puppet emperor in Rome. In A.D. 410 he came back, dismissed his puppet, and sacked Rome for three days, an event which powerfully impressed the imagination of the whole world ("Babylon the great is fallen!"), and led St. Augustine to begin his great work *The City of God*, a defense of Christianity against the charge that by prohibiting the worship of the ancient gods it had brought about the fall of the Roman Empire. The Alans, Suevi, and Vandals now passed into Spain. Constantine, the Roman officer commanding in Britain, crossed the Channel and seized Gaul. Honorius' generals were able to put him down, but the Visigoths were let into Gaul. These were soon disappointed by their treatment at the hands of their Roman allies. Seizing land for themselves in southwestern Gaul, by A.D. 419 they had established an independent principality. When Honorius died in A.D. 423, Britain, Spain, and southwestern and northwestern Gaul had been virtually lost to the empire. He was succeeded by his nephew Valentinian III, a boy under the tutelage of his mother, Galla Placidia. For some years what remained of the western empire was distracted by the rivalry of Aetius and Bonifacius for the chief military command. During a brief ascendancy of Aetius, Gaiseric, king of the Vandals of Spain, brought from forty to fifty thousand of his men to Africa. Mauretania and Numidia were soon lost, and Africa Proconsularis was invaded. When St. Augustine died in A.D. 430, Gaiseric was beseiging his episcopal city of Hippo. By A.D. 439 the Vandals were masters of Carthage.

These grim circumstances humbled the emperors and exalted the church with its message of subjective escape from a world which once again appeared to be slipping beyond control. After A.D. 378 Gratian and Theodosius were certainly not masters of the church, but at most its junior partners. In A.D. 379 and 380, decrees were issued against all heretics. In A.D. 381, the Constantinian policy of religious toleration was formally abandoned, and the emperors now at long last, almost seventy years after the conversion of their great predecessor Constantine, committed themselves fully to Catholic Christianity. In A.D. 382 the post-Actium Altar of Victory was removed from the Senate Chamber in Rome, pagan endowments were confiscated, and pagan worship prohibited. The emperors ceased to be *pontifices maximi* and thereby renounced by implication the ancient right of their predecessors to supervise religious activity in the interest of the secular state. This new phase in the relationship of emperor to Christianity was symbolized by St. Ambrose's determined efforts to reduce Theodosius to the status of a private soldier or at most a noncommissioned officer in Christ's spiritual army. From his vantage point as bishop of Milan, he held that all Christians, including emperors, must submit to the church's teaching and discipline, and that the first duty of every Christian, imperial or otherwise, was not to maintain order or defend a frontier but to save his immortal soul. Everyone knows of the penance which he imposed upon Theodosius for the massacre of the Thessalonians who had risen against the imperial representatives. In another instance the Christian population of Callinicum in Asia, inspired by their bishop, had burned a synagogue. When Theodosius ordered the punishment of the guilty and an indemnity for the Jews, St. Ambrose refused him the sacraments until he had rescinded the decree. If the imperial power had any value in the eyes of such men as St. Ambrose—and St. Augustine—it lay in the use which could be made of it to publicize, protect, and encourage Christian private virtues. Worldly security and prosperity, the original objectives of imperial activity, were, at best, things indifferent. The emperors were not exactly sinning when they pursued these ends; but such activity if taken too seriously was likely to distract them from weightier spiritual matters. In A.D. 395, after a short-lived pagan reaction under the usurper Eugenius, Theodosius destroyed some pagan temples and dedicated others to Christian uses. In the east, where the emperors of the fifth century managed to shore up the *civitas terrena* for another century and a half, the doctrine took hold that the empire should be regarded as an attempt under the emperor's leadership to realize, on earth, that Kingdom of God the pattern of which is laid up in heaven. But Theodosius' successors in the west (and Africa) did nothing to refurbish the imperial public image. The imperial savior god was now a devitalized shadow of his former self. Any hopes of conquering this material world were well and truly laid to rest. Man could only trust in God, strive for subjective peace, and hope for another life in a better world.

Aurelius Augustinus was born at Thagaste in the Roman province of Numidia on November 13 A.D. 354, to middle-class parents of modest means.[24] His father, Patricius, was at that time a pagan, but died a Christian some twenty years later. His mother, Monica, a committed Christian, "presented" him as an infant to the local church, but this formal introduction failed to tie him to Christianity in any significant way. He says that he always loved Christ; but it was not until he was thirty that he attached himself definitely to the church, and two more years passed before he was willing to take Christianity seriously as a rule of life. His father early recognized his intellectual potentialities and arranged for him to study grammar and literature in the neighboring town of Madaura. He admits to having been lazy and to having had trouble with the Greek text of Homer, but he developed a great and abiding love of Vergil.[25] His progress at Madaura seemed to warrant his going on to study rhetoric at Carthage, the capital city of Africa Proconsularis and the chief cultural center in Roman Africa. Here he discovered a passion for drama and the theater and began to live what he later regarded as a dissipated life.[26] But he soon drifted into something like a common-law marriage to which he remained faithful for fifteen years, and he apparently made a great success of his rhetorical studies.

[24] *Serm.* 356.12.
[25] *Conf.* i.9.4, 14.23, 13.22.
[26] *Conf.* ii.3.6.

When he was nineteen he read Cicero's *Hortensius* and was deeply stirred by its description of the happiness of a life devoted to the pursuit of wisdom.[27] This proved to be a "serious call," and left him with a lifelong need to grapple with the problem of man's place in the nature of things. At first he was moved to glance at the Christian scriptures, but like his contemporary St. Jerome at a similar stage of development he was put off by their lack of literary distinction. In his hunger for wisdom he fell into the hands of the Manichees, being challenged by their moral austerity and attracted by their claim to be above wishful thinking and willing to accept life in this world for the evil thing which it obviously is. He never joined the "Elect" who tried to escape from *all* worldly attachments, but for nine years he was a "Hearer," more or less committed to rules of conduct mild by comparison with those which bound the "Elect" but still austere by ordinary Christian standards.

When his training was complete, he began teaching rhetoric in his native town, and in A.D. 377 his outstanding ability was recognized when he was granted a prize by Vindicianus, the proconsul of Africa. Soon after this he decided to try his wings in Carthage itself; and his dedication at this time of a treatise on rhetoric to a prominent *Roman* rhetorician suggests that he was already considering launching himself in Rome. Meanwhile he was becoming disenchanted with the Manichees. Several incidents suggested that the morals of the "Elect" were not as lofty as he had been led to suppose. But more than this, he had come to see through their intellectual pretensions. Their frankness in admitting that the world is evil was more than matched by the gullibility with which they accepted a fantastic cosmic myth and a great deal of astrological nonsense. In A.D.383 Faustus, a renowned Manichaean "bishop" from whom St. Augustine had been led to expect great things, visited Carthage; he proved to be an amiable old man, but quite out of his depth in trying to resolve St. Augustine's intellectual problems.

Carthage was plagued with student disorders, and much against his mother's wishes St. Augustine decided that the time had come to try to establish himself in Italy. But after his arrival in Rome he found that the local students had the reputation of not paying their fees. He evaded this pitfall by persuading Symmachus, the *praefectus urbi*, to secure his appointment as Public Orator of Milan, the

[27] *Conf.* iii.4.7.

imperial capital of the west. He took up residence in Milan in A.D.
384 at the age of thirty and at once found himself in an elevated and
stimulating intellectual atmosphere. The Manichaean cobwebs were
soon blown away. He had never lost a friendly interest in Christianity—he had appreciated the Manichaean reverence for Christ—and
now he began to attend St. Ambrose's sermons, at first for their
style but in time for their content. He was sufficiently impressed to
become a catechumen or adherent. More important to him at this
time was his discovery of the Academic school of thought, with its
tradition of radical skepticism. He lost and never recovered his
"natural" confidence in knowledge derived from sensation and
reason, and he came to see the necessity under which all men labor
of living by faith in uncertainties. Meanwhile he was still hearing
St. Ambrose, and was introduced to the allegorical method of
scriptural exegesis. He saw that "unchristian" elements in the Old
Testament could be explained away and Christian meaning read
into every book and every verse. But he was still in much doubt and
depression and not ready for anything like a total commitment to
Christianity.

At this point he "discovered" the Neo-Platonists. Their intellectual respectability was a datum, and he found to his surprise that
they held doctrines strikingly similar to those of Christianity.
Christian doctrines could often be expressed in Neo-Platonic terms,
and this suggested that in addition to its long-standing emotional
attraction for him, Christianity might have intellectual respectability
as well. He learned of the conversion to Christianity of Victorinus,
an old and illustrious Neo-Platonist. At about the same time, he
discovered in Christian monasticism an ethical challenge comparable
with that which had been part of the attraction of Manichaeism.
Christianity began to seem comparable with Neo-Platonism in its
intellectual subtlety, and with Manichaeism in ethical austerity. In
A.D. 386 at the age of thirty-two he was effectively converted to
Christianity—a consummation to which he had been plainly drifting
—and subsequently spent some weeks with friends at a villa at
Cassiciacum, thinking out and talking out the implications of his
new commitment. That he tended to express himself in Neo-
Platonic terms is hardly surprising, and implies no deficiency in his
conversion. A Confucian converted to Christianity can discuss his
new faith only in Confucian idiom. In A.D. 387 St. Augustine was

baptized. Soon after, he and his mother shared a mystical experience at Ostia. Mystical experience is "nonsectarian" in essence if not in accidents, and there is not much point in debating whether this particular experience was "Christian" or only "Neo-Platonic." Certainly St. Augustine himself put a Christian interpretation upon it. His mother died soon after this incident, and nearly a year later he returned to Africa for life.

After a brief stay in Carthage he set up a small quasi-monastic establishment at Thagaste and before long was making a reputation in Christian circles with such works as *De Magistro, De Genesi ad Litteram,* and *De Vera Religione.* In A.D. 391 he visited Hippo Regius. The bishop Valerius was an old man and a Greek, who found difficulty in dealing with a flock whose languages were Latin and Punic. He was badly in need of help, and St. Augustine found himself virtually compelled to submit to ordination as a presbyter. He was brought to accept his virtual kidnaping as the call of God. After his ordination he was given leave of absence to prepare himself for his new role. In A.D. 393, for the first time, he preached to catechumens being prepared for baptism. He was given permission to set up beside the cathedral a monastic house of the sort to which he had become accustomed. In the same year he was invited to address a council of African bishops meeting at Hippo. In A.D. 394, after his scruples against two bishops in one see had been overcome, he was appointed coadjutor to Valerius, and on Valerius' death in A.D. 396 he succeeded him at the age of forty-two as bishop of the diocese.

For the rest of his life he sustained two complementary roles. As chief pastor he preached, taught, engaged in charitable works, and found himself involved in much legal business with Christians and non-Christians alike. As controversialist and "doctor" he defended his version of the Christian faith against specific attacks, and set forth what he held to be the Christian point of view on various questions of interest to his age. In A.D. 405, for instance, he was writing against the Manichees and defending the Christian scriptures against their criticisms. In the same year the government made another in a long series of attempts to discipline the schismatic Donatists, because of the antisocial behavior of their supposed secular arm, the Circumcellions.[28] They were proscribed and

[28] See below, pp. 139–141.

ordered to conform to Catholic Christianity. A council of bishops at Carthage in A.D. 410 supported this policy, and in his writing of this period St. Augustine strongly asserted the unity of the Catholic Church and condemned the sin against charity which schism implies. He came to see the case for compulsion in urging wanderers into the fold. After the sack of Rome in A.D. 410 he began his great work *De Civitate Dei contra Paganos*, in which he defended Christianity against the charge that it had ruined a healthy and prosperous empire by interfering with traditional religion. He went on to distinguish between the *Civitas Terrena*, which trusts in reason and hopes for material progress, and the *Civitas Dei*, which trusts God in *all* circumstances but looks for perfect happiness only beyond the grave. During most of what remained of his life St. Augustine was engaged against the Pelagians, who held that God has given every man grace sufficient to work out his own salvation, that each of us has Adam's chance to choose the right, and that every man is free to act upon or to reject Christ's offer of salvation. St. Augustine regarded this a sheer sentimentalism which ignored the fact that most men had never heard of Christ, let alone accepted him, and which failed to appreciate the absolute necessity of external help if any man was to be saved. In defending divine omnipotence he was led to stress determinism and predestination in terms which most Christians have thought incompatible with their belief in divine love. In A.D. 430 St. Augustine died at Hippo, while the city was under siege by the Vandals.

St. Augustine's philosophy of history is essentially that of his age. Like most educated men after the fourth century B.C., he doubts that knowledge of the truth can be got from sensation and reason. His skepticism is not just conventional. It was made conscious, immediate, and specific by his "discovery" of the Academics. These philosophers also made him aware of the role of faith in his own and in every man's daily life. Like so many others in the old age of Greco-Roman civilization, he wonders if revelation may not be an alternative and superior source if not of knowledge then at least of ideas to be accepted on faith. The fact that the Neo-Platonic philosophers accepted the doctrine of revealed *gnosis* added plausibility to the wishful belief of religious persons in divine revelation.

In his treatment of historical evidence he is controlled by the *a priori*. The doctrines of his Christian faith have more weight with him than any evidence which human science can produce. If secular evidence runs contrary to his *a priori* beliefs, so much the worse for the secular evidence. It must either be jettisoned or be reinterpreted to support dogma. His contempt for secular evidence reflects his age's generalized distrust of the powers of human reason. He shared with his fellows both Christian and pagan a predilection for *ancient* revelation, and like St. Ambrose and many others he tried to add the cachet of antiquity to his Christian faith by reading it into the Old Testament. He would probably have been driven to allegorical exegesis sooner or later; but at the very beginning of his Christian life he encountered a master of the technique in the person of St. Ambrose, and he learned his lesson thoroughly. Denigrate as he does non-Christian "wisdom," he is ready to "syncretize" with Neo-Platonism insofar as it seems to support and agree with his Christian faith—as it does to a remarkable degree—while writing it off completely where it fails to agree. Neo-Platonism helped him to an understanding of intelligible reality and of the nature of the immaterial Trinity. He freely acknowledges his debt, and is glad to find Neo-Platonism supporting his faith. But no human philosophy, however admirable, is allowed to shake his Christian premises.

His interpretation of the world of human experience reflects a pessimism not peculiar to Christianity and only partially mitigated for some people by the long-cherished hope that the emperor might find a way of salvaging something from this material world. St. Augustine does insist that the material world is good in itself, as against the Manichees, who thought it evil. But he is obsessed with the misery and hopelessness of most men's lives—how could he fail to be in such an age of civil strife, foreign invasion, rapine, and massacre, when simple security of life and limb had become a distant memory? He admits that one can be cheerful only by denying—in faith—that the world is what it *seems* to be, and by reading God's loving providence into what "natural man" might describe as grim and miserable chaos. Asceticism for him, as for so many, was an effort to achieve emotional detachment from a world beyond human understanding or control.

His world picture accepts the Christian version of determinism: everything follows God's *a priori* design. But like the astrologers and the worshipers of Isis, he seeks some mitigation of the rigors of complete determinism. In any event, man must have some measure of free will in order to relieve God of responsibility for human unhappiness in a world which he has created. St. Augustine accepts the Stoic and Christian qualification, and postulates an inner subjective world where man has some freedom at least to govern his reactions to the external world. But under Pelagian prodding he emphasizes ever more strongly the determinism which touches even this inner world and limits its effective freedom. The details of world history are important only to the extent that they can help him suggest and sketch the theme and purport of the Divine Comedy. As a Christian, he believes that the central event in world history was the coming to earth of *his* Savior Christ. He has no hope in the emperor; his ambitions are entirely spiritual and otherworldly. He shares the church's—and the age's—hope for eventual escape to a better world beyond the grave. As a Christian bishop he expresses in Christian terms the doubt, despair, detachment, and hopes of a whole society.

CHAPTER TWO

Theory of Knowledge

St. Augustine's interpretation of history is determined by his peculiar theory of knowledge. In his opinion, sensation and reason are necessary but very fallible guides to the world around us. In addition, the soul is directly aware of its own existence, will, and conceptual power, and of the distinctions between itself and body, and between subject and object. Divine revelation ratifies some of reason's findings, and tells man of God, universals, and the divine plan; but for most individuals revelation comes second hand, by hearsay, and can only be taken on faith.

Up to a point skeptics, conceived as men of "open mind," who are still looking, can follow him with sympathy. But much of which he was "directly aware" no longer seems self-evident. Divine revelation no longer seems the only possible source of the propositions which he attributed to it. And in the field of "revealed truth," he deliberately confuses *belief* and *knowledge*, in a way likely to bedevil his treatment of historical evidence and pervert his picture of the historical process.

I. SENSATION AND REASON

In this branch of St. Augustine's epistemology, skeptics can agree with his conclusions, if not perhaps for his reasons.

At one stage in his development, St. Augustine had a scarifying experience of doubt, not as a philosophical premise or intellectual pose, much less an emancipation from some sort of intellectual slavery, but as a frightening state of confusion and insecurity. He was overwhelmed by the skepticism of the Academy without being able to take much comfort from its probabilism. The arguments of the ancient Skeptics boil down to four. First, all thought is based ultimately upon sensation, and sensation is fallible.[1] Second, causal explanations assume causal connections which cannot be demonstrated.[2] Third, in appealing an issue, one goes to a third party, and then a fourth, and so on, in infinite regress.[3] Fourth, the disagreements of dogmatists suggest the relativity of all dogma.[4] The conclusion is that one should suspend judgment. As far as sensation and reason were concerned, St. Augustine remained a skeptic.[5]

His description of the *modus operandi* of the several senses is primitive and incomplete, but such as it is it supports his skepticism.[6] In each instance, the form and quality of the sensation is conditioned by intermediate factors, such as light, air, moisture, and the state of the sense organs; and St. Augustine thinks these factors too variable to permit assurance that any specific sensation is objectively true.

Vision is a faculty of the eye. A swift ray of light darts from the eye, and like a wand touches its object. This ray is weak, and its effectiveness varies with the quality of the external light which supplements it. Vision, incidentally, takes place in the eye, and not at the place from which the image seems to come. Thus when one shuts one's eyes after gazing at a bright object, like a candle flame, an afterimage remains, showing that what the soul perceives is not the ostensible object of vision but the state of the sense organ.[7] *Hearing* is effected through a mobile airlike medium, presumably present in the air. Percussion of this medium reverberates within

[1] For the earlier Skeptics and Agrippa, see Sextus Empiricus *Pyrrh. Hyp.* i.14.40–144; i.15.167; Diogenes Laertius *Pyrrh.* ix.11.79–82, 84–87, 89.

[2] For Aenesidemus, see Sextus Empiricus *Pyrrh. Hyp.* i.14.181–184.

[3] For Agrippa, see Sextus Empiricus *Pyrrh. Hyp.* i.15.169; Diogenes Laertius *Pyrrh.* ix.11.89.

[4] For the earlier Skeptics and Agrippa, see Sextus Empiricus *Pyrrh. Hyp.* i.14.145–161; i.15.165, 167–168; Diogenes Laertius *Pyrrh.* ix.11.83, 88–89.

[5] St. Augustine identifies corporeal perception with sensation, and spiritual perception with reason, and regards these as *natural man's* greatest faculties. Intellectual perception (divine revelation) comes only with external help; see *De Gen. ad Litt.* xii.4.15–21. Étienne Henri Gilson, *L'Introduction à l'Étude de Saint Augustin* (Paris: Vrin, 1929), p. 214.

[6] William Montgomery, *St. Augustine. Aspects of his Life and Thought* (London: Hodder and Stoughton, 1914), p. 111.

[7] *De Mus.* vi.4.5; *De Gen. ad Litt.* i.16.31; *Serm.* 277.10; *De Quant. Anim.* 43, 44; *De Trin.* xi.2.2–4; *Conf.* vii.10.16.

the membrane of the ear.[8] Through *touch*, exercised through an "earthy" medium, the soul extends itself and discerns and feels cold and heat, roughness and smoothness, lightness and heaviness. Pain serves as a useful warning of danger to the body-domicile.[9] St. Augustine is inclined to think that *smell* is transmitted either by direct contact or through a vapory medium, perhaps anticipating the modern idea that it is occasioned by the discharge of infinitely minute particles. *Taste* is conveyed in heavy moisture.[10]

There are further complications, and chances for distortion, before the soul perceives any of these sensations. The brain is the center of the soul's communications system. It has three ventricles, the anterior concerned with the senses, the posterior with movement, and the third with memory.[11] This may be oversimplification, but it is on the right track. Nothing is said of the distinction between sensory and motor nerves known to Alexandrian physiologists, and St. Augustine feels no obligation to devise or retail a complete theory of the nervous system. Brain and sense organs are alike the instruments of the soul.[12] But disturbances in the sense organs are not transmitted directly from them to the soul, because the difference between their corporeal nature, and its spiritual nature, is too great to allow for direct communication. The intermediary is a fine (but still material) substance, which can be influenced by the sense organs and observed by the soul. This medium, which is something like air, or fire, or a combination of these, is present in narrow tubes called *tenues fistulae*, or *tenuissimi rivuli*, which extend from the several sense organs to the brain. St. Augustine might seem inclined, here, to confuse soul with brain. The marrow in the spine and connecting bones is another medium of communication. So, perhaps, is the air allegedly pumped by the heart through the arteries, which in the liver becomes fiery but in the upper brain so lucent and sublimated that it gives rise to the rays which dart from the eyes.[13] The disturbance in the sense organ is transmitted to the medium, and from

[8] *De Mus.* vi.5.10–11; *De Ver. Rel.* 79; *Conf.* xi.7.8. *Cf.* James Morgan, *The Psychological Teaching of St. Augustine* (London: Elliot Stock, 1932), p. 130.

[9] *De Mus.* vi.5.10; *De Quant. Anim.* 33.71; *De Lib. Arb.* iii.8.23.

[10] *De Mus.* vi.5.10; *Epist.* 137.6.

[11] *De Gen. ad Litt.* vii.18.24.

[12] *De Quant. Anim.* 33.71, 58; *De Trin., passim.*

[13] *De Mus.* vi.5.10; *De Gen. ad Litt.* vii.20.26.

the medium it is translated by the soul into a non-material *sensation*. This version is then translated back into the medium, and from this it is imposed upon the sense organ from which the impetus first came. A replica of the sensation, as formulated by the soul, is filed for future reference in what St. Augustine calls "the caverns of memory." [14] There are difficulties. If body and soul need a middle-man (*tenuissimi rivuli*), then so will body and middleman, and soul and middleman, and so on, in infinite regress. In any event the *tenuissimi rivuli* can hardly be thought a proper middleman, because the brain to which they come is no less material than the sense organs. The soul is still left face to face with an organ of different substance—if not the eye, then the brain.

Sensations which have been stimulated in, or by, the sense organs, and formulated by the soul working in some way through the brain, are processed by the *sensus interior*. The brains of both men and animals possess this faculty. [15] *Sensus interior* judges whether the several sense organs are operating efficiently. It can combine in-dividual sense impressions to form a composite sensation. Thus sensations of sound and depth may be combined to produce a sensation of great size or depth. [16] The *sensus interior* does much that we might be inclined to attribute to instinct or induction. It distinguishes between the innumerable differences of taste, smell, sound, and shape. It knows what is good, and rejects what is bad, for the body. [17] It relies heavily upon memory: each sound and syllable of a word must be remembered and kept in order if the sensation is to be meaningful. [18] *Sensus interior* seems to draw, or be aware of, analogies; it obviously generalizes, and applies these generalizations in identifying new sensations and in authorizing (or initiating?) responses. But it apparently does this more or less unconsciously, and only to the degree necessary for brute survival.

[14] *De Quant. Anim.* 58; *De Trin.* ii.5.7; xi.2.2–3, 8.14; xiii.1.2; *De Ver. Rel.* 10; *De Anim. et eius Orig.* iv.5.6; *Conf.* x.6.9, 8.13, 10.17.

[15] *De Lib. Arb.* ii.5.12. *Cf.* Meyrick Heath Carré, *Nominalists and Realists* (London and New York: Oxford University Press, 1946), p. 16; Gilson, *Introduction à l'Étude de Saint Augustin*, p. 18.

[16] *De Lib. Arb.* ii.5.12. Carré, *Nominalists and Realists*, p. 15.

[17] *De Quant. Anim.* 33.71.

[18] *De Mus.* vi.8.21. Carré, *Nominalists and Realists*, p. 17; Martin Cyril D'Arcy, "The Philosophy of Saint Augustine," in D'Arcy and others, *A Monument to Saint Augustine* (London: Sheed and Ward, 1930), p. 177.

This theory of the role of the *sensus interior* provides St. Augustine with a tentative explanation of the paradox that while *ex christiana hypothesi* man alone has been given reason, animals seem to have some quasi-reasoning power to learn from experience.

But at best sensation conveys no certain knowledge of the nature of an external reality. Sensations are "true" in the sense that they exist as conditions of the soul; but this is no guarantee of the accuracy of their supposed account of non-self.[19] At most, sensation provides stimulus and material for higher faculties which alone can authenticate the information which it conveys.[20]

Reason, supported by its auxiliary faculties, memory and imagination, is man's highest intellectual power unaided by revelation.

Memory supplies the raw material for the rational process, as it does for the implicit comparisons and generalizations of *sensus interior.*[21] Replicas of any and every condition of the soul (i.e., sensations, thoughts) are stored up. First, there are replicas of sensations. The incorporeal nature of the replicas is shown in the fact that pictures of great cities and high mountains are retained in the narrow confines of the human organism.[22] Second, there are replicas of the products of imagination and of reason itself. Third, there is the contribution of revelation. This consists not of replicas but of universal and eternal ideas revealed in the soul itself through divine illumination. These are present in the soul, and when once they have been discovered they can be inspected repeatedly.[23]

Information gained by the soul is handed over to memory; later it can be summoned for re-examination, consciously and discriminately.[24] The objects of memory vary in vividness. Some are made more vivid by repetition, others by association, whether

[19] *Contra Acad.* iii.11.26; *cf. De Trin.* xi.3.6.

[20] *De Gen. ad Litt.* xii.5.14; *De Quant. Anim.* 22; *Epist.* 13.4; *De Mag.* 12.39; *De Immort. Anim.* 6.10. *Materia pura* could not impinge directly upon the sense organs; see *Conf.* xii.3–5.3–5. For creation *ex nihilo,* see *Conf.* xi.5.7; xii.7–8.7–8.

[21] *Conf.* x.11.18. *S.I.* immediately precedes *M.* in hierarchy of powers.

[22] *De Trin.* xi.8.14; *De Doctr. Christ.* ii.27.41, 30.47; *Conf.* x.14.21, 16.25f.; *De Ver. Rel.* 10.

[23] *Conf.* x.8.12–14, 12.19. *Cf.* Montgomery, *St. Augustine,* p. 119. Emotions are not re-experienced, but their replicas can be dispassionately examined; see Morgan, *Psychological Teaching of St. Augustine,* pp. 204–205.

[24] *De Trin.* xv.21.40.

through contiguity or through similarity. The soul can summon particular replicas, or Ideas in the Platonic sense, and still be aware of their places in series. This will to remember something cannot arise if the memory has completely faded.[25]

Imagination uses remembered material to construct new images, which may (but need not) correspond to pre-existing ones. If I have seen white swans, I may "imagine" swans like the ones which I have seen. Or I may garble memories, and picture a black swan, or a bird with four legs, or without a head. Hence the comment that imagination has "a certain faculty of subtracting or adding." The operation may be voluntary, or involuntary as in the case of hallucination.[26] Despite the fact that it manufactures counters useful in higher thought, by visualizing numbers, measures, Ideas, literary characters and plots, and so on, St. Augustine is inclined to think of imagination as above all a disturber of data and a creator of illusions.[27] Its primitive character is shown in the fact that we share it with animals. He seems to recognize neither its essential role in all inductive generalizations nor the possibility that it not merely visualizes but creates the numbers, measures and Ideas elsewhere supposed to be created and revealed by God, in the same way that it is responsible for black swans and four-legged birds.

Discursive reasoning is our mode of dealing with the material made available by sensation, the interior sense, memory, and imagination. It springs from an act of will, and is to the soul what vision is to the eye—and no closer to objective certainty. Discursive reason generalizes, leaping from specific instances to general principles; it tests its own generalizations, rejecting some and keeping others for its purposes; it identifies sensations by applying generalizations to them; by the use of its generalizations it reconstructs the past and prognosticates the future.[28]

---

[25] *De Trin.* xi.7.12; xiv.13.17; *Conf.* x.19.29; *De Mus.* vi.8.22; *De Quant. Anim.* 62, 72. (Sister) Mary Patricia Garvey, *Saint Augustine, Christian or Neo-Platonist?* (Milwaukee: Marquette University Press, 1939), p. 193.

[26] *De Mus.* vi.11.32; *Epist.* 7; *De Trin.* xi.8.14, 10.17. For comment on delirium and "second sight," see *De Gen. ad Litt.* xii.17.35.

[27] *Epist.* 7; *Conf.* x.8.14; *Solil.* ii.11.20, magna cautione vitandae.

[28] *De Quant. Anim.* 52–53; *De Ord.* ii.12.30; *De Trin.* ix.6.9; xii.2.2; *Conf.* x.40.65; *Solil.* i.6.12. Carré, *Nominalists and Realists*, p. 7; Gilson, *Introduction à l'Étude de Saint Augustin*, p. 101; Morgan, *Psychological Teaching of St. Augustine*, p. 160.

The point of immediate interest is St. Augustine's distrust of the discursive reason. For him it has serious limitations. We use it not because it is accurate but because it is the way in which our minds naturally work. But reason cannot give us certainty. Nor can it show us purpose, and therefore meaning and significance, in life as a whole.[29] Its generalizations are never more than patterns in the specific groups of particular instances where they have been observed, and they lack the universal and eternal character which St. Augustine, following Plato, thinks that truth must possess. The universal and eternal Forms of Man, Red, Triangularity, and so on, cannot be discovered by this process of observation, comparison, and abstraction, because nothing that we observe can be seen by us to be universal or eternal. The discursive reason searches; but something more is needed to find, and know.[30] But apart from this limitation, even within its own limited field reason cannot draw conclusions more reliable than the unreliable sensory evidence with which it must work. It is a stream which cannot meander higher than its source.

A modern skeptic would agree completely that the "knowledge" which is the final product of sensation and reason is at most hypothetical. But he is likely to train his fire not upon the sensory evidence but upon fundamental weakness in the reasoning process itself. Whatever the quality of the evidence with which it works, this weakness renders all its conclusions and judgments tentative. This is evident in the empirical, deductive, and social sciences, and equally so in the province of common sense.

In all conscious thought there is an invincible tendency to generalize, most plainly seen in the empirical sciences. Let any unknown impetus (A, B, or C) to a new state in the stream of consciousness be called a sensation. Let each new state in the stream of consciousness (x, y, and so on) be a quality of sensation (with x^1, x^2, and so on, as states differing little, if at all, from x); and let any subsequent state (α, for instance) or states of the stream of consciousness, for which some observed quality of a sensation seems to be a pre-

[29] *Conf.* x.11.18; *De Ord.* i.1.2; *In Johan. Evang.* 99.4; *De Mor. Eccl. Cath.* 7.11.

[30] *De Quant. Anim.* 52–53; *De Gen. ad Litt.* xii.31.59. Carré, *Nominalists and Realists*, p. 26; D'Arcy, in D'Arcy and others, *Monument to Saint Augustine*, p. 130; Gilson, *Introduction à l'Étude de Saint Augustin*, p. 103.

requisite, be called the sequel of that sensation. Imagine a sensation A, with quality x, and sequel α. Imagine next a sensation B, with quality x^1. The mind is struck by a sense of familiarity. It argues a complete from a partial likeness, and by an act of imagination assumes that Bx^1 is, or will be, followed by α. If this faith proves justified, then when a sensation C displays the quality x^2, the mental machinery leaps the more readily to the conclusion that α will follow. A given generalization, that a sensation with quality x, x^1, or x^2, and so on, will be followed by the sequel α, may be based upon one, five, or five hundred instances.

Obviously there is a large element of risk. The quality x may not have been necessary to the appearance of α. We do not know how, if at all, x^1 and x^2 differ from x and from each other, or how these differences may affect the sequel. Furthermore, there may be other sequels unnoted by us, but more important empirically to us than α. But as the number of successful identifications and predictions increases, the more confident (perhaps quasi-mechanical) becomes the imaginative extrapolation of the generalization, although the element of risk will never be eliminated.[31]

Explanation, prediction, and confirmation involve what is substantially the same *modus operandi*. From observation of $Ax\alpha$, $Bx^1\alpha$, and $Cx^2\alpha$, we generalize that a sensation with the quality x, x^1, x^2, and so on, will be followed by the sequel α. A new situation, α, will be *explained* as having followed upon a sensation with quality x, x^1, or the like, because such a sensation is always (according to the generalization) followed by α, and α (one hopefully assumes) is always preceded by such a sensation. It is possible that the sequence was purely coincidental, in this and in every case known to us. But rightly or wrongly, we are likely to explain α by a formula, Dx^3-*followed-by*-α, assuming that α must have been preceded by Dx^3 or its like, with the latter circumstance making the former in some way inevitable. In *prediction* the emphasis is upon the effect to be expected of given conditions. If we are confronted with a sensation E with quality x^4, we conclude, by applying our rule, that the sequel α will follow. In *testing* the generalization, we watch for such new sensations as Fx^5 and Gx^6, and so on. If we find them followed by α, we consider that the generalization has been strengthened. Explanation,

[31] Morris Raphael Cohen and Ernest Nagel, *Introduction to Logic and Scientific Method* (2nd ed.; Madison: Harcourt Brace, 1949), pp. 267–268, 277.

prediction, and confirmation can be closely associated. Gardiner notes that the behavior of the planet Uranus seemed, in light of certain astronomical generalizations, to imply the existence of another planet, and in a sense predicted the discovery of another planet. The actual discovery of Neptune explained the behavior of Uranus, verified the prediction, and confirmed the relevent generalizations.[32]

All generalization depends upon imagination, which falls short of knowledge.[33] There is no way of proving that one is generalizing upon "similarities" (general likenesses with minor differentiation) rather than upon "analogies" (major differences with superficial likenesses). In any event, all generalization implies an act of imagination.[34] The procedures of natural science are described in inductive logic. One makes observations, notes uniformities, and extrapolates these into unknown territory, explaining the unknown in terms of the known. According to Carnap, all concepts of empirical science are founded upon remembrance of similarity between moments of direct experience. Nothing has significance which cannot be brought into some familiar context. Knowledge is the perception that two propositions do, or do not, agree. Each man, in his scientific aspect, assumes that nature repeats herself frequently and closely enough to make comparative studies worth while.[35] When he does not see

---

[32] Patrick L. Gardiner, *The Nature of Historical Explanation* (London: Oxford University Press, 1952), pp. 1–2.

[33] Daniel Heinsius, *The Value of History*, trans. by G. W. Robinson from the edition of 1613 (Cambridge, Mass.: privately printed, 1943); F. Gundolf, "Historiography," in Raymond Klibansky and Herbert James Paton (eds.), *Philosophy and History. Essays presented to E. Cassirer* (Oxford: Clarendon Press, 1936), pp. 8–9.

[34] Gardiner, *Nature of Historical Explanation*, pp. 130–131; Cohen and Nagel, *Introduction to Logic and Scientific Method*, p. 326; Robin George Collingwood, *The Idea of History* (Oxford: Clarendon Press, 1946), pp. 247, 269–270.

[35] Collingwood, *Idea of History*, pp. 223, 234, 250; Rudolf Carnap, *Der Logische Aufbau der Welt* (Berlin-Schlachtensee: Weltkreis-Verlag, 1928), cited by Lizzie Susan Stebbing, *Logical Positivism and Analysis* (London: Humphrey Milford, 1933), p. 25; John Hick, *Faith and Knowledge. A Modern Introduction to the Problem of Religious Knowledge* (Ithaca, N.Y.: Cornell University Press, 1957), p. 118; Werner Heisenberg, *Physics and Philosophy. The Revolution in Modern Science* (New York: Harper, 1959), p. 77; William Henry Walsh, *An Introduction to the Philosophy of History* (London and New York: Hutchinson's University Library, 1951), p. 52.

coherence in a mass of material, he tries to read coherence into it by means of *a priori* hypotheses. He *assumes* certain uniformities, and then tests to see if experience will bear him out. Unamenable facts are then explained by other assumptions, and common ground is sought on which the various assumptions can be shown to be consistent with one another and so to form a system. There is a more or less constant appeal from the hypotheses to the experiential evidence. If many facts escape the net of these *a priori* explanations, the scientist concludes that the latter were ill chosen. He cuts his losses and looks for new assumptions to test.[36] Our logical conclusions may turn out to have been concretely justified in specific cases; but the induction itself is a leap in the dark. Inductive generalization is our way, successful or not, of dealing with the unknown on the basis of a calculated risk. It is less risky when we regard it as pointing not to certainties but only to more or less likely possibilities. In most cases the generalizing process is probably unconscious. One can only hope that one's mental machinery is subtle enough to be jolted into skeptical restraint by very small signals of difficulty in identifying, explaining, or predicting circumstances, and that our miscalculations will not prove too costly.[37]

Scientific classification of uniformities involves limitation of prospective. If chemistry seems more precise than practical farming, and practical farming than the art of government, this is not due to a fundamental difference in the experiential stuff, which may be the same in all three cases. The various sciences represent three different approaches to what may be the same material. If they see different things, they are in the position of men whose eyes are such that they see different patterns in a single color chart. Each man notes only "certain selected invariant relations of things." A scientific law deals *only* with certain aspects of situations. A scientist combining hydrogen and oxygen to form water cannot let himself be distracted by questions relating to how the glass in his test tubes was formed,

[36] Gaetano Salvemini, *Historian and Scientist. An Essay on the Nature of History and the Social Sciences* (Cambridge, Mass.: Harvard University Press, 1939), p. 77; Cohen and Nagel, *Introduction to Logic and Scientific Method*, pp. 39–40; William Kluback, *Wilhelm Dilthey's Philosophy of History* (New York: Columbia University Press, 1956), p. 52.

[37] Cohen and Nagel, *Introduction to Logic and Scientific Method*, p. 14; Salvemini, *Historian and Scientist*, p. 76; Karl Raimund Popper, *The Poverty of Historicism* (London: Routledge and Kegan Paul, 1957), pp. 134–135; 138.

or to the religious and political significance of water in the Jordan and Ganges rivers. To take all factors, in any way relevant, into account, if this were possible, would be to classify the unique and to formulate a law for a single instance, which would be absurd.

But with the deductive sciences we may seem to attain precision. Deduction is a sort, or degree, of induction from which the risks have been eliminated. Suppose that every sensation with the quality x, x^1, or the like, *must* be followed by the sequel α: suppose, further, that sensation H has the quality x^7: then sensation Hx^7 must be followed by the sequel α. Whatever else may be said of this syllogism, it is a tautology. The second term is included in the first, and the third is included in the first and second. "All men in this room are white: John is a man in this room: therefore John is white." This seems airtight, and so it is, if the first and second terms are really correct. But have all men in the room, including John, been correctly identified as such? Are there other objects in the room, which on other grounds might have been identified as men, had they not lacked the color deemed essential? We are safe only as long as we stick to symbols, and avoid translating the symbols in terms of empirical phenomena. Two plus two equal four; but in the phenomenological field two spiders plus two are likely to leave *one*. Mathematics is a logico-deductive affair, a game in which certain conclusions inevitably follow *if certain indemonstrable propositions are true*. "All men are white: John is a man: therefore John is white." This is simply induction minus a caveat, assuming without question that the first and second propositions are objectively true.[38] In the deductive sciences we stick to our premises, right or wrong; and that is true which follows from them. We proceed from indemonstrable assumptions to conclusions unanchored in time and space. Deductive systems remain abstract. We do not know the precise range or degree of their applicability to the phenomenal world— which is not to affirm that they convey no useful *hints* and serve no useful purpose.[39]

In the field of the social sciences there are factors which seem

[38] Cohen and Nagel, *Introduction to Logic and Scientific Method*, pp. 7–8, 133.
[39] Collingwood, *Idea of History*, pp. 4, 25, 234; Heisenberg, *Physics and Philosophy*, pp. 83–84; Stebbing, *Logical Positivism and Analysis*, pp. 26–27; Bertrand Russell, *The Analysis of Mind* (London: Allen and Unwin, 1921), p. 104.

constant enough to permit generalization, although the statistical basis may be decidedly narrower than in the case of chemistry.[40] If astronomers can predict eclipses, sociologists can and do predict revolutions. The probability quotient is lower with the sociologist, because he admits more factors as directly relevant, and because he has studied fewer revolutions than astronomers have eclipses.[41] Neither can speak with absolute assurance of particular instances. The natural scientist cannot tell, by applying generalizations, exactly what a particular toad, biological cell, or atom will do.[42] He can say only that there are 499 chances to one that the toad, cell, or atom will behave in such and such a way. For the sociologist, the odds in favor of revolution in Peru by 1970 may be a miserable four to five—though still high enough to warrant the attention of Peruvian statesmen. If he reduces his prospective from revolution *in toto* to some more limited and easily controlled facet of the subject, he can achieve chemical if not quite mathematical precision. Thus the odds are perhaps 499 to one that *if* revolution breaks out in Peru by 1970 the leader will be in the under-eighty age group—and perhaps 1,000,000,000 to one that he will be under one hundred and ten!

Common sense is shown in swift, quasi-mechanical decisions. These are taken by applying "extra-ordinarily successful hypotheses" which have been justified in the long experience of the individual or of the race. Science differs from common sense by self-consciously and deliberately making and applying generalizations. Common sense involves little or no deliberation, and has no significant interest in the background of the generalizations, or in the testing which these automatically receive in each application. When common sense becomes self-conscious and cautious, it ceases to be mere common sense and becomes science.[43] Common sense has a less conscious grasp of the generalization, and of the particular to which it is applied. It uses words whose associations are likely to

[40] Salvemini, *Historian and Scientist*, p. 7.

[41] *Cf.* Popper, *Poverty of Historicism*, pp. 36–37.

[42] Cohen and Nagel, *Introduction to Logic and Scientific Method*, p. 279; *cf.* Russell, *Analysis of Mind*, pp. 104–107, 303; Herbert Arthur Hodges, *Wilhelm Dilthey. An Introduction* (London: K. Paul, Trench, Trubner, 1944), p. 318.

[43] Cohen and Nagel, *Introduction to Logic and Scientific Method*, p. 394; Gardiner, *Nature of Historical Explanation*, pp. 16–21.

be vague and variable.[44] But in practice, the time-tested precepts of common sense are likely to work very well.[45] They tend to be causal in the classical sense, picking out factors which will precipitate, prevent, or terminate some state of affairs. Some persons describe common sense as philosophy "somewhat hurried and hardened by practical needs," and science as "organized common sense." This is true enough, in the sense that all three employ what is basically the same psychological *modus operandi*.[46]

Neither science nor common sense claims to be infallible. A scientific hypothesis is got by abstracting certain specific factors from broader contexts, and it states how these factors are likely to behave and what they imply. There is no attempt to sum up all the interrelations of all the factors in any given situation in a single causal statement. "Insistence on the postulates of a complete logical clarification would make science impossible."[47] The words *position* and *velocity*, *i.e.*, of electrons, seemed within the Newtonian framework to have some permanent significance. But in light of the quantum theory, no physical or geometrical picture of phenomena can be identified with the "real" nature of things. Physical concepts may manage to "save the appearances," without themselves having the same kind of physical reality as the phenomena. But their correlation with an objective nature can never be defined precisely. Nor can we know in advance whether nor not our generalizations may seem less applicable as our acquaintance with nature is extended. Sometimes concepts will seem in retrospect to have been unjustified, though they may have seemed reasonable at one time.[48] Scientific laws which are empirically verifiable are only approximate; if they are exact, they are not empirically verifiable.[49] Temperamental

[44] *Ibid.*, pp. 6f., 23, 63; Gustaaf Johannes Renier, *History, Its Purpose and Method* (London: Allen and Unwin, 1950), pp. 142–143; Walsh, *Introduction to the Philosophy of History*, pp. 63–64.

[45] Gardiner, *Nature of Historical Explanation*, pp. 11, 25.

[46] *Ibid.*, pp. 5, 11, 16–17.

[47] Heisenberg, *Physics and Philosophy*, pp. 78–79.

[48] *Ibid.*; Walsh, *Introduction to the Philosophy of History*, p. 36; Maurice H. Mandelbaum, "Can There be a Philosophy of History?" in *American Scholar*, IX, 1 (1940), p. 76; Cohen and Nagel, *Introduction to Logic and Scientific Method*, pp. 132–133; Eric Lionel Mascall, *Christian Theology and Natural Science. Some Questions in Their Relations* (London: Longmans, 1956), p. 59.

[49] Bertrand Russell, *Mysticism and Logic, and Other Essays* (New York: Longmans Green, 1918), p. 197; Collingwood, *Idea of History*, p. 254.

Platonists fancy that in the tautologies of mathematics they have hold of certainties which can deliver them from the horrors of universal doubt. But pure science and mathematics are not directly concerned with whether or not their axioms are concretely true of the phenomenal world of our experience. Deduction explores the logical implications, not the phenomenological basis, if any, of generalizations. Mathematical truths are "true" only in the sense that they follow from premises which the mathematician arbitrarily agrees to accept as true.

Whether because of the relativity of sensory evidence, or because of the element of risk in all generalization, one can agree whole-heartedly with St. Augustine that sensation and reason together afford no *knowledge*, recognizable as such, of the world of appearances.

2. DIVINE REVELATION

We entertain certain propositions which in St. Augustine's opinion could spring neither from sensation nor from reason. He attributes them to divine revelation, which we can regard as one of several plausible hypotheses.

The ideas which St. Augustine attributes to revelation are the very ones which count for most in his interpretation of history. In the first place, *there is a world order, in which every circumstance has a predestined place.* This determinism is expressed in Christian terms. An omnipotent God created all things visible and invisible, and no single event stands outside His divine plan.[50] Second, although all external events are predetermined, *we can choose, up to a point, how we shall interpret and react to the inevitable.*[51] If we can accept this as consistent with the foregoing determinism, then we will have allowed some scope for free will. Third, *the most important thing in life is that a man should adopt, or be brought to adopt, the right attitude toward the world of experience.* Every blessing will follow the man who is ideologically sound. This theory may lead to missionary work, and this in turn, where feasible, to benevolent efforts at thought control. The agents of the latter, with the most kindly intention, may come to see value, at times, in paternal coercion. In

[50] *De Doctr. Christ.* i.22.20; *Solil.*, i.1.3; *Conf.* x.41.66; *De Trin.* xii.4.4.

[51] See below, p. 150. *Cf.* Seneca's remark, ducunt volentem fata, nolentem trahunt.

the fourth place, *all revealed propositions will find support in the Canonical Scriptures.* This suggests, nor is the suggestion belied, that supposed evidence will, if necessary, be forced to support an *a priori* interpretation.[52] In the fifth place, *there are certain laws of universal and eternal scope.* These include the (Platonic) Forms of entities and patterns of processes, the laws of mathematics, and certain moral principles.[53] The laws of social and economic change are implicitly included. Our observations and inductions point the way to this intelligible world by showing us caricatures and approximations, but the universal and eternal scope of these principles could never be learned from observation or induction, and suggests a higher source. These patterns or laws or Forms are not simply the bright ideas of men, to be tried and tested. They are ideas existing in the mind of God, finding expression in the visible world when and to the extent that He wills.[54]

These and other truths, in St. Augustine's opinion, first came to men by revelation, and may be revealed afresh to any one of us. But to most of us they come indirectly by what amounts to hearsay, and like inductive propositions they must simply be taken on faith. But he is certain of the truth of some few of his beliefs, and since neither sensation nor reason seem to him to justify certainty, he assumes that this *psychological certitude comes from God.*[55] This assumption, that if one is sure of something one must be right, may have been safe in the hands of St. Augustine, who seems to have been sure of very little; but it can be adduced to lend blanket support to any subjective dogmatism.

[52] *De Fide Quae non Videntur* 2.

[53] *De Quant. Anim.* 22–23; *De Immort. Anim.* 17; *cf. Conf.* x.12.19. Carré, *Nominalists and Realists*, p. 30.

[54] *De Lib. Arb.* ii.15.39, 16.42, 16.44; *De Div. Quaest.* 83.46; *De Quant. Anim.* 5. *Cf.* Morgan, *Psychological Teaching of St. Augustine*, p. 72; D'Arcy, in D'Arcy and others, *Monument to Saint Augustine*, p. 168; Prosper Alfaric, *L'Évolution Intellectuelle de St. Augustin* (Paris: Nourry, 1918), p. 462; Dom Edward Cuthbert Butler, *Western Mysticism* (2nd ed.; London: Constable, 1951), p. 38; Étienne Henri Gilson, "The Future of Augustinian Metaphysics," in D'Arcy and others, *Monument to Saint Augustine*, p. 297, and *Introduction à l'Étude de Saint Augustin*, p. 110.

[55] *Conf.* vi.4.6; x.40.65; *De Lib. Arb.* ii.2.4, 8.22–23; *Contra Acad.* iii.11.25. D'Arcy, in D'Arcy and others, *Monument to Saint Augustine*, p. 182; Vernon Joseph Bourke, *Augustine's Quest of Wisdom* (Milwaukee: Bruce, 1945), p. 117.

As for the mechanics of revelation, in works written shortly after his conversion he seems sympathetic to the Platonic doctrine of reminiscence. Gilson believes that at this stage he was thinking in a Platonic way, although no text precisely affirms the pre-existence of the soul.[56] Man is said to recognize "instinctively" the "meaning" of sun, moon, and stars by "looking within" rather than relying upon sensation and abstraction. The Ideas can only be fully grasped with the help of our "Maître interieur," "la Verité cachée au plus fond de notre âme."[57] But later, St. Augustine says that it is not to be inferred from these early statements that, in his considered judgment, the soul brings knowledge forward from a previous existence.[58]

God reveals his truth to those who see it, rather than merely hear about it, in various ways. In some cases, like that of Abraham, men are instructed by angels who come in human form and deliver oral messages.[59] This is a straightforward way to convey ideas, but may leave the recipient in doubt as to whether his visitor was really an angel. In other cases, the revelation is insinuated into the stream of consciousness by beings of aërial or etherial nature, who can pass into and through our bodies, deliberately playing upon our physical apparatus so as to affect our thought processes.[60] In other cases, perhaps in most, truth comes through *divine illumination*. The recipient may become assured of the truth of some proposition which he has already entertained, or encountered through sensation (*e.g.*, by reading) or reason. Or he may be brought to recognize some idea already dimly present in his thought, or implicit in it; or he may see universal and eternal implications in some generalization heretofore tied to the specific particulars from which it was abstracted. The Platonic Ideas, or Forms, are cases in point. This illumination

[56] *De Quant. Anim.* 20.34; *Solil.* ii.20.35; *Epist.* 7. Gilson, *Introduction à l'Étude de Saint Augustin*, p. 94; Morgan, *Psychological Teaching of St. Augustine*, p. 22; Montgomery, *St. Augustine*, p. 126; Garvey, *Saint Augustine, Christian or Neo-Platonist?* p. 153.

[57] *De Mag.* 10.32; *De Ver. Rel.* 72. Henri Irénée Marrou, *S. Augustin et la Fin de la Culture Antique* (Paris: Boccard, 1938), p. 292.

[58] *Retract.* i.3.2. *Cf.* Garvey, *Saint Augustine, Christian or Neo-Platonist?* p. 159.

[59] *De Civ. D.* xi.4.1; xvi.6.1.

[60] *Epist.* 9.3.

is made by an Interior Light which either comes from, or is, God.[61]

Neither psychological certitude nor the propositions cited above could spring, St. Augustine thinks, from sensation or from reasoning upon sensory evidence. No man sees God creating the world, much less bringing the historical process to a foreordained conclusion. No man can grasp the universal plan by induction, because the historical process is unique and does not lend itself to the making or applying of generalizations. Free will is a hypothesis which can be defended or attacked. Every event in the world of experience is *not obviously* the expression of a wise and loving purpose. The Canonical Scriptures, and notably the Old Testament, do not give *obvious* support throughout to the Christian interpretation of experience. Laws assumed to hold universally and eternally are not shown by eternal and universal observation to do so. If these ideas cannot spring from our experience, where do they come from?

One may believe, *in faith*, that they come by divine revelation. One may prefer to attribute them, in faith, to intuition or to the operations of the subconscious mind.

Many persons use the diploma word *intuitive* to confer authority upon various propositions of obscure origin. Once canonized as intuitive, these are taken to embody naked truth, superior to the dull stuff assembled by plodders content to make do with the fruit of sensation and reason. Intuition in this sense is used to sanctify all sorts of guesses and bright ideas: the relationship of the part to the whole, secret motivations, "the inside story," the meaning of history,[62] and other mysteries too deep for those who prefer to base their conclusions upon conscious induction. The hypothesis that one may have immediate perceptions of truth is no easier to defend from a purely rational point of view than the theory of divine revelation. In either case one is moving on a different plane from reason. Revelation, or intuition, is a way of getting information beyond the

[61] *De Trin.* xiv.15.21; *De Div. Quaest.* 83.1–2; *De Gen. ad Litt.* xii.31. Gilson, *Introduction à l'Étude de Saint Augustin*, p. 61; D'Arcy, in D'Arcy and others, *Monument to Saint Augustine*, p. 181; Butler, *Western Mysticism*, p. 54.

[62] Popper, *Poverty of Historicism*, pp. 20–21; Russell, *Mysticism and Logic*, pp. 14–15; Douglas Clyde Macintosh, *The Problem of Religious Knowledge* (New York: Harper, 1940), p. 5.

province of reason and therefore not subject to reason's authentication.

Others prefer to think that all thoughts have their origin in sensation and reason, but that a very great deal of the process is beneath the level of consciousness. The Freudians sometimes seem to visualize the subconscious as a chained, ravening beast. Others less picturesquely see it as an unconscious tendency of the human organism toward certain courses of physical or mental activity, conditioned by behavior, temporarily thwarted by other and stronger tendencies, always as ready to express itself as water to find its level, but no more "conscious" in any way than water. Freudian "censorship," in this view, is simply the momentary triumph of the fat man over the thin in a narrow doorway, or of the levee over the flood. The "frustrated" impulses, which sometimes "break out," are depersonified,[63] and "subconscious thinking" seems to be a more or less mechanical process. Some thoughts which appear in the stream of consciousness, and which have no obvious connection with *conscious* experience, may simply be eruptions from this subterranean world. Eruption may be explained in terms of association and habit.

After it has been in any way stimulated, an organism enters upon a new equilibrium, and the difference between its earlier and later stages is called an engram. An engram is the product not just of an isolated stimulus, but of *all the stimuli at a given time*. The repetition of *some* of the stimuli may, by association, precipitate repetition of the whole engram. Responses with pleasant outcomes are more likely to be repeated. Semen thinks that engrams can be inherited.[64] He does not say that the engram is in substance a material alteration, but the fact that brain lesions disturb memory gives some support to this view, which Russell tends to favor on the basis of analogies and general scientific maxims. Habitual knowledge is a matter of acquired habits of response. If we are asked the capital of France, we reply "Paris," because of past conditioning. We learn to speak, write, do mathematics, and govern empires in the same way that a rat learns to find its way out of a maze.[65] Ordinarily we are not

[63] Russell, *Mysticism and Logic*, pp. 31–34, 37–38.
[64] Russell, *Analysis of Mind*, pp. 53, 80–86.
[65] *Ibid.*, 52–53, 77, 79–80, 85.

conscious of applying general laws in our continual judgments upon daily circumstances, but proceed in this way by habit.[66]

Instinct seems to have affinities with both the physical and the mental, and suggests a certain mechanical common denominator between the two. Instinctive reactions, especially in their first appearances in an individual's behavior pattern, seem to be independent of the individual's past experience, tend to the physical well-being of the individual and the preservation of the species, and are the same in all members of the species. These earliest instinctive reactions seem to follow a principle like that shown in physical growth. Plants and animals grow into extremely complicated yet predictable shapes, without conscious thought and in accordance with some natural law of their organisms. On the other hand, the higher we rise in the evolutionary scale, the greater is our power of modifying instinctive reactions, consciously and deliberately, in the light of personal experience; and this suggests a close relationship between what we perhaps superficially distinguish as mechanical and thoughtful operations respectively. In practice, it is very hard to distinguish between what one does by instinct and what one does as the result of a process of learning. James, but certainly not every psychologist, thinks that children walk and birds fly by instinct, when they have reached a certain age. Even in the case of so obviously acquired a habit as speech, some instinct toward making sounds seems needed to get the educational process under way. One might say that in the case of more delicate mechanisms, like man, instinctive and virtually mechanical processes are honed and refined by experience into "thoughtful" activity, whereas in the lower animals and plants instinct is, and remains, crude, aimed at the usual, and easily confused by unusual circumstances.[67]

Conscious thoughts believed by some to have a subconscious origin have much in common with those which Newman thought

[66] Gardiner, *Nature of Historical Explanation*, pp. 25–26, says that when we are told that X has slipped on a banana peel, we understand the situation not by applying general laws about banana peels, but from our familiarity with situations of a certain sort, i.e., from "habitual response." But "habitual response" is in itself a matter of applying general rules to particular situations, and Gardiner's instance suggests only how mechanical the process can become.

[67] Russell, *Analysis of Mind*, pp. 50–51, 54; 14–15, citing Henri Bergson, *Introduction to Metaphysics*, trans. by Thomas Ernest Hulme (New York and London: Putnam, 1912), pp. 2, 6, 8.

must be held on "illative faith." According to Newman, one surveys a large field of evidence, and by an unconscious sorting process makes generalizations. There is no conscious induction here—how often is there?—but the results are of the order which one might expect from a conscious consideration of the evidence. The "illative" process resembles in its mechanical quality the operation of an electric letter-sorter.[68]

Some may think that ideas attributed to the subconscious operations of the mind should not be thought in the same category as those attributed by St. Augustine to divine revelation. Both sets may have in common the fact that neither set seems to have been *consciously* derived by reason from experience. Do they perhaps differ in that the allegedly revealed thoughts could never, whether consciously or unconsciously, have been derived from experience? But a similar going beyond experience is implicit in every act of induction. When I assume that what is true of two cats will hold for others, and when I assume that a third and unseen cat possesses the quality in question, I am leaping from the seen to the unseen; and whether I extend the generalization to cover one unseen cat, or five, or every cat which I or anyone else will ever encounter in time and space, I have formulated a thought which is beyond my experience. It is also possible, as St. Augustine himself admits, for the imagination to garble evidence, mixing memories to produce such pictures as "black swan" and "four-legged bird," which are certainly not *experienced* but which nevertheless arise out of experience. Every identification of an object or process, and every acceptance and application of a generalization, involves the same passage from the seen to the unseen, and could equally well be attributed by St. Augustine to divine revelation. Indeed in a sense he does this, in his doctrine that God made us what we are and gave us such mental capacities as we possess. If he sees reason to doubt, as he does, what God reveals in the ordinary way of induction, why a greater confidence in what God reveals no more miraculously by means of angels, demonic insinuations into our thought processes, and divine illumination?

Concepts attributed on one hypothesis to divine revelation, on

[68] John Henry Newman, *An Essay in Aid of a Grammar of Assent* (London: Burns, Oates, 1870), cited on this point by Hick, *Faith and Knowledge*, p. 96.

another to the operations mechanical or otherwise of the sub-conscious mind, have two things in common. It cannot be shown that they were consciously drawn by reason from experience—and they are even more liable to dispute, in the light of subsequent experience, than those drawn by straightforward conscious in-duction. Many "intuitive truths" later seem to have been halluci-natory. It seems, too, that psychology has become a more useful science since it gave up "intuitive insights" for "scientific re-searches." [69] Dogmas attributed by some persons to divine revelation may, and often do, seem unsatisfactory, implausible, disingenuous, or impious to others, who make their own claims to possessing revealed truth. It will generally be found more useful to employ what wits we have than to identify sudden brainstorms with moments of truth. A rational piety might suggest that we confine the term *divine* revelation to what comes to us through the more, rather than the less, reliable medium.

3. BELIEF

We believe a proposition if we are willing to act on the assumption that it is true. We can believe with varying degrees of faith, ranging from tepid and doubtful acceptance to something falling just short of certainty. If we are certain, then in our own opinion at least we no longer merely believe but know. But St. Augustine is aware that we know very little. We live for the most part according to beliefs held in faith, and this is no less true of religious than of secular assumptions. Belief in this sense, whether in relativity or in revela-tion, has in St. Augustine's opinion two chief props, authority and plausibility, although we will later suggest that the argument from authority is really only a special instance of the argument from plausibility. [70]

[69] Russell, *Mysticism and Logic*, p. 16: our "intuitive knowledge" of those whom we love is notoriously shaky. Walsh, *Introduction to the Philosophy of History*, p. 45.

[70] *De Util. Cred.* 25, nam in alio vitae actu, prorsus nescio quo pacto possit homo nihil credere. quamquam in illis etiam qui se in agendo probabilia sequi dicunt, scire possem, quam nihil credere, votunt videre. quis enim probat non credit ? Hick, *Faith and Knowledge*, pp. 31–32; Cohen and Nagel, *Introduction to Logic and Scientific Method*, p. 157. For basis of authority in plausibility, see below, p. 187.

At this point we shall take them to be two arguments, and even follow St. Augustine in giving authority the pride of place. He assumes that authority is the normal basis of belief. Our opinions and rules of conduct in nearly every situation are taken on authority, and conveyed to us through sensation, *i.e.*, hearing or vision. We begin by trusting the word of parents and teachers. We rely upon hearsay for our personal history, including the identity of our fathers. We accept what we hear, or read, about geography and history. We gamble upon the good faith and good will of our supposed friends. Beliefs *de rerum natura* are usually taken on authority.[71] The almost universal hope of personal survival after death is supported only by pronouncements which it is hoped are authoritative, and not by experience.[72] Reliance upon authority is a universal phenomenon. St. Augustine can conceive of men living without intellectual certainty, but not without this willingness to trust authority.[73]

In the religious field, it is not surprising to find St. Augustine impressed by the authority of the Holy Catholic Church, an authority which leads men to take seriously the beliefs which she professes. Her prestige arises, he thinks, from the memory of the great councils which established her doctrines; from the sanctity of sees founded by the Apostles and presumed to preserve their teachings in pristine purity; from the apologetical efforts of great theologians who have helped to make her creed seem intellectually plausible; from the miracles recorded of her saints; from the number and ubiquity of her adherents; from her hope of immortal happiness; from her demonstration of love; from her antiquity and continuity shown in the succession of bishops and priests, especially in the apostolic Roman see; and from the very name "Catholic" which

---

[71] *De Ord.* ii.9.26; *De Ver. Rel.* 7.13; *Contra Acad.* iii.20.43; *Conf.* i.6.10, 8.13; *De Fide Rerum Quae non Videntur* 2,4; *De Civ. D.* xix.22; *De Cons. Evang.* i.22.30; *Ennar. in Ps.* 8.5; 10.3; *Serm.* 43.1; *In Johan. Evang.* 40.9; 79.1; *De Fide Spe Car.* 7.20; *De Util. Cred.* 26. D'Arcy, in D'Arcy and others, *Monument to Saint Augustine*, pp. 159–160; Gilson, *Introduction à l'Étude de Saint Augustin*, p. 31; Alfaric, *Évolution Intellectuelle de Saint Augustin*, pp. 472–473. *Cf.* Montgomery, *St. Augustine*, p. 48, and Morgan, *Psychological Teaching of St. Augustine*, p. 59.

[72] *De Trin.* xiii.9.12.

[73] *De Util. Cred.* 25, 26, 33–35; *De Ord.* ii.9.26. *Cf.* Henri Xavier Arquillière, *L'Augustinisme Politique* (Paris: Vrin, 1934), p. 28.

she retains in the teeth of heresy and schism. Her successes urge adherence, and caution one against the arrogance which would reject her help.[74] He says, "I would not believe the Gospel unless the authority of the Catholic Church compelled me thereto," [75] and it is plain that he has in mind the authority with which the Church testifies, and not simply the fact that the Church is the medium through which certain information, to be judged on its own merits, has come to him.

He also thinks that Jesus' miracles added authority to his teaching. The Canonical Gospels were the work of men who believed that they had lived with the Son of God and had seen miracles which could only have been of divine origin. These miracles should lead one to take seriously the creed whose Author performed them.[76] Christ himself, in St. Augustine's opinion, sought to impress the imagination of his followers so strongly by means of miracles that they would unhesitatingly adopt his teachings in general. His miracles were intended to enhance his credit with his hearers. Similarly, the greater miracles of the Resurrection and Ascension strengthen faith in his doctrine of another life.[77] The present prosperity of a church founded by a condemned felon, and propagated by ignorant fishermen, is in itself a miracle to touch the imagination.[78] St. Augustine might at first seem to be weakening his case when he asserts that a miracle is not really a violation of natural law, and that occasional raisings of the dead are no more and no less remarkable than the process of birth. But certain events *seem* to run counter to our limited knowledge of the laws of nature, and it is this *arresting* quality in the event which counts.[79]

The other great prop of belief on faith is plausibility. This term is often given a pejorative meaning, but here is intended to signify that a proposition described as plausible seems reasonable in light

---

[74] *Ep.* 118.32: heretical groups appeal to *ratio* because they lack *auctoritas*. *Contra Epist. Man. Fund.* 4.5; *De Util. Cred.* 31, 35. John Neville Figgis, *The Political Aspects of S. Augustine's "City of God"* (London: Longmans Green, 1921), p. 7; *cf.* John H. S. Burleigh, *The City of God* (London: Nisbet, 1949), p. 62.

[75] *Contra Epist. Man. Fund.* 6.

[76] *De Util. Cred.* 34; *De Lib. Arb.* ii.2.5. Elsewhere demons are said to have some power from God to perform miracles.

[77] *In Johan. Evang.* 17.1; 49.1; *De Doctr. Christ.* i.15.14.

[78] *De Fide Rerum Quae non Videntur* 10.   [79] *In Johan. Evang.* 8.1; 24.1.

of appearances. This criterion of credibility underwrites authority itself, by telling us why particular sources of information seem authoritative. In addition, St. Augustine was the happier when pronouncements of authority could also be shown to be reasonable in themselves. He had been attracted by the sweet reasonableness of the Manichees, and even after his conversion seems to have felt a compulsion to seek a reason for what he had already accepted on authority.[80] But faith is needed for belief in professedly scientific hypotheses no less than in articles of religion.

A proposition seems reasonable if it conforms to the rule of coherence, and is consistent with what else we accept, as for instance the "well-established principles of natural science."[81] We accept such and such a statement of Thucydides as a datum because it is consistent with what else we are prepared to accept about Pylos-Sphacteria, the siege of Syracuse, or whatever the subject may be. Data are simply alleged facts, which the historian, or scientist, is able for the time being to regard as "coherent." Personal experience will affect the historian's, or scientist's, decision as to what is credible. Would he or people known to him have done such and such a thing? Is it consistent with what he thinks that he knows of life? The facts first in the field need not prevail against all later comers. New propositions may accord better with wider systems and with the total picture, and old "facts" may have to be modified or dropped. To narrate is to explain in terms of the principle of coherence. One explains a body of evidence by showing that it can be arranged to constitute a coherent story. Subsequent detail can be explained by expanding the story to accommodate it.[82] The aim of all historical work is to build a coherent picture of the past as a

[80] *De Ver. Rel.* 7.13; 24.45; *De Util. Cred.* 1.2; *Contra Acad.* ii.9.23; iii.20.43.

[81] Renier, *History, Its Purpose and Method*, p. 163; Walsh, *Introduction to the Philosophy of History*, pp. 76f.; *Theory and Practice in Historical Study: A Report of the Committee on Historiography* (New York: Social Science Research Council, 1946), p. 137, Proposition xiii; Gardiner, *Nature of Historical Explanation*, pp. 75, 129. Archaeology is to be taken into the reckoning; see Robin George Collingwood, *The Philosophy of History* (Historical Association Leaflet No. 79 [London: Bell, 1930]), pp. 12–13.

[82] Renier, *History, Its Purpose and Method*, pp. 173–174; Gardiner, *Nature of Historical Explanation*, pp. 68, 97; Walsh, *Introduction to the Philosophy of History*, pp. 185–186; Benedetto Croce, *Logic as the Science of the Pure Concept*, trans. by Douglas Ainslie (London: Macmillan, 1917), p. 325.

concrete whole, a unified structure with each part shown in its relationship to the total context. The coherence of the story provides the final test of each part.[83] The historian who relies on the principle of coherence is concerned not so much with "what really happened" as with what the present evidence, *i.e.*, the appearances, seems to imply. The fact that present evidence is all that we have to work with is certainly no guarantee of its authenticity. Coherence, not only for the historian but for everyone else who relies upon reason interpreting appearances, is the criterion of *what could have happened* or *what may be the case, granting the truth of the evidence.*[84]

An instance cited by St. Augustine is the supposed coherence of Old Testament prophecy with New Testament events. He claims that most pagans who are converted are brought around by the demonstration that the basic beliefs of the Church are foreshadowed in ancient Hebrew prophecy. St. Augustine himself, before his conversion, was very much impressed by St. Ambrose's figurative interpretation of the Old Testament.[85]

Coherence is a rule of thumb; it carries no guarantee of objective authenticity. Its advocates are right when they assert that truth cannot be established piecemeal. But for them to affirm that truth must therefore be seen as a whole is a *non sequitur*, for we have no necessary reason for believing that truth can be established on any basis whatever. In any event, to identify the coherent with the true is to give up the idea that the essential factor in "truth" is objectivity.[86] On the coherence principle, we can retain a proposition by excluding from our picture all propositions which disagree with it.

[83] Renier, *History, Its Purpose and Method*, pp. 87–88, 169–170; Maurice H. Mandelbaum, *The Problem of Historical Knowledge. An Answer to Relativism* (New York: Liveright, 1938), p. 258.

[84] Michael Joseph Oakeshott, *Experience and Its Modes* (Cambridge: Cambridge University Press, 1933), p. 106; Walsh, *Introduction to the Philosophy of History*, pp. 65, 88–89, 106–107; Gardiner, *Nature of Historical Explanation*, pp. 105, 130; Edgar Wind, "Some Points of Contact between History and Natural Science," in Raymond Klibansky and Herbert James Paton (eds.), *Philosophy and History*, p. 129; Benedetto Croce, *History as the Story of Liberty*, trans. by Sylvia Sprigge (London: Allen and Unwin, 1941), p. 129; Collingwood, *Idea of History*, pp. 238–240.

[85] *Conf.* v.14.24; *De Fide Rerum Quae non Videntur* 5, 7f., 10–11; *De Cat. Rud.* 27.53; *In Johan. Evang.* 35.7.

[86] Oakeshott, *Experience and its Modes*, p. 133; Walsh, *Introduction to the Philosophy of History*, pp. 79, 86.

Suppose ourselves faced with two mutually exclusive sets of propositions, each internally self-consistent. We cannot say that both are true without falling foul of our principle of coherence. Should we choose the one approved by contemporary scientists? Then which is true, the system which contains the proposition that it is accepted by contemporary scientists, or the one actually so accepted? If the former, each may pass muster. If the latter, we are abandoning the criterion of coherence for mere observation with all its pitfalls. There is no obvious reason why a consistent system cannot be built upon propositions some or all of which are objectively false.[87]

For those who think that reason working upon sensation is our only guide to the nature of things there is a strong case for suspending judgment. A reasonable proposition is one which is plausible in the light of sensory appearances, which St. Augustine considers unreliable, and in addition to this we have noted an element of risk in the most trifling induction. Authority offers no better guarantee of truth, because authority itself is no more than plausible in the light of appearances. But suspense of judgment can be achieved only deliberately, self-consciously, and very occasionally. Whether we like it or not we live by assumptions, without as a rule being fully aware of what they are, let alone able to demonstrate their truth. Everyone, including the skeptic, brazenly distinguishes "real" from "imaginary," and "truth" from "falsehood." Educated and uneducated persons alike are highly credulous in everyday life, and have no trouble in swallowing the most contradictory ideas.[88] The senses are known to deceive us at times; but we continue to rely upon their evidence ninety-nine per cent of the time. We are continually forced into making decisions, and the assumptions on which we make them are either demolished, or more or less justified, by experience. Hence Croce's opinion that historical skepticism is shallow, naïve and stupid. The skeptic to whom this judgment applies is simply not facing the implications of his own compulsive tendency to generalize.[89]

[87] Alfred Jules Ayer, *The Foundations of Empirical Knowledge* (London: Macmillan, 1955), pp. 91–92; Russell, *Analysis of Mind*, pp. 267–268.

[88] Renier, *History, Its Purpose and Method*, pp. 128–129; Gardiner, *Nature of Historical Explanation*, pp. 70–71; Croce, *History as the Story of Liberty*, p. 111, and *Logic as the Science of the Pure Concept*, p. 289.

[89] *Ibid.*, p. 289, and *History as the Story of Liberty*, p. 111; Renier, *History, Its Purpose and Method*, pp. 149–150; Ayer, *Foundations of Empirical Knowledge*, p. 1.

St. Augustine thinks that most, if not quite all, our decisions in this life must be made in accordance with beliefs held on faith. Faith is of course a diploma word, applied at one time or another, and by various persons, to every degree of assent from a conscious trust in what is acknowledged to be unseen and indemonstrable, up through cold-blooded gambling on plausible hypotheses, to psychological certitude. St. Augustine distinguishes faith from knowledge and would presumably agree with the Voluntarists, for whom faith implies a conscious choice. As St. Thomas has it, one chooses, by an act of intellect moved by will, to assume the truth of one proposition rather than of another.[90] Thus William James takes a sporting view of faith and speaks of "the will to believe"; we can "believe" any useful proposition which is not demonstrably false, that is to say inconsistent with the appearances and with what else we agree to accept.[91] This sort of faith is implicit in inductive thinking.[92] A. J. Balfour notes that religious and scientific knowledge alike are based upon plausibilities and incertitude.[93] It works out reasonably well to believe in electrons and to believe in God, and either proposition may be, and often is, accepted with something less than psychological certitude.

So far, the skeptic who believes that he lives by indemonstrable assumptions, and who is ready, in principle at least, to examine and alter these in response to new evidence, has no quarrel with St. Augustine.

4. KNOWLEDGE

But difficulties arise over St. Augustine's idea of knowledge. The word seems to imply, or pretend to imply, an objective accuracy which the man of skeptical temperament thinks unattainable or indemonstrable. The man who thinks that he knows something is ready to accept, as certain, propositions which the skeptic is committed to taking as uncertain. St. Augustine claims *to know* very little: that he himself exists with a spiritual soul and a material body; that he has free will; that God exists. But certainty here—as for instance that God exists—confers, by association, a disposition

---

[90] *Summa Theologica* 1.2.4.2.

[91] Hick, *Faith and Knowledge*, pp. 46, 56–57.

[92] *Ibid.*, p. 55.

[93] I.e., *The Foundations of Belief* (New York and London: Longmans, 1895).

to accept without question various related "religious" propositions, as for instance that the God who exists has revealed his purpose in the Canonical Scriptures and through the Church which claims to be his continuing mouthpiece. It is worthwhile to examine the possible bases of the "knowledge" which supposedly strengthen these hypotheses in themselves tentative.

Psychological certitude is the highest degree of assent. St. Augustine distinguishes this kind of assent (*knowledge*) from more or less hearty acceptance of hypotheses admitted to be tentative (*belief*). Ryle expresses this traditional view when he calls *belief* a task or "try-" word, and *knowledge* an achievement or "got it-" word, and even more plainly when he says that knowledge is something more than belief which happens by chance to be correct.[94] When we *know*, we are right, and conscious of being right. Unfortunately, certitude does not in itself prove the objective truth of any particular proposition. One may be sure of a proposition and later come to think it mistaken. Truths are not always obvious to the same person at different times, or to different persons at the same time.[95] There is no empirical criterion for distinguishing knowledge from belief, as far as objective truth is concerned, and knowledge is in effect nothing but a diploma word which we award to beliefs which at the moment we hold in psychological certitude.[96] Experience shows that all Examiners do not give First Class Standing to the same papers. What one man accepts tentatively on authority another may think more or less plausible, and a third "know" for truth.

How does one advance toward this highest degree of assurance? We may begin by accepting *on faith* certain working hypotheses which we neither know nor think that we know to be true. If we apply these consistently in the making of judgments, and if we lay ourselves open to the influence of authority and reason, our faith is likely to increase, and our belief grow stronger. If a hypothesis seems to be confirmed by experience over a long period of time, we may become "morally certain" of its truth. This moral certainty is not

[94] *The Concept of Mind* (London: Hutchinson's University Library, 1955), p. 133.

[95] Hick, *Faith and Knowledge*, p. 55; Ayer, *Foundations of Empirical Knowledge*, p. 96; Russell, *Analysis of Mind*, p. 272.

[96] Ayer, *Foundations of Empirical Knowledge*, p. 80; Hick, *Faith and Knowledge*, pp. 15–16.

the same thing as intellectual conviction. The argument, as an argument, might still not convince an "inadequately experienced ... doubter." [97] What has happened is that we have fallen into a sort of stupor, in which our skepticism is locally, perhaps temporarily, stunned not by argument but by imagination. Sometimes an association of ideas suddenly grasped, or some striking experience "on the road to Damascus," seizes the imagination so forcefully that one hardly stops to ask for its reasonable basis, but accepts without cavil the truth which it seems to illustrate. Conscious certitude, or knowledge, is only the highest degree of assurance, and so-called knowledge has no more than what Hick nicely calls "the somewhat austere virtue of logical possibility." [98]

St. Augustine thinks that he knows something, and that his knowledge comes from direct awareness of self, and from divine revelation. The sum total of his "knowledge" from both sources is small, and we may think that in any event what he regards as knowledge is no more than strongly held belief.

St. Augustine thinks that he is *directly aware* of his own existence, of his free will, of his power to think, and of distinctions between soul and body, subject and object. These "truths" may no longer seem self-evident to us. But this much can be said for St. Augustine's position. Even though we no longer "know" them, and may entertain other propositions as equally plausible or more so, we still act upon these assumptions, and treat them as indisputable in the somewhat qualified sense that we never dispute them except when we are deliberately philosophizing.

St. Augustine was not exhilarated by skepticism, practical or theoretical. He came to think that he could enjoy peace of mind only if he could confront his doubt with some incontrovertible fact, however small. Like Descartes, he found this solid fact in the soul's direct consciousness of its own existence, gained by a turning inward upon itself differing from ordinary sensation and inference. [99] The

[97] Macintosh, *Problem of Religious Knowledge*, pp. 163–176.

[98] Hick, *Faith and Knowledge*, p. 165.

[99] *De Civ. D.* xi.26; *De Lib. Arb.* ii.3.7; *De Trin.* xiv.6.8; *De Ver. Rel.* 72, noli foras ire, in teipsum redi. Carré, *Nominalists and Realists*, p. 11; Gilson, in D'Arcy and others, *Monument to Saint Augustine*, p. 295; D'Arcy, in D'Arcy and others, *Monument to Saint Augustine*, p. 171; William John Sparrow Simpson, *St. Augustine's Conversion* (London: Society for Promoting Christian Knowledge, 1930), p. 46.

soul is not obliged to prove its own existence, or to search for what
is present.[100] To ask, "Do I exist?" is to imply an affirmative
answer. Doubt is turned against itself. If one doubts, there must be
something which is, and which is in a state of doubt. The skeptic
who wishes neither to affirm nor to deny, but to remain in a state of
suspended judgment, must accept the existence of that which
would neither affirm nor deny, but would remain in a state of
suspended judgment.[101] In this perspective, St. Augustine cannot
doubt his own existence, and believes that in primary self-consciousness he has found his incontrovertible fact.[102] Certainty on this
point may not take one far, but for St. Augustine it exorcizes
the demon of universal skepticism and restores his intellectual
morale.

But am I directly aware of self-existence? Consciousness is
generally conceived to have an object.[103] I may say that I am conscious of an external object, insofar as I have an image which I
believe to be an image of such an object. Similarly I may say that I
am conscious of an image A when I have a second image A^1, not
of the supposedly external prototype of the image A, but of A itself,
and associated with A in my mental process. I may be conscious
both of the sun, and of the fact that I am conscious of the sun, and
so on *ad infinitum*.[104] But am I really aware of the conscious self
per se? It is inferred that where there is a photograph there must
also have been a photographer. In fact I can only contemplate the
process, never the agent, who remains hypothetical. I am conscious
of consciousness, and self is *postulated* as the agent of consciousness
without in itself being self-evident.[105]

[100] *De Trin.* x.9.12.

[101] *De Trin.* xv.12.21; *De Lib. Arb.* ii.3.7; *De Civ. D.* xi.26, si enim fallor,
sum; *De Ver. Rel.* 39.73. Erich Przywara, "St. Augustine and the Modern
World," in D'Arcy and others, *Monument to Saint Augustine*, p. 253.

[102] *De Beat. Vit.* 7; *Solil.* ii.1.1; *De Lib. Arb.* ii.3.7; *De Ver. Rel.* 72; *De Trin.*
x.10.14.

[103] Russell, *Analysis of Mind*, p. 294; *cf. ibid.*, pp. 299–300: sense datum
terminologists would say that we are conscious of our own sensations, and not
of the objects supposedly sensed.

[104] Russell, *Analysis of Mind*, pp. 123, 291–292, and *Mysticism and Logic*,
p. 212; Ayer, *Foundations of Empirical Knowledge*, pp. 63–65.

[105] Russell, *Mysticism and Logic*, p. 212, and *Analysis of Mind*, p. 296; Ayer,
Foundations of Empirical Knowledge, pp. 61–62.

The soul is also conscious, St. Augustine thinks, of a *vis quaedam* or dynamic quality in itself. This *will* is "an uncoerced movement of the mind toward obtaining or retaining something," and is free, subject to such limitations as reason or revelation may disclose. No distinction is drawn between the capacity for choosing and the capacity for acting upon choice.[106] The will, in St. Augustine's opinion, is the very core of personality. Men are *nihil aliud quam voluntates*.[107] The soul is aware that it feels, perceives, remembers, and reflects—but each such operation must follow upon an act of will.[108]

Will, like force in mechanics, is a hypothesis used to explain occurrences of a certain sort. Will may be said to characterize, or cause, a movement which is likely to have some specific result; which, if not interrupted, continues until that result is reached; which, if completed, is followed by quiescence. In hunger, we are moved by internal discomfort, and attracted by certain odors, and we may, and usually do, act to satisfy hunger before we are *conscious* of the end toward which our activity is tending. Other animals, and even plants, behave in the same way. We, and they, act as if we wished to satisfy our hunger. But we do not say that the plant *wills* to reach toward the sun, or that the river "desires" the sea, and if we knew more of physiology we might choose to avoid such poetic language in describing our own behavior. Certainly many physical courses of action are initiated unconsciously.[109] When we are conscious of desires, and have the will to satisfy them, it is not that we assume control of the machine with a view to driving it toward a destination voluntarily determined, but that we come to recognize and accept, with more or less grace and enthusiasm, natural movements or tendencies initiated before we become aware of them. Whether or not this belittling view of will appeals to us, there is no doubt but that it offers an intelligible alternative to St. Augustine's "self-evident" hypothesis of will as a capacity for spontaneous and free choice.

[106] *De Ord.* ii.7.18; *De Quant. Anim.* 17; *Conf.* vii.3.5; *cf. De Trin.* x.10.13; *De Duab. Anim.* 14, voluntas est animi motus, cogente nullo, ad aliquid vel non amittendum vel adipiscendum; *De Div. Quaest.* 83.8.

[107] *Conf.* vii.4.6.

[108] *De Trin.* x.10.13f., xiv.17.18; *Conf.* xiii.11.12; *De Lib. Arb.* ii.3.7; *De Quant. Anim.* 72,75; *De Civ. D.* xi.27.

[109] Russell, *Analysis of Mind*, pp. 32, 63–76.

So far as it can judge, St. Augustine continues, the soul occupies, but is not identical with, a body which is of a different and material substance. Unlike Descartes, St. Augustine thinks that this connection with a material body is as obvious as self-existence.[110] The soul rules the partnership and, largely unconsciously, gives the body vitality and sensation. It incites to propagation, and cares for the unborn. It holds together and maintains the body. It is no mere harmony, *temperatio*, or *entelecheia*. The body is its instrument or servant.[111] But soul and body form one essential whole.[112]

But what is the substance of the soul? Here St. Augustine's direct awareness fails. He admits that there is no way of knowing whether it is composed of atoms, air, fire, or of some fifth element.[113] If, as he sees no reason to believe, it is material, then its matter is incomprehensible, and different from the matter which we recognize in the body.[114] The soul's incorporeality, in the usual sense at least, is shown in the fact that if the body is pricked in two places simultaneously, the soul is aware of each incident separately, and of both at the same time.[115] Also, if it were like the body, and its thoughts a function of matter in the usual sense, it could not contain so many and such large "memory pictures."[116] It seems to have neither length nor depth as these are generally conceived, but is present in its entirety in every part of its body-domicile.[117]

St. Augustine thinks that he is directly aware of a distinction between matter and non-matter. But is this distinction self-evident? The further "down" we go with animals and plants, the more regular, predictable, and in fact mechanical appear the actions

[110] *De Gen. ad Litt.* vii.24.35–36: refuses to dogmatize regarding soul's origin and relationship to body.

[111] *De Civ. D.* x.16; xi.23; *De Mor. Eccl. Cath.* 1.52; *De Quant. Anim.* 22.70–71, and *passim*; *Conf.* x.11.18: it is the soul, qua vivifico carnem meam; *De Anim. et eius Orig.* 46; *De Ord.* ii.7.19; *De Immort. Anim.* 10.

[112] *De Civ. D.* i.13; xi.23.

[113] *De Trin.* x.10–11. 13–16; *cf.* x.7.9.

[114] *Epist.* 159.1; *cf. De Trin.* x.7.10; *Epist.* 166.4, if by *corpus* we mean something that exists, then the soul is "corporeal." *De Anim. et eius Orig.* iv.12.17–18, but if *corpus* is conceived as a measureable, extended entity, whose whole exceeds its parts, then the soul is not corporeal. *De Trin.* vi.6.8; *De Immort. Anim.* 16; *De Gen. ad Litt.* vii.6.9.

[115] *De Immort. Anim.* 16.

[116] *De Anim. et eius Orig.* iv.12.17.

[117] *De Quant. Anim.* 69, 71; *Conf.* x.11.18; *Epist.* 155.4.

which in ourselves we might attribute to a spiritual will. The hungry animal and the egg-laying hen seem merely to be yielding to an internal (physical) restlessness or instinct. In animals we can observe only behavior, never desires or wishes. A horse will react in a mechanical way when he smells bear, even if it is only a bearskin. Is he conscious of a universal? Animals, it is assumed, are impelled by an instinct not much different, perhaps, from whatever it is in plants which makes them grow toward the sun.[118] We do not trouble to describe animals as rational, virtuous, or vicious in the sense of being truly responsible agents, and are ready to dismiss *their* behavior as a function of matter. God, or nature, has wound them up, and like mechanical toys they go until they run down.

But since there is no great gap in structure or physical behavior between protozoa and man, it might be inferred that there is probably no great mental gap. If a new element, a soul for instance, has been injected to give us a peculiar character, this has been without noticeable effect upon structure or behavior. Should we argue from our opinion of ourselves to the nature of animals? Or should we ourselves level down, and assume that what seems probable in the case of the lower animals is probably true of us too? Behaviorists prefer the latter approach, and think our behavior no less mechanical, if admittedly more complex, than that of the lower forms of life.[119]

Voluntary, reflex, and mechanical movements can be superficially distinguished. A physiologist, however, will locate all three in the nervous system, and may even find their several seats in different areas of the brain tissue. He sees nothing suggesting a special seat, or physical medium, for will or consciousness, and is inclined to regard these as functions of matter, reducing physiology to chemistry. Certainly *external* observation cannot distinguish voluntary from mechanical movements. Nor is the distinction between living and

[118] Russell, *Analysis of Mind*, pp. 43–44, 61–62, 207, 27–28.

[119] Mascall, *Christian Theology and Natural Science*, p. 251: differences in size and proportion of brain are in degree, not kind. Mascall, p. 272, cites Solly Zuckerman, in *The Physical Basis of Mind* (P. Caslett, ed.; Oxford: Blackwell, 1951). Russell, *Analysis of Mind*, pp. 41–42; Georgii Valentinovich Plekhanov, *In Defence of Materialism. The Development of the Monist View of History*, trans. by A. Rothstein (London: Lawrence and Wishart, 1947), pp. 146–147: man is *par excellence* a tool-maker, but Darwin has shown that every feature of human behavior has animal parallels, *e.g.*, in this context, the elephant breaking off a tree branch to serve as a fly-swatter.

dead matter as obvious as some think. Magnetized steel behaves in a manner characteristic of what we usually call "live matter." Dynamite is excessively sensitive to shock. Perhaps the human brain carries this sensitivity to a still greater degree, and can be shaken from equilibrium by so small a disturbance as a spoken word. Perhaps the distinction between the vital and the mechanical is superficial only, and would disappear under sufficiently intensive microscopic examination.[120]

In light of these considerations, the modern Realist claims that the primary stuff is physical, and "mental" a mere property of the physical.[121] He asserts that "the only realities in the development of the historical complex are the movements of the primary elements and the laws which regulate these movements,"[122] a statement reminiscent of Democritus' dictum, "There is only atoms and void." To these men of faith, the laws of physics can explain everything, including thought. Perception of an object is simply its effect upon certain nervous tissue. Mental images are small movements in a physical medium; even though they cannot at the moment be explained in physical terms, the materialist believes, in faith, that this will be possible in time, and that the causal laws which govern mental and physical phenomena will be shown to differ only as do those which severally govern gases and solids.[123]

Materialism in this sense is a plausible hypothesis, but certainly nothing more. There are no coercive empirical reasons for believing that living and dead matter exemplify in their behavior the same laws. It is at most probable, or plausible, that they do so, and there is no demonstration.[124] Indeed an anti-materialist might take the offensive and ask if matter is in fact more than a logical fiction, postulated to explain the qualities of certain mental states.[125] In point of fact, when perceptions have one or more of the following three characteristics they *are said* to have a material cause. First, members of a set of perceptions may show a marked "visual" and

[120] Russell, *Analysis of Mind*, pp. 44–48, 78.

[121] *Ibid.*, p. 10.

[122] Nicholas Johannes Spykman, *The Social Theory of Georg Simmel* (Chicago: Chicago University Press, 1925), p. 66.

[123] Russell, *Analysis of Mind*, pp. 36–37, 118, 120–121, 129–131, 149, 152, 303.

[124] *Ibid.*, pp. 36–37.

[125] Ayer, *Foundations of Empirical Knowledge*, pp. 238, 242.

"tactile" similarity, although this impression may require the writing off as irrelevant of certain dissimilar qualities of the perceptions. Even so, the similarities are at best imprecise.[126] Second, there are sets which occur in a single context, and show continuity, leading into one another with no appearance of a break, contrasting in this regard with other perceptions. But the context is continually changing, and material things once hypothesized may appear differently to you and to me, and to the same observer at different times.[127] Third, there are sets which I believe to be, or which imply, such and such, whether or not I am looking at them, and these implications do prove to be fairly predictable. But all the evidence for or against the existence of material things will be in terms of hypothetical perceptions, and will be for or against the possible future occurrence of hypothetical perceptions.[128] In any case, predictability is no proof of the objectivity of one's observations, let alone of their material cause.

We do not know whether there is a material world, much less whether it corresponds to our perceptions. Matter, *as we conceive it,* is itself an intellectual hypothesis, sound or unsound, to account in part at least for the origin of certain perceptions which are themselves mental phenomena. The data of physics, whether or not they are objectively true, are thoughts in the mind of the physicist, and subject to psychological "laws." No experience of sense data establishes anything whatsoever with regard to an external factor different in substance from the "spiritual" medium of the sense data themselves.[129] There is no compelling reason for holding that there is a material cause for any perception, and it is not self-evident that mind is distinct from matter. Perhaps it is, but this is not, as St. Augustine claims, a piece of knowledge of which we are directly aware, which is beyond doubt or dispute.

This much must be conceded: that ninety-nine per cent of the time we are unimpressed by any agrument which questions the existence of matter, or denies a distinction between the mental and the material. Sense data either belong to material objects or are

[126] *Ibid.,* pp. 249–259, 271; Russell, *Analysis of Mind,* p. 152; *cf.* pp. 127, 149.
[127] *Ibid.,* pp. 101, 192; Ayer, *Foundations of Empirical Knowledge,* pp. 3, 240–241, 251–265.
[128] *Ibid.,* pp. 226, 229, 257.
[129] *Ibid.,* pp. 229–241; Russell, *Analysis of Mind,* pp. 308–309.

taken to do so. It has been suggested that one can perceive "one thing as behind another, although it is so hidden that there is no sensible appearance of it." Moore says that when we sense a table, we sense something more than a mental hypothesis, whatever may be the case when mathematical points and physical electrons are at issue. This invincible feeling acknowledged by Moore does not provide a coercive argument for the reality of matter, and each of us has had invincible opinions proved illusory. But it corresponds with our habitual belief,[130] and will certainly be accepted by us, if not as self-evident truth, at least as a working proposition in which we have an exceedingly high degree of faith.

In addition to what he regards as direct awareness of self-existence and of will and matter, St. Augustine thinks that the soul is directly aware of the existence of an objective reality distinct from the ego, however conceived.

It is very evident that I cannot *prove* that there is an objective external reality. Solipsists argue that I can never break out of the circle of my experience, and become aware of more than self. Anything that I experience is *ipso facto* my experience, a datum of my self-consciousness.[131] It may all be internal to me, and my thought a subjective closed circuit. If I seemed aware of something external, that awareness in turn would be part of my thought process. I can prove nothing about the existence, much less the experience, of other beings like myself, however strong my belief that there are such beings existing in a common world.[132] This belief is part of my experience, and if to know an external reality I must be aware of something beyond the confines of my thought process I am obviously asking for the impossible, and am condemned to solipsism.[133] From the point of view of rational proof, belief in an external reality is an arguable hypothesis and not self-evident knowledge.[134] It is worth remembering, if we think it improper to use arguments from sensation and reason against truths "directly

[130] Ayer, *Foundations of Empirical Knowledge*, p. 235; *cf.* p. 231; Stebbing, *Logical Positivism and Analysis*, p. 34.

[131] William Terence Stace, *Theory of Knowledge and Existence* (Oxford: Clarendon Press, 1932), p. 67: solipsism can be escaped only if one is unwilling to see.

[132] Ayer, *Foundations of Empirical Knowledge*, p. 136.

[133] Russell, *Analysis of Mind*, p. 142.

[134] Heisenberg, *Physics and Philosophy*, p. 133.

perceived," that a proposition which is disputable cannot be held to be self-evident and manifest truth, whatever its alleged source. Any principle, whether frankly hypothetical or professing to be indisputably true, which is offered as a guide to experience must be able to stand scrutiny in the light of experience.

Even if one did have mysterious intimations of an external reality, could one think it or describe it? The language which I understand and use is given meaning for me by *my* experience, and can express nothing which is not meaningful in terms of my experience.[135]

Perhaps in all consciousness there is an implicit distinction between subject and object. The boundary may shift alarmingly, but it is doubtful if object is ever totally swallowed by subject this side of Nirvana. If we profess that Self comprehends the All, we are deliberately awarding the diploma word "true" to a proposition which, true or false, we Occidentals find difficulty in taking seriously.[136] The objective world, the world external to the conscious subject, may be material or spiritual or a combination of the two, or a product of imagination for all that one can prove to the contrary. What is constant is my strong belief, justifiable or otherwise, that there is a reality distinct from my *ego* and that I can to some extent examine this.

Certainly the subjective-objective distinction cannot be *proven*, or demonstrated in terms of sensation or reason. The opponents of solipsism offer little more than a profession of faith. They suggest that because I can not only successfully foresee a course of events, but can also visualize the events in reverse order, there must be an objective reality. Similarly, because other people behave and respond as I should expect, they must really exist.[137] But subject and object may here be different elements in a continuum. It is also suggested

---

[135] Ludwig Wittgenstein, *Tractatus Logico-Philosophicus* (London: Routledge and Kegan Paul, 1922), 5.62; Stebbing, *Logical Positivism and Analysis*, pp. 24–25: W.'s apparently complete solipsism begins with this linguistic difficulty. But Carnap insists that the Logical Positivist position calls for no more than "methodological solipsism," a linguistic and argumentative cul-de-sac with no necessary metaphysical implication.

[136] Ayer, *Foundations of Empirical Knowledge*, p. 144: solipsism is born not of inner conviction but of the difficulty in bridging the gap between "self-inclosed experience" and a common social world.

[137] *Ibid.*, pp. 66–67, 155–161, 247–263; *cf.* pp. 163–170.

that I can know an external object directly, without benefit of the direct acquaintance deemed necessary by solipsists. When I see a table, I am really receiving intimations of an external object. It is not necessary, in logic, that I should experience only feeling located in myself; and the privacy of sense data is only a verbal convention of philosophers, not accepted by the laity, who persist in saying that two persons are listening to the "same noise." The antisolipsists go on to ask why I should not have, or share, an experience said to be "owned" by someone else.[138] But these are bald assertions, if more than mere suggestions, and their strongest point is simply that they are not necessarily false. The limits of self are still left undefined, and the assertions and feelings employed in the delimitation remain part of my experience and, for all that can be proven, completely subjective.

Antisolipsists also argue that thought is not just another sort of immediate experience, like "feeling" and "sensation"; it is *about something*. It involves an awareness of *other* mental states, which as the objects of thought, and classifiable, are in some sense *objective*.[139] In the act of thought, the soul is conscious, and the act is auto-conscious, and this implies distinction between subject and object, universal and particular, theory and practice, thought and will, imagination and intellect, utility and morality, however these may be defined.[140] If that which is the object of thought is *ipso facto* objective, then the thoughts which are the stuff of historical studies, for instance, must be objective.[141] What the antisolipsists succeed in showing is how within the perhaps closed circuit of my mental experience there can be a sort of intramural contrast of subject and object.[142] But the distinction may be between not the world and me but between my different moments.

Unlike St. Augustine, we do not *know*, but we remain invincibly prejudiced against both solipsism and Collingwood's idea that the essence of the subject-object relationship is a sort of contemplation

[138] *Ibid.*, pp. 140–146, 153–161, 168–170; Stebbing, *Logical Positivism and Analysis*, p. 228; Gardiner, *Nature of Historical Explanation*, pp. 63–64.

[139] Collingwood, *Idea of History*, pp. 291–292, 294.

[140] Benedetto Croce, *Theory and History of Historiography*, trans. by Douglas Ainslie (London and Sydney: Harrap, 1921), pp. 118–119.

[141] Collingwood, *Idea of History*, p. 290.

[142] Giovanni Gentile, "The Transcendency of Time in History," in Klibansky and Paton (eds.), *Philosophy and History*.

of one's navel. I assume an external world, and other observers with whom I can communicate. I also assume that I possess distinct and continuous personal identity, that my body is part of me and distinct in this respect from other matter. [143] These beliefs are not appreciably affected by the strength of the argument of the solipsists or by the weakness of their opponents, although one can easily conceive of an artificial and learned desire that Self might be absorbed in the All. Miss Stebbing says that any view leading to solipsism is "manifestly false." [144] Whether true or false, solipsism seems irrelevant to my mental experience, which is characterized by a constant feeling for the subject-object relationship. But what we have here is not something self-evident, of which we are "directly aware," and which continues under scrutiny to seem indisputably true, but rather a debatable proposition to which we happen to be invincibly attached.

The importance of the doctrine of direct self-awareness, for St. Augustine, lies not so much in the propositions which it supposedly conveys or authenticates, as in its effect upon his intellectual morale, releasing him from the paralysis of suspended judgment, and persuading him that some facts, however few, are *beyond question true*, that mental effort is worth while despite the skeptics. Similarly there are persons who take comfort from the universally and eternally true tautology that $2+2=4$, although in the phenomenal world as opposed to the fanciful world of mathematics two bits of mercury plus two are likely to equal one. His doctrine of direct self-awareness gives St. Augustine assurance that he not merely believes but actually *knows* the truth of certain propositions, and this heady assurance has the effect of increasing his credulity with regard to certain other propositions which he would have been well advised to continue to regard skeptically.

Another stimulus to "knowledge" lies in what St. Augustine might describe as the experience of the presence of God. This experience does not convey propositions, but is likely to have the indirect effect of seeming to underwrite much of what is attributed by some people to divine revelation. Mystical experiences are familiar in most religious traditions, and being essentially nonintellectual, they are hard to describe.

[143] Ayer, *Foundations of Empirical Knowledge*, pp. 142–143, 163.
[144] *Ibid.*, p. 24.

St. Augustine says that in his own case he begins with *an intense longing* for something not clearly envisaged.[145] The next step is *recollection*, not in this case a summoning of memories, but a calling of the soul away from all that could distract it from the business in hand, and back to the inner sources of its strength. One must try to eliminate perturbations, material concerns, and images,[146] and even the axioms of geometry and physics which were regarded by Plato as rungs in the ladder by which one ascends to the Idea of the Good. The experience we seek is to be found, if at all, in absolute Inner Quiet.

When extraneous material has been stripped away, *introversion* follows,[147] conceived as a self-hypnotic fixation upon the idea of Permanence, by which St. Augustine seems to mean the thought "God always within me." Finally one *may* pass from this still conscious fixation to an experience different in kind from thought, and therefore a far cry from Plato's Idea of the Good, in which the principles of subordinate sciences are seen in their relationship to each other and to the whole. The divine vision is not, however, the automatic result of following a prescribed procedure. But even if one fails to reach the goal, one may have a sense of having approached an experience of a highly unusual sort.[148]

What happens in the moment of climax? In the first place, the soul has an unquestioning sense of living presence. This presence is identified out of hand with the God of Christianity. Though found within the soul, he is distinct from it, although non-Christian mystics are usually inclined to identify the subject with the Object. One does not recognize God through a private anamnesis nor through racial memory,[149] but only through His special grace. In the second place, the soul senses the timelessness and eternity of this Being.[150] Third, the experience of the presence of God is happy.

---

[145] *Ennar. in Ps.* 41.2.

[146] *De Quant. Anim.* 73–76, 79–80; *Ennar. in Ps.* 41.3, 7; *Conf., passim.*

[147] Butler, *Western Mysticism*, p. 29.

[148] *Conf.* i.3.3; iii.6.11; iv.9.14; vi.1.1; vii.10.16, 17.23; x.25.36–37; *Ennar. in Ps.* 135.8; 41.7, 10; *De Nat. Bon.* 19; *Contra Faust. Man.* xxii.53; *De Cons. Evang.* i.5.8; *De Doctr. Christ.* i.12.12. The experience does not lend itself to precise description; see *Conf.* vii.10.16; ix.10.24.

[149] *Conf.* x.20.29, 21.31; vii.10.16, 17.23; *Contra Faust. Man.* xxii.54; *Ennar. in Ps.* 41.7; *De Mor. Eccl. Cath.* 66; *De Trin.* xiv.15.21.

[150] *Ennar. in Ps.* 41.10; *Serm.* 52.16; *Conf.* x.16.25; *Contra Faust. Man.* xx.54.

The soul is filled with warmth. It experiences what St. Augustine calls "a holy inebriation," "a strange secret delight, a sweet melody in a heart overcome with longing for God's inwardly experienced sweetness."[151] The soul is filled with love and awe, and can imagine nothing better than an eternity of such happiness. But the soul in its present state could hardly bear a prolongation of so intense an experience.[152] Fourth, the passing of what can at best be no more than a fleeting moment leaves the soul in a Dark Night, where no other experience, it seems, can have reality or value.[153]

Mystical experience may come in varying degrees of intensity and elaboration, although in every case the soul is aware at the time of nothing else.[154] At the lower end of the scale, if one may use such language, the soul may experience a sense of the Divine Presence. Perhaps "cosmic rapture" should be considered a still lower degree. At the other end of the scale, one hears of visions and extraordinary graces, and the subject may believe, in retrospect, that he has experienced an *excessus* of the soul from the body. St. Augustine believes that Moses "saw God," and that St. Paul was rapt up to the "third heaven," and he seems to think such experiences typical of the highest sort of wisdom. But he himself can hardly be said, on his own evidence, to have passed the first stages of mystical experience. He gives an account of his experience of the presence of God. But this is only the first stage in the mystical experience of contemplatives more richly endowed with extraordinary graces.[155] Burnaby thinks the term *ecstasy* misleading if applied to St. Augustine's experience, and so it is, if taken literally. Watkin agrees, and thinks that St. Augustine claims nothing more than "infused contemplation." But, if limited in range, his mysticism is real; he believes, on the basis of his experience, that

[151] *Ennar. in Ps.* 41.9–10; *Contra Faust. Man.* xii.42; xxii.56; *Conf.* xi.9.11.

[152] *Serm.* 52.16; *Conf.* vii.10.16; ix.10.25; x.40.65; *De Quant. Anim.* 76; *Epist.* 20.4.

[153] *Conf.* vii.17.23; ix.10.24–25; x.40.65; *Ennar. in Ps.* 41.10.

[154] *Ennar. in Ps.* 30.2.

[155] *Ennar. in Ps.* 67.36; *Serm.* 52.16; *De Gen. ad Litt.* xii.5.14, 12.25, 26.53f.; II Cor. 12.2–5. Butler, *Western Mysticism,* p. 51; Edward Ingram Watkin, "The Mysticism of St. Augustine," in D'Arcy and others, *Monument to Saint Augustine,* pp. 110, 112, 117.

it is possible in this life to have an experimental perception of God.[156]

The mystical is a species of the intuitive. It may refer to a particularly intensive, obsessive, hypnotic quality of certain sensations whose origin, like that of all sensation, is beyond our ken. In this sense it is perfectly genuine, and if not entirely without nonreligious precedents is certainly highly remarkable, and argues an unusual stimulus. But "mystical" may be a diploma word, used to confer authority upon certain concepts associated in our minds with, but not actually arising from, the mystical sensation itself. The mystic is likely to believe that he has a direct knowledge of a reality beyond ordinary appearances—a sudden, coercive knowledge superior to the findings of sensation and reason because more direct. But it seems impossible to attribute any knowledge content to the mystical experience. When we examine the latter, we find an assortment of glosses, more or less unwittingly gathered around a core which vanishes to nothingness as we look at it.[157] At the heart of the mystical experience is a sensation which obviously has something in common with the sensational basis of hypnosis, and which can be induced in similar ways. Julian of Norwich sought the mystical sensation by gazing at a crucifix, the followers of St. Gregory Palamas by contemplating their navels, the Yogi by repeating the monosyllable "OM" while looking at the tips of their noses. Great mystics such as St. John of the Cross have in fact maintained that some less gifted mystics suffer from, or are guilty of, hallucinations and self-hypnosis. The condition may sometimes approach the pathological, and even so authentic a dévote as Mme Guyon was concerned by the frequency of her lapses into what in a nonreligious context might have been regarded as spontaneous self-hypnosis.

[156] *De Gen. ad Litt.* xii.26.54. John Burnaby, *Amor Dei* (London: Hodder and Stoughton, 1938), p. 33; Watkin, in D'Arcy and others, *Monument to Saint Augustine*, p. 110. *Cf.* Butler, *Western Mysticism*, p. 51; thinks that St. Augustine, however noncommittal his words, probably thought that he had seen the Divine Essence. But St. Augustine admits to seeing through a glass darkly—see *In Johan. Evang.* 1.24.5—and says that contemplation in this life must for the most part be taken as a possibility, on faith, with some few persons granted an enigmatical view of truth; see *De Cons. Evang.* i.3.5. *Cf.* Terrot Reaveley Glover, *Life and Letters in the Fourth Century* (Cambridge: Cambridge University Press, 1910), p. 194.

[157] Russell, *Mysticism and Logic*, pp. 8–10.

Probably most persons, and not just individuals of unusual sensitivity or abnormal character, have had experiences similar in kind, if not in degree, to those of self-confessed mystics, but without identifying them as such or putting a religious interpretation upon them.[158]

I should be inclined to agree that mysticism is "little more than a certain intensity and depth of feeling in regard to what is believed about the universe." This depth of feeling is aroused toward certain beliefs by an intense sensation which, rightly or wrongly, is associated by the conscious mind with the beliefs in question.[159] For religious persons, who think of God immediately before and after the experience, and who are predisposed to find God in it, belief in God is likely to be strengthened.[160] Christian, Neo-Platonist, and Hindu each associates the experience with his *a priori* idea of God, and while the Christian, responding to his theological indoctrination, experiences His presence, the Hindu believes that he has achieved identification with the Absolute.

Because of the intensity of the mystical experience, certain characteristic inferences are frequently drawn, all of them based on the negative hallucination that what we do not see must be unreal.[161] First, the intensity of the mystical sensation makes it seem unique in a sense more impressive than that in which every experience can be considered unique, and one concludes that God, or whatever is supposed to be its Object, must therefore be indescribable.[162] Second, concentration upon one Object has the effect of making everything else seem illusory; hence the mystical inference that only God, the Cause and Object of this experience, is real, and that everything else is illusory.[163] Third, in the mystical experience time ceases to count; hence the inference that, judged in the blinding light of the mystical experience, time is unreal.[164] Fourth, in the mystical experience, there is a temporary lapse from self-consciousness; hence the inference of many non-Christian mystics that self is

[158] Macintosh, *Problem of Religious Knowledge*, pp. 31–32, 34f.; St. John of the Cross: "Such a one has only been speaking to himself."

[159] Russell, *Mysticism and Logic*, pp. 3, 28.

[160] Macintosh, *Problem of Religious Knowledge*, pp. 43–44.

[161] *Ibid.*, pp. 23–24, 36.

[162] *Ibid.*, p. 17.

[163] *Ibid.*, p. 21; Russell, *Mysticism and Logic*, p. 10.

[164] Macintosh, *Problem of Religious Knowledge*, pp. 22–23; Russell, *Myticism and Logic*, pp. 10, 21–22.

unreal.[165] Fifth, no ugliness or evil has a place in the mystical moment; hence the inference that evil is unreal.[166] Often it is not so much a matter of drawing inferences as of finding confirmation for ideas already accepted.

This mode of thinking often, though not always, tends to encourage a contempt for the more sober procedures of conscious induction, without offering any real alternative source of knowledge.[167] Mysticism, like opium-smoking and other practices which wring their devotees dry, often leads to quietism by making all other activity seem tame and uninteresting in comparison. It is not so much a matter of deliberately rejecting reason, or physical work, as of having something vastly more interesting on one's mind. But mystical experiences can galvanize someone like St. Teresa, already committed to the belief that the God who is the Cause and Object of the mystical experience demands a strenuous life of service.[168]

Mysticism's contribution to "knowledge" is to intensify, perhaps to the point of psychological certitude, propositions associated rightly or wrongly with the experience. But even if the mystical experience adds nothing to the content of knowledge, it would appear to be stimulated by a sensation of unusual force, which may in turn be the product of an unusual Cause.

5. PRIVILEGED POSITION OF CHRISTIAN HYPOTHESES

How and what did St. Augustine "know"? He claims to be assured of his own existence, and to have experienced the presence of God. For the rest, he seems to have learned to live with uncertainties. He says very little of knowledge, but constantly expresses approval of what he regards as the almost universal habit of faith, that is to say of accepting propositions either on authority or because they seem to be more or less reasonable. The Manichees and the Academics, in their several ways, finished for all time his confidence in reason as an avenue to truth. At Cassiciacum, shortly after his conversion, he may have had temporary hopes that

[165] Macintosh, *Problem of Religious Knowledge*, pp. 23–24.
[166] *Ibid.*, pp. 26–27; Russell, *Mysticism and Logic*, pp. 10–11.
[167] Cohen and Nagel, *Introduction to Logic and Scientific Method*, pp. 400–401; one must *sometimes* put one's faith in surmises. (What else is there for one to do?)
[168] Macintosh, *Problem of Religious Knowledge*, pp. 29–30.

Christian dogma could be *proven* true; soon he was willing to accept his creed on faith, looking for certainty only in the next life. We find him admitting that he knows nothing for certain (his own and God's existences excepted), and that the wrangles of the philosophers show the vanity of looking to reason for a demonstration of truth.[169] He is free from the *misery* of doubt, and can accept, on faith, the teachings of revelation whether or not he can make them seem plausible. For him faith is the normal basis of living. He differs from the professional skeptic in his willingness to act on mere assumptions. He does not have "the faith of a little child." He is an intelligent and sophisticated adult, seeking by a deliberate, conscious acceptance of authority (and plausibility) an escape from the frustration of skepticism.

St. Augustine says that he himself once thought that the truths of religion, which govern his interpretation of history, should be accepted in the same way as the proposition that three plus seven equal ten. But in time he came to adopt the Catholic opinion, based upon recognition of the facts of mental life, that some propositions, including for most Christians the articles of their creed, must simply be taken on faith, without psychological certitude, *as if* they were true.[170] Heretics and Manichees who offer a "reasonable basis" for religious beliefs deceive themselves and others. The average Christian must begin by taking a chance.[171] No one, by an effort of will, can immediately become convinced of the truth of a proposition. But one can agree to act as if that proposition were true, unless or until experience forces the conclusion that it is false or improbable. There is, or need be, no hypocrisy here. The Christian freely admits that he is acting upon an assumption which he does not know to be true. St. Augustine assumes that when he has tasted and seen he will agree that the Lord is good.[172] Skepticism will be transformed by degrees into unquestioning acceptance.

[169] Simpson, *St. Augustine's Conversion*, p. 243; Gilson, in D'Arcy and others, *Monument to Saint Augustine*, p. 303; John Joseph O'Meara, *The Young Augustine* (New York: Longmans, 1954), p. 197.

[170] *Conf.* vi.4.6, 5.7: reaction against Manichaean intellectual pretentiousness. *De Util. Cred.* 24: some propositions, but not those of the Creed, may *not* be found justified by experience. *De Trin.* xiii.1.3, aliquando autem et rebus falsis accomodatur fides.

[171] *De Util. Cred.* 21; *De Symb. ad Catech.* 4; *In Johan. Evang.* 3.20; *De Fide et Symb.* 1.1; *De Trin.* xv.2.2; *De Fide Spe Car.* 1.5.

[172] E.g., *Contra Faust. Man.* xii.46.

Most persons are ready to admit, if only in principle, that most of their beliefs, however strongly held, might be mistaken. For those who hold their religious beliefs in this spirit, theology becomes, as in the eighteenth century, a branch of natural philosophy. But many religious persons not merely refuse to bring their religious beliefs under scrutiny, but go on to insist that they hold, and must hold, these beliefs in psychological certitude. For them, "I believe" means "I know." Mascall actually says that "only a person who was either pathologically sophisticated or a complete moron" would devote his life to the service of a God of whom he was not sure.[173] Are those who pray for a stronger faith ("Lord, I believe; help thou my unbelief") either pathologically sophisticated or complete morons? Are scientists, who regulate their activity by hypotheses which they know to be tentative, complete morons or merely pathologically sophisticated? The fact is that not just in religious matters but in practically everything else we build our lives upon assumptions which, as we freely admit, are not absolutely certain.

Non-Roman Catholics seldom maintain that the existence of God can be logically proven; there is no coercive argument for an objective universe, a material world, or moral obligations. At most, some persons find themselves acting upon these assumptions.[174] When they say that they know God by faith, they mean that they interpret their experience in theistic terms. But the theist's arguments are permissive, not coercive, and not verifiable within the historical process. Only time, or rather eternity, can test their truth. Apologetical argument can at most make a creed seem more plausible. Experience can almost be regarded as *materia pura*, as easily used to support the atheistic as the theistic hypothesis. Mascall admits that the Christian faith must seem to outsiders to be "unnecessarily complicated and fantastically devious," particularly in its explanation of why a loving, all-wise and all-powerful God tolerates evil in the world.[175] No reasonable person will begrudge a man tentative religious beliefs, or charge him with hypocrisy or superstition if he tries seriously to apply them in his life and test them against his experience. Religion in this sense a skeptic can understand and perhaps share. What puts one off is the frequently prickly insistence

[173] Mascall, *Christian Theology and Natural Science*, pp. 292–293; Hick, *Faith and Knowledge*, p. 55.

[174] *Ibid.*, pp. xvi, 132.

[175] Heisenberg, *Physics and Philosophy*, pp. 72–73.

that the *dévot* is, and should be, certain, and that those who are not are somehow beyond the religious pale. These persons who make a psychological certitude a requirement for salvation have got beyond St. Paul, who saw "through a glass, darkly." But as Montaigne says, "L'impression de la certitude est un certain tesmoignage de folie et d'incertitude extrême."[176]

St. Augustine *knows* of his own and God's existence. For the rest, he is skeptical in the manner of the scientist who is ready to act in accordance with unproven assumptions. *But St. Augustine gives exceptional treatment to one class of hypotheses, that which goes to make up what he regards as the Christian creed.* Believing as he does that virtually all his hypotheses are tentative, and must be accepted in faith, whether in authority or in their intellectual plausibility, he deliberately refuses to treat these particular ones as tentative. He chooses to treat them as beyond question. Presumably he believes that the peace of mind to be had from following this determination is worth the strain of having to deny or distort appearances, that is to say the natural testimony of experience, where the latter may seem to contradict the Christian propositions. This need involve no hypocrisy if one does not pretend—and St. Augustine did not—to a psychological certitude which one does not actually possess. But in St. Augustine's case it leads to, and is shown in, his cavalier treatment of evidence, his denial of nature, and his subjective interpretation of the historical process. The skeptic who has followed with sympathy the development of St. Augustine's theory of knowledge will now find himself at a parting of the ways. St. Augustine insists that beliefs which most persons can hold only on faith are to be treated as intrenched, exempt from modification in the light of experience.

[176] M. de Montaigne, *Essais* (ed. M. Rat; Paris: Classiques Garnier, 1962), II, 604: Hick, *Faith and Knowledge*, pp. 30, 33, 135, 137; Mascall, *Christian Theology and Natural Science*, p. 305.

CHAPTER THREE

Procrustean Treatment of Evidence

1. THE APOLOGETICAL APPROACH

Theological, philosophical, and historical studies, like most other departments of science, have three grand divisions: pure, applied, and apologetical. The pure scientist follows the rule of faith in his interpretation of fresh evidence, whether relating to intellectual cruces or to moral crises, to civilizations or to city-states. He holds his premises and his conclusions to be tentative, subject to constant testing and possible revision or repudiation. He is not irrevocably committed, intellectually or emotionally, to his current interpretation of experience, and is willing to change to any other interpretation which from time to time may seem to his deliberately open mind to be more plausible.

The practical scientist accepts the findings of his "pure" colleague at more or less face value, and tries to apply them fairly uncritically for the benefit of society.

The role of the apologist is ambiguous. At first glance he resembles the pure scientist, for he seems to be testing the ideas with which he is concerned. But closer acquaintance shows that the result of his intellectual maneuvers is a foregone conclusion. Doctrine is always found to be sound. The apologist is like a little dog on a leash. He runs up and down and barks; but when he darts too far the leash pulls him up short. With the apologist, his *a priori* hypotheses replace the leash. He is seeking not to investigate but only to illustrate the soundness or plausibility of his beliefs.

It is not hard to sympathize with the patently honest pure scientist searching for maximum plausibility, or with the practical scientist who tries in an unpretentious way to put at his clients' service the tested conclusions of the specialist. But what about the apologist? Must we dismiss him as a hypocrite? Only if he pretends,

83

as he sometimes may, that in making his hypotheses seem possible and plausible he has somehow proven them to be true. The apologist's own knowledge, if he "knows," depends not upon the intellectual "proofs" which appear in his apologetical demonstration, but upon some sort of intuitive assurance which if he is religious he may attribute to divine illumination. Even if he lacks intuitive assurance, but lives only by faith, he may in all sincerity want to propagate the faith by which he himself lives, and which seems to him to be plausible and satisfying. In either case he believes that others can profit by his creed if only they can be induced to give it a trial. If he can persuade them to adopt and apply his premises on a tentative basis, they may come in time to hold them with as high a degree of assurance as he does.

St. Augustine is an apologetical historian. The *De Genesi ad Litteram* and the *De Civitate Dei* are certainly not the fruit of free inquiry into the meaning of creation and history. His method has been criticized as antihistorical because of the rigid theological system which controls it.[1] His Christian creed is treated as beyond question true, and experience and the historical process, if they are not found therein, are made to conform to its prescription. It may be that St. Augustine is not intellectually or intuitively certain of the truth of every clause and subsection of the Christian creed, but he is willing to try to accept it complete, as a working principle.[2] His study of history is intended not *to discover* patterns or lines of development, but *to demonstrate* God's love everywhere expressed. He has time only for detail serviceable for this theme. What he tells is told, and in such a way, so as to arouse and strengthen Christian faith.[3] Nor is he a professional philosopher; he is a Christian bishop,

[1] John Neville Figgis, *The Political Aspects of S. Augustine's "City of God"* (London: Longmans Green, 1921), pp. 5, 29; Christopher Dawson, "St. Augustine and his Age," in Martin Cyril D'Arcy and others, *A Monument to Saint Augustine* (London: Sheed and Ward, 1930), pp. 43–48; James Morgan, *The Psychological Teaching of St. Augustine* (London: Elliot Stock, 1932), p. 48.

[2] W. Cunningham, *S. Augustin and His Place in the History of Christian Thought* (London: Clay, 1886), p. 114; Hubert Murray Burge, *Discourses and Letters* (London: Chatto and Windus, 1930), p. 213; William John Sparrow Simpson, *St. Augustine's Episcopate. A Brief Introduction to his Writings as a Christian* (London: Society for Promoting Christian Knowledge, 1944), p. 62.

[3] At the least, the study of history serves to refute the pagan fancy that all great calamities are the result of the triumph of Christianity. *De Cat. Rud.* 3.5. Gustave Combès, *S. Augustin et la Culture Classique* (Paris: Plon, 1927), p. 48; John H. S. Burleigh, *The City of God* (London: Nisbet, 1949), p. 195.

and he never forgets it. He uses the great secular philosophies of antiquity as an intellectual quarry. As for Canonical Scripture, he agrees with Irenaeus and St. Athanasius that the Bible is the first and greatest historical source; but he will be found as ready to distort this as he is the secular evidence, to secure his apologetical purpose.[4] He opposes to "l'amer lyricisme antique" and to modern "philosophies de l'absurde" a dogmatic optimism.[5] It is easy to agree with Babbitt that we have here a humbling of the intellect and of the critical spirit, and an opening of the way to obscurantism.[6] It has been suggested that St. Augustine wrote not a philosophy of history but a theology of history.[7] But the distinction is likely to be a hard one to maintain. Theologians will claim that theological premises are no less and no more true than "philosophical truth"; and skeptics will assert that secular hypotheses are no more and no less tentative than those proffered by religion.

St. Augustine begins with certain *a priori* premises which he attributes to divine revelation. These premises control both his attitude toward the historical evidence and his specific interpretation of the historical process. They are held on faith, but everything is interpreted as supporting them. Sacred and secular literature alike are forced to bear witness, willing or otherwise, to the plausibility of the original premises. Where this seems impossible even for St. Augustine's ingenuity, the evidence is declared to be either false or figurative. He is frank in his adherence to this Procrustean principle. His justification, if he thought that he needed one, would lie in his apparent assurance that every man would be the happier for adopting the Christian approach to experience. Any technique of exegesis, however high-handed, which can make the Christian creed seem more plausible, attractive, and worth trying is not merely excusable but highly commendable. Nothing in human speculation, *or in the historical record*, must be allowed to destroy Christian faith or even call it seriously into question. Not just the interpretation of the fact, but on occasion the fact itself, may have

[4] But *cf. ibid.*, p. 153.

[5] Henri Irénée Marrou, *S. Augustin et la Fin de la Culture Antique* (Paris: Boccard, 1938), p. 16.

[6] *Democracy and Leadership* (Boston and New York: Houghton Mifflin, 1924), p. 177; Charles Norris Cochrane, *Christianity and Classical Culture* (Oxford, New York, and Toronto: Oxford University Press, 1939), p. 378.

[7] Jacques Maritain, "St. Augustine and St. Thomas Aquinas," in D'Arcy and others, *Monument to Saint Augustine*, pp. 200, 220.

to be arbitrarily determined, if Christian truth is to be seen to prevail.

Christian propositions must be held for the most part, and by most believers, on nothing more than faith. They are tentative, like those of chemistry and astronomy, to say nothing of sociology and political science. But instead of letting them be tested by experience, and allowing for their possible failure in this test, St. Augustine insists upon putting them in an intrenched position where, in the event of a contradiction, not they but experience must yield.

2. APPROACH TO SECULAR STUDIES

Many disciplines contribute to our understanding of the historical process. Each is justified, in St. Augustine's eyes, by its contribution to a Christian understanding.

Non-Christian evidence for historical studies proper comes from sensation and inference. One can expect unintelligibility and factual error; but when divine revelation has supplemented and read sense into the secular evidence, the latter can be accurate and useful.[8] When St. Augustine insists, as he often does, upon the distinction between true history and false, his touchstone of truth is agreement with the Christian faith.[9]

St. Augustine's approach to historical studies proper, that is to say to factual details in the human record as distinct from the grand pattern of the cosmic process, is neither broad nor deep. It suggests the Roman grammarian rather than the disinterested historian. In the schools of the empire the various liberal arts, variously identified, were taught in connection with the study of grammar. Vitruvius includes history in a list of seven *disciplinae* commended to the attention of future engineers. But Quintilian makes it clear that the grammarian can hardly be expected to be erudite in such peripheral matters.[10] Historical works were read, if at all, for style, and for

---

[8] *Epist.* 101; *De Doctr. Christ.* ii.41.62; ii.43.64, narratione historica praeterita hominum instituta, *and* historia narrat facta fideliter atque utiliter. *De Ord.* ii.12.37, curarum plenior quam iucunditatis aut veritatis.

[9] *De Civ. D.* iii.31; vi.4; xvi.8,9; *Epist.* 143.12; *In Johan. Evang.* 90.2.

[10] Vitruvius *De Architectura* i.1.3; Quintilian *Instit. Orat.* i.2.14, 8.18–21; Varro, see Dahlmann, in August Friedrich von Pauly and Georg Wissowa, *Real-Encyclopaedie der classischen Altertumswissenschaft*, Supplement vi, 1256.

specific anecdotal illustrations of human qualities and modes of behavior. Augustus is said to have had a rich store of historical *exempla* at his own and his friends' disposal, and Valerius Maximus dedicated to Tiberius a veritable gold mine, or gravel pit, of "instances" in his *Memorabilia*. Such antiquaries had no very lively scruple against improving an illustration by stretching a point. For them, historical writing was closer to the "true parable" than to the scientific report.[11]

St. Augustine resembles his grammarian compatriots in his great use of *exempla* both Roman and Greek. The simplicity of the ancient Romans is illustrated in the careers of Cincinnatus, Regulus, Mucius Scaevola, Fabricius, Scipio Africanus, and others. Camillus, Fabricius, Scipio, Romulus, Numa, and Brutus are specimens of civic virtue. Catilina typifies the great criminal. Such illustrations were common coin with the orators of the imperial age.[12]

But certain factors led St. Augustine to a more profound consideration of history than that usual with the grammarians and their disciples. But it is an exaggeration to suggest that the Donatist controversy made a "modern historian" of him.[13] His great objective in dealing with the history of the Donatist heresy, as with any other part of the human record, is to reconcile the record with the Christian faith, and to place secular data in a sacred context. His account of Near Eastern history is little more than a chronological pairing off of local worthies with Old Testament figures and Greek heroes. He does not bother to adapt or supplement Eusebius' chronological tables so as to deal with the period before Abraham, a period of relevance to his theme.[14] He is particularly keen on

[11] Suetonius *Divus Augustus* 89.2; Cicero *De Divinatione* i.50, plena exemplorum est historia; and *Brutus* 42, concessum est rhetoribus ementiri in historicis ut aliquid dicere possint argutius; *cf.* Cicero *Epist. ad Fam.* v.12.3.

[12] *Epist.* 104.6; 138.10; 167.7–8; *De Civ. D.* v.18.2; *Contra Jul. Pelag.* iv.3.17; *De Op. Monach.* 25.32. J.-P. Trudel, *Saint Augustin, Humaniste* (Trois-Rivières, Que.: Bien Public, 1954), p. 46, says with reason, "Pour Augustin, l'histoire fait donc partie du 'labeur grammatical;' elle est 'une filiale' de la grammaire; mais elle est parfois aussi l'humble servante de la rhétorique à laquelle elle sert d'ornement en fournissant une collection d'exemples."

[13] *Cf.* Paul Monceaux, *Histoire Littéraire de l'Afrique* (Paris: Leroux, 1901–1923), VII, 197, 205, 243, cited by Marrou, *S. Augustin et la Fin de la Culture Antique*, p. 419.

[14] William MacAllen Green, "Augustine on the Teaching of History," in *University of California Publications in Classical Philology*, XII, 18 (1944), 327.

chronological studies of an unambitious sort, which can help to maintain Christian claims to priority in ideas. Thus St. Ambrose is said to have shown by his historical researches that Plato is more likely to have plagiarized Jeremiah than Jesus Plato. He notes, too, that the letters alleged to have been written by Jesus to Sts. Peter and Paul cannot be authenticated.[15]

There is a disproportionate reliance upon the Old Testament, but St. Augustine shows a considerable acquaintance with Roman historians from Ennius (mythology is not distinguished from history) to Eutropius.[16] In each case he uses them as a source of *exempla* to illustrate his *a priori* theory: never as a source of material which might with critical care be woven into a coherent objective record. Varro is his chief authority for pagan history and religion, and in every field he is made to testify to pagan folly. He is praised as the most learned of the Romans, as a source for all secular learning— and as trustworthy. Regret is expressed that he lived too early to be converted to Christianity.[17] He is the great guide to Roman institutions, and with Eusebius serves as a source for the great eastern monarchies. St. Augustine has read Eusebius' *Historia Ecclesiastica* in Rufinus' translation, and relies upon St. Jerome's translation of that great study of comparative chronology, the *Praeparatio Evangeli*. Marrou thinks that he may be forgiven for relying upon "the best contemporary authorities" for historical data.[18] The point is that his purpose does not seem to demand a disinterested search for factual accuracy, but tolerates the work of any historian to the extent that the latter purveys information appearing to support his own *a priori* interpretation of the historical process.

Sallust is said to weight his words carefully, to give a full account, to have penetrating insight and good judgment, and to be completely impartial. This confidence is not shared by Sallustian scholars. The work of Sallust is cited twelve times in the first decade of the *De*

[15] *De Cons. Evang.* i.10.15f.; *De Doctr. Christ.* ii.28.42.

[16] Burleigh, *City of God*, pp. 196–197; Samuel Angus, *The Sources of the First Ten Books of Augustine's "De Civitate Dei"* (Princeton: Princeton University Press, 1906), pp. 9–49; F. G. Maier, *Augustin und das Antike Rom* (Stuttgart: Kohlhammer, 1955), p. 78.

[17] *De Ord.* ii.20.54; *De Civ. D.* vi.2; xviii.2.2; xix.22.

[18] *De Civ. D.* 18, *passim; Epist.* 222.2. Marrou, *S. Augustin et la Fin de la Culture Antique*, p. 466.

Civitate Dei.[19] In one case he is carelessly misquoted, the name of Cato being substituted for that of Caesar.[20] He testifies to the horrors of pagan warfare, and to the moral degeneracy which followed Roman victory and accompanied prosperity—and to nothing else, as far as St. Augustine's use of him is concerned. Livy is mentioned twice, and Angus has shown him to be a major source for the first decade of the *De Civitate Dei*, sometimes through the medium of the epitomes.[21] Here again St. Augustine's use of materials is not antiseptically meticulous, and in one instance he lowers a figure cited by Livy.[22] From Florus he borrows *exempla*, and here too he is capable of carelessness.[23] Eutropius is used in the same way, and his *Breviarium* is almost contemporary.[24] On two occasions St. Augustine seems to follow Eutropius into careless errors, stating in contradiction of Livy that Lucius Valerius died during his consulship instead of in the following year, and adding a year to the duration of the Social War, an error in which Eutropius is inconsistent with his own account, as St. Augustine would have noted had it occurred in the Canonical Scriptures and therefore been worth noting.[25] Almost certainly he thinks the secular account insufficiently important to warrant much expenditure of critical energy.[26] There are only three reminiscences of Tacitus and one of Suetonius.[27] Each would have corroborated St. Augustine's opinion

[19] *De Civ. D.* i.5; ii.18, 19: iii.10, 18; *De Beat. Vit.* 31.

[20] *De Civ. D.* i.5. *Cf.* Sallust *Coniur. Catil.* 51.

[21] *De Civ. D.* ii.24; iii.7. Angus, *Sources of the First Ten Books of Augustine's "De Civitate Dei,"* pp. 26–35; 49.

[22] *De Civ. D.* ii.17, decem as against quindecim (Livy, Valerius, Plutarch).

[23] *De Civ. D.* ii.16. *Cf.* Florus *Epit.* i.1.2, following Livy *Ab Urbe Condita* i.19.5.

[24] Angus, *Sources of the First Ten Books of Augustine's "De Civitate Dei,"* p. 49; Marrou, *S. Augustin et la Fin de la Culture Antique*, p. 418.

[25] (a) *De Civ. D.* v.18, and Eutropius *Brev.* i.11.4 as against Livy *Ab Urbe Condita* ii.16.7. (b) *De Civ. D.* v.22, and Eutropius *Brev.* v.3.3 as against Eutrop. *Brev.* v.4.

[26] Blunders for which no external source can be found, e.g., number of Metellus' sons, see *De Civ. D.* ii.23, and Angus, *Sources of the First Ten Books of Augustine's "De Civitate Dei,"* p. 277.

[27] *De Civ. D.* xx.19; xxi.5, 25. Angus, *Sources of the First Ten Books of Augustine's "De Civitate Dei,"* pp. 49–50; Marrou, *S. Augustin et la Fin de la Culture Antique*, p. 481, note 1.

of the degeneracy of pagan society, and his neglect of them in favor of epitomists and antiquaries suggests that he did not think that the development of his historical theme called for any very detailed study of the secular evidence. He knows in advance what he will find, and what conclusions he will draw, and sees no need to go far afield in pursuit of illustrations and *exempla*.

Cicero is used, for political science if not for historical evidence. His definition of *populus* as *multitudo iuris consensu et utilitatis communione sociata* is quoted to show how far short the Roman Republic fell of its own defective ideal.[28] Apuleius, in addition to giving evidence as a Platonic philosopher, is made to testify to the natural disasters which befell the world before Christianity had begun to interfere with the worship of the pagan gods.[29] Seneca testifies to the absurdity of the Roman civic theology and its rites, the official worship of the Roman state.[30] Justin is quoted referring to the Roman monarchical period as a "golden age"; St. Augustine doubts its golden quality, from the *Christian* point of view, and notes that other "more trustworthy" but unnamed authors do not share Justin's enthusiasm. Justin's untrustworthiness would probably not have warranted mention if he had managed to avoid reference to a pre-Christian golden age.

It is doubtful if St. Augustine had any direct acquaintance with the Greek historians.[31] The history of the later empire is not completely overlooked; he discusses Constantine, Julian, Valens, Valentinian, that model Christian prince Theodosius the Great, and Honorius' pagan-harrying counts Gaudentius and Jovius, as we shall see, but only with regard to their relations with the Christian community.[32] He shows a generalized contempt for the work of pagan authors, but is ready to accept their testimony at face value when it can be used to put pagan society in a bad light.

The subject of the historian should always be the evolution of the Divine Plan, *the main lines of which are to be taken as a datum.* The

[28] *De Civ. D.* ii.21.2; ix.4.

[29] *De Civ. D.* iv.2; viii.4, 14.

[30] *De Civ. D.* vi.10.3.

[31] For his knowledge of Greek, see pp. 102–105 below. Reminiscences of Herodotus perhaps springing from "common knowledge" rather than personal reading, see *De Civ. D.* i.14 (Herod. i.23–24; *cf.* Ovid *Fasti*, xi.80); *De Civ. D.* xviii.2 (Herod. i.181); *De Civ. D.* x.13 (Herod. i.65).

[32] *De Civ. D.* v.21, 26; xiii.52; xviii.40, 54; xxi.6.

historian should reserve his ingenuity for wresting the record into conformity with the data of faith, and the test of truth for pagan writers must always be agreement with the Biblical account. St. Augustine says that he gives the catechumens an outline of God's plan from Creation to the present time,[33] marking off epochs, *and not burdening his hearers with too many details*, but aiming at showing them how the love of God is revealed in history, and at awakening in them a reciprocal love. God's great design is adequately revealed in the Canonical Scriptures, properly interpreted; secular historical studies at best supply unneeded but interesting corroboration, which may strike the imagination of men whose education has for better or worse been secular. The secular scientist here as everywhere must justify himself by serving as a hewer of wood and a drawer of water for the Christian exegete. From the point of view of the modern professional historian, St. Augustine's approach must seem strangely limited, if not disingenuous. From his own, he is not indifferent to truth; but not all truth is equally worth knowing. The purpose of historical studies is not to discover but to illustrate the truth that is important.

In a world where every experience is part of the realization of the Thought of God, any branch of learning, and not merely historical studies so called, might be expected to contribute to our understanding of the process of realization, the historical process.

St. Augustine has a thorough grounding in Latin classical literature.[34] He received a conventional grammatical training at Madaura, and learned the rules of language and of meter.[35] But after the beginning of his episcopate, his time and energy were absorbed by the spiritual needs of his diocese. At one time, he had read half a book of Vergil a day; now this went by the board.[36] Apart from the problem of time, he formed the opinion that much in the field of belles-lettres was an unhealthy "literature of escape." Who but a fool would weep for Dido's misfortunes while his own soul faced the possibility of damnation? Philological learning which worries about

[33] *De Cat. Rud.* 3.5.

[34] Greek? See pp. 102–105 above.

[35] Figgis, *Political Aspects of S. Augustine's "City of God,"* p. 44; Trudel, *Saint Augustin, Humaniste,* p. 45; John Joseph O'Meara, *The Young Augustine* (New York: Longmans, 1954), p. 41; Gennadius *Script. Eccl.* 46, vir acer ingenio, in divinis scripturis doctus, Graeca et Latina lingua scholasticus.

[36] *De Ord.* i.8.26; *Epist.* 72.23; 75.6; 101.3; 110.6; 118.9; 213.5–6.

solecisms and false quantities reveals false pride. It is stupid to be more interested in the rules of grammar than in those of salvation, and one gathers that all one's time is not too much to devote to these. At any rate, they should always have priority over matters not essential to the survival of either body or soul. It is true that he writes to the deacon Deogratias, and offers to help in the latter's teaching program; but his contribution would certainly be designed to serve an apologetical purpose.[37]

St. Augustine shows a meager and elementary knowledge of mathematics.[38] He thinks that this study can have three justifications, none of which, except perhaps the last, would appeal strongly to professional mathematicians. First, it can bring us to Platonic-Christian idealism, by introducing us to eternal and universal truths which have a real existence independent of their sensational expressions.[39] Second, mathematics can sometimes supply the Christian exegete with a timely metaphor or simile. Thus the will of the sage is like a circle, where everything depends upon a central point—in this case, the sage's Christian faith. The mathematical axioms—eternal, universal, immaterial—offer for finite minds a feeble analogy to the existence and nature of God himself.[40] Third, mathematical studies can sharpen the wits. But mathematical proficiency must never become an end in itself.[41]

St. Augustine shows little knowledge of astronomy, although he admires the technical skill of astronomers and contrasts their mathematical calculation of solstices, equinoxes, and eclipses with the fables of the Manichees. The more he knew of astronomy the less regard he had for astrology. But apart from this indirect contribution to enlightenment, it is said to add nothing to human happiness and to be a waste of time. Scientific knowledge for its own sake has no value in St. Augustine's eyes.[42] He attaches little importance to nature in itself, though the stars, like every work of God, can convey intimations of His purpose, and can provide illuminating "figures." For instance, the moon, in reflecting the sun and in

---

[37] *De Cat. Rud.* i.2; *Conf.* i.13.21, 18.29; *De Doctr. Christ.* ii.13.20.

[38] Marrou, *S. Augustin et la Fin de la Culture Antique*, pp. 273, 287.

[39] *De Immort. Anim.* 2.2, quid enim tam aeternam quam circuli ratio ?

[40] *De Doctr. Christ.* ii.38.56; *De Ord.* i.1.2; *De Quant. Anim.* 16.27–29.

[41] *De Ord.* ii.5.14, talis enim eruditio, si ea moderate utitur, nam nihil ibi quam nimium formidandum est.

[42] *Conf.* v.3.6, 4.7–8.

suffering eclipses, offers an analogy to the soul, or the church, which reflect with sinful interruptions the Sun of Righteousness.[43]

St. Augustine's demonstrated knowledge of physics is equally negligible.[44] He shows caution with regard to contemporary theories, and confesses that he has not had time to plumb the difficult depths of cosmology. He adheres to the doctrine of the four elements: earth at the bottom, and water, air, and fire ranged above it.[45] He gives much thought to the quasi-theological question of primitive matter. What is meant by the saying, "The earth was without form, and void"? He conceives of a formless substance endowed with some life, underlying not merely the form of things, but underlying the four elements themselves. It is the substratum of all diversity and change, and like everything else it was created by God. The structure of the world reveals an internal logic and a perfect order which bolsters faith in Providence.[46]

St. Augustine shows a certain passing interest in biology by dissecting some kind of legged worm at Cassiciacum, and recording that each separated segment seems capable of acting autonomously. He is ready to accept various current notions. Bees, he says, spring from the bodies of dead oxen. Elsewhere he offers an alternative or supplementary theory that their young are produced from wax. One can hardly blame him for not being more advanced than his contemporaries in scientific knowledge. But the real value of biology lies for St. Augustine in the light which it can throw upon God's purpose. St. Augustine wishes that someone would do for botany what Eusebius has done for history, by preparing a concordance for the use of exegetes. An elementary knowledge of how a serpent sloughs his skin would add point to the injunction to put off the old man and put on the new. In commenting on the sentence *justus ut palma florebit*, he says that as the palm tree lifts its leaves toward the sky, the just man reaches out and expands toward the heavenly Christ, realizing his beauty.[47]

[43] *Ennar. in Ps.* 10; *Epist.* 55.58. Meyrick Heath Carré, *Nominalists and Realists* (London and New York: Oxford University Press, 1946), p. 23.

[44] Pierre Maurice Marie Duhem, *Système du Monde* (Paris: Hermann, 1913–1917), II, 410.

[45] *De Civ. D.* xxii.11.

[46] *Conf.* xii.6.6; *De Ord.* ii.4.12, 5.14.

[47] *De Mor. Manich.* 2.63; *De Trin.* iii.8.13; *De Quant Anim.* 62; *De Doctr. Christ.* ii.16.24, 29.45.

Some interest has been shown in St. Augustine's implicit opinion of evolution, a theory of which he had no explicit conception. Genesis itself offers two accounts of creation. In the first chapter it is said that God created all things in an instant; but in the second, a temporal succession of creations is described—hardly a deliberate anticipation of the theory of the progressive modification of species.[48] St. Augustine reconciles the two accounts by suggesting that Creation is in two stages: 1. All flora, fauna, and inanimate objects were created by God simultaneously, some taking form immediately, and others not yet appearing but being the predestined products of processes set in train at the moment of Creation. These latter creations *in posse* are said to exist from the beginning as *rationes seminales*, germs of the seeds of all beings destined to appear in time. The germ of potentiality does not contain the individual in condensed form, any more than the acorn contains a tiny oak, but rather in a causal potency.[49] 2. All things actually *appear*, and the *rationes seminales* are "realized," in due succession and order. The voluntary activity of created beings cannot create any truly new thing, but can be used by God to further the appearance of something already created by Him and existing *in seminali ratione*. When an apparently new being appears, in horticulture for instance, this is simply the development of a latent potentiality present *ex origine*.[50] Will the *rationes seminales* develop in a way consistent with modern evolutionary theory ? He says that a bean cannot come from a grain of wheat, nor wheat from a bean, because each thing has its "well-defined force and proper quality." But over against this vaguely encouraging remark, he says, "It is not impossible for Him to change the natures of His own creatures into whatever He pleases." This would seem to allow for the possibility of developments likely to startle scientific evolutionists. He has an open mind with regard to lycanthropy and other forms of shape-shifting. But these transformations perhaps affect only the "outer man," and are not genuine instances of transmutation of species. But one must certainly disagree with Bourke's suggestion that St. Augustine would have denied the possibility of Adam's having begun with an animal

---

[48] Carré, *Nominalists and Realists*, p. 23.

[49] *De Gen. ad Litt.* vi.11.18; v.23.44–46. Ernest Charles Messenger, *Evolution and Theology* (London: Burns, Oates and Washbourne, 1931).

[50] *De Trin.* iii.8.13–19.

body which later "turned human."[51] The *ratio seminalis* of man could presumably have existed in hominids. Whether St. Augustine would have liked this suggestion is an open question! But his expressed views are at least consistent with the idea of an evolution of human beings from lower types. The fact that man is said to have been made in the image of God is not really to the point. St. Augustine's thought is at least waveringly consistent with the modern theory of the modification of species. He may have been a conscious evolutionist to the extent of having a sense of "the plasticity of things." But the evolution which he accepts is teleologically conceived, whatever its *modus operandi*, and here he parts company with modern secular evolutionists.[52]

Rhetoric, queen of the ancient "social sciences," can serve in the propagation of the faith. But useful as it can be, St. Augustine feels that he himself would have been better advised to have spent his youthful energy in praising God rather than in cultivating and preening himself upon his skill in public speaking. The applause of the world is smoke and wind. He could have sharpened his wits sufficiently in studying Scripture, without sacrificing to the rebellious angels by seeking worldly applause.[53] His parents were so concerned that he acquire a rhetorical education which might fit him for a lucrative career that they failed to study his more immediate physical and moral needs, which might have been better served, though at some risk to his education, by an early marriage.[54] He replies most ungraciously to a young Christian, who has written asking his advice with regard to a study of the rhetorical books of Cicero, that he, a Christian bishop, can neither take a fee nor waste his time gratis in giving instruction in such "childish trifles." He would show himself a "contemptible trifler" if he tried to comment on these books.[55] The fact that his correspondent frankly admits that he is seeking advice on how to make an impression of great scholarship in the town to which he is moving may help to explain

---

[51] *De Civ. D.* xxi.8; *De Gen. ad Litt.* v.23.44. Vernon Joseph Bourke, *Augustine's Quest of Wisdom* (Milwaukee: Bruce, 1945), p. 235; Carré, *Nominalists and Realists*, p. 21.

[52] He hardly knows what to think about stories of shape-shifting.

[53] *Conf.* i.11.17, 17.27.

[54] *Conf.* ii.2.4–5.

[55] *Epist.* 118.2.9, 5.34.

St. Augustine's asperity. The fact that he did in the end condescend
to give some helpful advice in no way indicates a retreat from his
first expressed position. It might of course be argued that St.
Augustine's practice has had a greater effect than his preaching, and
that the example of erudition and eloquence shown by him and
other Fathers of the Church had a much greater cultural effect upon
their Roman and medieval successors than had their professions of
distaste for eloquence and erudition.

Logic can help in disentangling scriptural knots, but can lead to
wrangling, quibbling, and pride in intellectual one-upmanship. The
man with dialectical skill is likely to have an exaggerated impression
of his own intelligence. What profit is there in understanding
Aristotle's *Categories* if one is ignorant of the Source of such truth
as Aristotle may have stumbled upon? The rules of logic in themselves are useful instruments. But a logical syllogism, however
accurately formulated, is as objectively true as the premises upon
which it is based. For a Christian, truth means consistency with the
Christian faith.[56]

St. Augustine confesses to a considerable sensuous pleasure in
music, and recognizes that listening even to the music of the church
can be an aesthetic rather than a devotional experience.[57] In the
De Musica he is nearly led astray into the field of aesthetics. But
righting himself, he confesses that the teaching of music is chiefly
to be valued because the harmonies of sensation may lead the spirit
to discovery of the universal harmonies in the thought of God.
Christ's own death, conquering the double death to which sin had
condemned us, reflects, in this marvelous "accord," the perfect
consonance of the octave.[58]

In nearly every case the value of the various practical skills is
reckoned in terms of their ability to throw light upon words,
expressions, or ideas in Scripture. Such skills as medicine, farming,
and sailing can have some use in this way; and in addition the
Christian may practice them, if not for profit then at least for a
living.[59] Reading, writing, and even shorthand can help one in

[56] *De Doctr. Christ.* ii.31.48–49, 35.53, 37.55; *Conf.* iv.16.28.
[57] *Conf.* x.33.49.
[58] *De Trin.* iv.2.4; *De Doctr. Christ.* ii.16.26.
[59] *De Doctr. Christ.* ii.30.47.

learning and in spreading the Gospel.[60] Some knowledge of geography, mineralogy, and other such matters can be useful in a small way on occasion.

But is there any justification for the not uncommon view that St. Augustine contrived in some way to reconcile sacred and secular learning? Reeves says that in becoming a Christian he repudiated his former sins and nothing else, and had no regrets for a memory well stocked with pagan poets, playwrights, and philosophers. When he condemns vain curiosity, it is sometimes obvious that he is thinking of magical and other occult inquiries; and when he says that the angels have contempt for the knowledge which devils vaunt, he is really castigating the devils' lack of charity,[61] shown in their vaunting. Figgis even suggests that there was an element of pose in his frequent expressions of contempt for secular learning.[62] In the next section we shall consider the extent to which his thought was influenced by Neo-Platonism.

But it would seem that in a very real sense he did repudiate his pagan learning. No one would claim that on his conversion he forgot his classical education and his former preoccupations. That old seminarian, Marshal Stalin, is said never to have emancipated his speech from such expressions as "God willing." But far from glorying in his past, and recommending a similar training for others, St. Augustine seems only to hope to realize something from what he has come to regard as a dubious investment of youthful time and energy, and to suggest how others in a similar predicament can put their educational lumber to some use. In his eyes, secular education has value insofar as it helps to develop habits of obedience and industry, and provides a linguistic and grammatical basis for the study of Scripture, and makes one more critical of such pretentious nonsense as that put forward by the Manichees.[63]

It would be wrong to think that while St. Augustine could see only a limited *exegetical* value in mathematics, biology, and so on, he was ready to concede that for ordinary Christians they can have a practical value which can justify a lifetime spent in mastering

[60] *De Doctr. Christ.* ii.26.40; *Conf.* i.13.20.
[61] *Conf.* x.35.54–55; *De Civ. D.* ix.22.
[62] Figgis, *Political Aspects of St. Augustine's "City of God,"* p. 44.
[63] *Conf.* v.3.3. Cochrane, *Christianity and Classical Culture,* p. 394.

them. In point of fact, he says that worldly learning offers little real advantage to anyone. An elementary knowledge of natural science might have some value, both exegetical and for purposes of making a living; but all that a Christian need know for happiness is that a good God created everything in nature.[64] For earthly purposes, very little knowledge will suffice for earning a living, *and detailed specialization would distract from more important things.* St. Augustine speaks slightingly of empirical knowledge, and while, as Carré says, that is not identical with disparaging a scientific understanding of nature, it tends to give one's understanding an *a priori* character.[65] Technical progress is occasionally noted, but it is always distinguished from *real* progress, which has to do with one's growth in Christian faith.[66] Wisdom takes precedence over science, the chief service of which is to furnish figures and similes for the elucidation of Scripture.[67]

Granted, then, that secular studies can have a certain slight value; but they are more likely to afford danger and distraction. Interest should be heavily concentrated upon eternal things, and curiosity about temporal matters is to be discouraged; *curiosus* is a term of abuse. Secular studies should be pursued, at most, in discreet moderation.[68] In the end, St. Augustine comes to think that he has overstated the case for philosophy and the liberal arts. Knowledge of any sort out of the ordinary tends to puff up the student.[69] Such secular knowledge as the Christian needs can be predigested for him by the Church.[70]

3. Treatment of Philosophy

The western Christian tradition was not overly friendly to secular philosophy taken as a key to the meaning of reality and of the cosmic process. Tertullian describes philosophers as publicity-hunting

[64] *De Fide Spe Car.* 3.9.

[65] *De Anim. et eius Orig.* iv.10.14; *De Fide Spe Car.* 9.

[66] *De Civ. D.* xviii.3, 6, 8, 12–13, 22, 24, etc. Henri Irénée Marrou, *L'Ambivalence du Temps de l'Histoire chez Saint Augustin* (Paris: Vrin, 1950), pp. 28–29.

[67] *De Doctr. Christ.* ii.16.23–24; *De Ord.* i.8.24. Marrou, *S. Augustin et la Fin de la Culture Antique*, p. 280.

[68] *De Ord.* i.8.24, eruditio disciplinarum liberalium modesta sane atque succincta; i.11.31; ii.5.17; *De Mus.* vi.13.39.

[69] *De Doctr. Christ.* ii.42.62.

[70] *Conf.* i.15.24. Dawson, in D'Arcy and others, *Monument to Saint Augustine*, p. 58, on Tychonius.

corrupters of virtue; he says further that dialectics is the mother of heresy and, in effect, that the pure milk of the Gospel can only be soured by the approach of a philosopher.[71] Even St. Ambrose maintains that the Christian faith is sufficient in itself, and that whatever is valuable and true in secular thought has been stolen from the Judaeo-Christian tradition.[72]

St. Augustine himself believes that the Christian faith contains everything which a man need know for salvation. But he seeks assurance that his Christian beliefs make sense in terms of what he takes to be the best thought of his day, fallible as that thought may be,[73] in principle. Of all the disciplines, philosophy especially should lead to the contemplation of *intelligibilia*.[74] But God may conceal his nature from men of intellect, and reveal himself to very humble persons.[75] Furthermore, the disagreements of philosophers suggest to St. Augustine, as to Timon of Phlius, the folly of relying upon them for the highest knowledge; and the fact that no pagan city has ever dared to emulate the Jews and set up a canon of "Wisdom Literature" is taken as a confession of the limitations of non-Christian intellect.[76] The role of philosophy should always be secondary to that of revelation. Reason by itself, even in the most brilliant men, cannot discover unquestionable truth without divine illumination. Faith must precede reason. Before one can apply reason to the explanation of an object, one must have faith in the latter's existence and in the powers of reason. *The real use of philosophy is to show how reasonable are the pronouncements of authority.* It is complementary to the Christian faith, serving to make the latter seem more plausible to intelligent, educated men.

St. Augustine says that after his revulsion from Manichaeism he adopted Academic suspense of judgment, and drifted listlessly and lazily with the wind.[77] One need not assume a special study of the original sources for either Pyrrhonism or the ideas of the New

[71] Tertullian *Apol.* 46, and *De Praescript. Haeret.* 7.

[72] Carré, *Nominalists and Realists*, p. 5.

[73] *De Ord.* i.1.2; ii.9.26; *Contra Acad.* iii.6.13; *De Ord.* ii.28; i.3.9, 11.31. (Sister) Mary Patricia Garvey, *St. Augustine, Christian or Neo-Platonist?* (Milwaukee: Marquette University Press, 1939), p. 94.

[74] E.g., *Epist.* 101.3; *Retract.* i.6.

[75] *Conf.* v.3.5; *cf. De Civ. D.* ii.7.

[76] *De Civ. D.* xviii.41.3.

[77] *Conf.* v.14.25; *Contra Acad.* ii.9.23; *De Beat. Vit.* 4.

Academy. The question of St. Augustine's grasp of Greek will be discussed below. In any event, he would hardly have been recognized as a skeptic by the Skeptics *ipsissimi*, for he says that he never doubted that seven plus three make ten, that God exists, that the soul is mortal, and Christian ethics valid.[78] He has too high an opinion of the sagacity and dexterity of the human mind to think that it has no chance of seizing upon any truth. In a very short time he recovered his capacity for "assenting." He came to think that he could be, and was, certain of some things, but never, be it noted, of information drawn from sensation and reason, without a higher guarantee. On issues where his adopted Christian faith gives no lead, he continues to display Academic suspense of judgment. He professes a wholesome "scientific" skepticism with regard to the findings of pagan science and the pronouncements of scientific authorities. The inferences made by physicists, astronomers, zoologists, botanists, mineralogists, physiographers, chronologists, and others are not to be taken as proven facts: usually they are more or less intelligent guesses, to be accepted tentatively, if at all, and with no really worth-while end to justify the risk.[79] Skepticism drives him into subjective idealism, or at any rate cuts all other ground from under his feet. His concession to Carneades is that, for all his "belief" in revealed and intuitive truth, ninety-nine per cent of the time he lives by faith, taking a chance with the merely plausible.[80]

He freely admits ignorance. One need not believe all that one hears of monstrous races; but it would be equally rash to deny *the possibility* that where there are monstrous births there may be monstrous races.[81] In one instance he departs from this admirable suspense of judgment and says flatly that it is quite incredible that men should exist on the other side of the earth. But he is led to this uncharacteristically dogmatic stand by the positive dogmatism of those who insist that there *must* be land, and Antipodes to inhabit it, on the other side of the earth.[82] He will not affirm as a known fact the existence of *incubi*, but says that it would be impudent to deny

[78] *Conf.* vi.4.6–8, 11.18.
[79] *De Fide Spe Car.* 9.
[80] *De Util. Cred.* 20.
[81] *De Civ. D.* xvi.1–2.
[82] *De Civ. D.* xvi.9.

out of hand so many apparently trustworthy witnesses.[83] Varro
tells of various shape-shiftings: Ulysses' companions were changed
into animals by Circe; Arcadians become wolves when they share
in certain rites and swim in a certain pool, and become men again if
they keep from human flesh for nine years and then swim back across
the same pool; Demaenetus, an Arcadian, turned wolf after he had
tasted the flesh of a boy offered in sacrifice to Zeus Lycaeus, and was
changed back into a man ten years later, went into training, and won
a victory at Olympia.[84] Are such stories to be credited? And what
of the transformations "told of or feigned" by Apuleius? They are
either false, or so extraordinary as to excuse disbelief. But they are
not dismissed as impossible.[85] St. Augustine suggests that they may
have been hallucinations. He goes on to report various travelers'
tales which he cannot explain scientifically. Salt from Agrigentum
melts when thrown in the fire, and crackles when thrown in water;
the Garamantae have a fountain whose water is too cold to drink by
day, and at night is too hot to touch; there is a fountain in Epirus
which lights quenched brands and quenches lighted ones; Egyptian
figwood sinks in water, but once soaked it rises and cannot be sub-
merged again; the interior brilliancy of Persian selenite varies with
the phases of the moon; Cappadocian mares impregnated by the
wind bear colts who live for three months only.[86] He assumes that
the story of the Epirote fountain is probably true, because he has
heard of another similar one at Grenoble. As for the others, he states
unequivocally that *he neither affirms nor denies*, showing an open-
mindedness, particularly with regard to the Cappadocian mares,
which few modern skeptics would care to imitate. He is skeptical in
the sense that he carefully avoids either positive or negative
dogmatism.[87]

He ventures to tilt in desultory fashion with the Skeptics. According to Cicero, they held that nothing could be perceived to be
certainly true, but St. Augustine thinks that he can make true
statements. In physics, for instance, he can assert that "The number

[83] *De Civ. D.* xv.23.1.
[84] *De Civ. D.* xviii.17.
[85] *De Civ. D.* xix.18.1f.
[86] *De Civ. D.* xxi.5.1.
[87] *De Civ. D.* xxi.7.2, caetera vera sic habeo, ut neque affirmanda neque
negam decreverim. *Cf. De Civ. D.* xxi.6.

of worlds is either one or not one," and that "The number of worlds is either finite or infinite." But these statements make no positive assertions about the nature of the world, or the number of worlds, and the term "world" is itself left undefined and unexplained. To pose alternatives is not to describe the thing in itself.[88] We have already noted his superficially more impressive claim that the fact of doubt, and of suspended judgment, implies the real existence of an agent who doubts and can suspend judgment.[89]

St. Augustine seems to have thought that Plato, the Academics, Aristotle, the Peripatetics, and the Stoics form one more or less consistent School, *in una verissimae philosophiae disciplina*,[90] although he acknowledges that on occasion they differ, and in these instances he prefers the Platonic position.[91] Julian of Eclanum sneeringly calls him "the Punic Aristotle," probably with reference to his claim to have read the *Categories* without difficulty.[92] It has been suggested that Aristotle had considerable influence upon him, and reinforced his common sense against the fantasies of the Manichees.[93] If so, the reaction was delayed for a decade if, as he claims, he read the *Categories* when he was about twenty, before he had taken up with the Manichees. His psychology has elements suggestive of Plato, the Neo-Platonists, Aristotle, the Peripatetics, and the Stoics, and he makes passing references to Anaxagoras, Anaximander, Anaximines, Antisthenes, Carneades, Epicurus, Pythagoras, and Zenocrates, but never, except in the case of (Neo-) Platonism, in such a way as to suggest extensive personal acquaintance.[94]

To what extent did St. Augustine understand Greek? Opinions on his proficiency range from confidence in his ability to read all the *Enneads* in the original to the view that he could at most translate easy sermons, if indeed he could deal with any Greek text without a

[88] O'Meara, *Young Augustine*, p. 112.

[89] Morgan, *Psychological Teaching of St. Augustine*, p. 165.

[90] *Contra Acad.* iii.19.42. Morgan, *Psychological Teaching of St. Augustine*, p. 25; Burleigh, *City of God*, p. 68. Was he led to this by following Victorinus alone?

[91] *De Civ. D.* viii.7.

[92] In Latin? See p. 104.

[93] *Op. Imperf. Contra Jul.* iii.199; *De Quant. Anim.* 72; *De Trin.* xiii.9.12.

[94] Morgan, *Psychological Teaching of St. Augustine*, pp. 16, 23.

Latin translation at hand.[95] At one time, most Romans had begun their grammatical training with a study of Greek, and St. Augustine tells us that as a boy he spent painful hours with a Greek text of Homer.[96] Judging by its scant effect upon his later writings, his acquaintance with classical Greek must have made very little impression upon him. His own claims are modest in the extreme. He says, *et ego quidem graecae linguae perparum assecutus sum, et prope nihil.*[97] But Marrou suggests, agreeing with Angus, that this is only "une plaisanterie, un artifice de rhétorique," intended to disarm critics. "I'm no Greek scholar, but even I can see that your interpretation of *katholikos* is wrong."[98]

He shows a certain low technical knowledge of Greek. He compares Greek and Latin versions of Biblical passages, and shows a superficial interest in the differences between the Greek versions.[99] He uses such Greek terms as "historical," "aetiological," "analogical," and "allegorical" in describing the methods and results of exegesis.[100] He explains many Greek terms, frequently repeating himself. Nor are these explanations particularly *recherché*. He will show simple equivalents, such as *epi = super, tis = quis*; or etymologies, such as *philosophia = amor sapientiae, Cynici = canini philosophi*. Or he will explain simple technical terms both pagan (e.g., *analogia, rhythmos*) and Christian (*chrisma = unctio*, whence *Christus; ousia = essentia*).[101]

St. Augustine reveals some knowledge of Antiochene theology. He appeals on occasion to St. Gregory Nazianzus, to St. John Chrysostom, to St. Basil the Great, and to various other Greek Fathers; and seems actually to have had before him the Greek text of St. John Chrysostom, *Homilies to Neophytes*, and to have

---

[95] Paul Henry, *Plotin et l'Occident* (Louvain: "Specilegium Sacrum Lovaniense" Bureaux, 1934), p. 133; Pierre Paul Courcelle, *Les Lettres Grecques en Occident* (Paris: Boccard, 1948), p. 161; Gennadius *Script. Eccl.* 46; Combès, *Augustin et la Culture Classique*, pp. 4, 16.

[96] *Conf.* i.14.23; Quintilian *Instit. Orat.* i.1.12, 14.

[97] *Contra Litt. Petil. Donat.* ii.28.91.

[98] Marrou, *S. Augustin et la Fin de la Culture Antique*, p. 29; Angus, *Sources of the First Ten Books of Augustine's "De Civitate Dei,"* p. 239.

[99] *De Doctr. Christ*, ii.12.18.

[100] *De Util. Cred.* 5.

[101] Marrou, *S. Augustin et la Fin de la Culture Antique*, p. 30.

translated a few lines of St. Basil's *Homily on Fasting*.[102] But much of what he reports could have been absorbed from Latin intermediaries, and he himself says that he could not really understand the Greek texts of eastern works on the Trinity. He also asks St. Jerome to suggest a good Latin book on the eastern heresies for those (himself included?) who would have trouble with Greek originals.[103]

It cannot be proven that he himself read a single Greek book for which there was not available a Latin translation, and he frequently quotes Greek authors in Latin translations. He had certainly read Aristotle's *Categories*, for which there was a translation and commentary by Marius Victorinus.[104] He cites Plato's *Timaeus*, once in Cicero's translation, and eight times in the translation of Chalcidius; he cites the *Phaedo*, which Apuleius had translated, four times; all other Platonic references are from Cicero.[105] Neo-Platonic works had great influence upon him at about the time of his conversion, and Henry and Marrou agree that the portions of the *Enneads* which he studied were those translated by Marius Victorinus.[106] There is no proof that he read *only* translated works, but it is suggestive that we find him criticizing translations but never a Greek text *seul*.[107]

Marrou thinks that St. Augustine's episcopal duties would have left little time for the study of Greek in his later years. He continued to read the Bible in Latin: would he have done more for Plato or Plotinus? Furthermore, it is in later life, when writing the *De Trinitate*, that he confesses his inability to handle Greek treatises on the Trinity. The knowledge of which we have evidence is on an elementary level.[108] We may perhaps conclude with Angus that St. Augustine has a modest working knowledge of Greek, chiefly

[102] *Contra Jul. Pelag.* i.5.15.

[103] *Epist.* 40.6; *De Trin., prooem.* 3.1. Morgan, *Psychological Teaching of St. Augustine*, p. 26.

[104] Marrou, *S. Augustin et la Fin de la Culture Antique*, p. 34.

[105] *De Civ. D.* xiii.16.2. Marrou, *S. Augustin et la Fin de la Culture Antique*, p. 34; Angus, *Sources of the First Ten Books of Augustine's "De Civitate Dei,"* p. 241.

[106] *Conf.* vii.9.13; viii.2.3. Henry, *Plotin en l'Occident*, p. 19. Plotinus *Enn.* 16.5.1.

[107] Marrou, *S. Augustin et la Fin de la Culture Antique*, p. 33.

[108] *Ibid.*, p. 35: O'Meara, *Young Augustine*, p. 45.

of the Septuagint, the New Testament, and to a much less degree Greek patristic literature, but that in secular fields he is almost completely dependent upon translations.[109]

Of the philosophers known to St. Augustine, the Neo-Platonists made by far the greatest impact upon him. He says simply that he read "certain books" of the Neo-Platonists. His approach was probably through Victorinus' translations of one or more of the treatises of Plotinus and perhaps one of Porphyry.[110] It has even been suggested that St. Ambrose's sermons gave St. Augustine a predigested synthesis of Christianity and Neo-Platonism,[111] but by his own account he got at least as close as Victorinus could take him to the original sources.

Plotinus is St. Augustine's favorite secular philosopher, whatever the basis of his acquaintance, and Inge actually asserts that it was Plotinus who brought him to Christ, and that in St. Augustine we have, in effect, Neo-Platonism plus the Incarnation.[112] Burnaby calls him the greatest disciple and the profoundest critic of Plotinus.[113] It has been suggested that through his influence upon St. Augustine, Plotinus has had more influence upon the development of Christian theology than any other writer with the possible exception of St. Paul.[114] Burnet says that Plotinus provided St. Augustine with the basis of his Christian philosophy,[115] and Inge that Augustinianism is the next logical step after Neo-Platonism, and the last creative achievement of classical civilization.[116] St.

[109] Angus, *Sources of the First Ten Books of Augustine's "De Civitate Dei,"* p. 273.

[110] *Conf.* vii.9.13. For the influence of Victorinus on St. Augustine, see Bishop Gore, "Victorinus," in *Dictionary of Christian Biography*: double procession of Holy Ghost; Holy Ghost as bond of Trinity; unity of Christ and Church; strong predestinationism; strong assertion of grace; priority of faith over reason. *De Ord.* ii.5.16; *Contra Acad.* ii.11.25; *cf.* ii.1.1, and iii.2.3.

[111] Pierre Paul Courcelle, *Recherches sur les Confessions de Saint Augustin* (Paris: Boccard, 1950).

[112] William R. Inge, *The Philosophy of Plotinus* (London and New York: Longmans Green, 1918), I, 12; II, 207.

[113] *Amor Dei*, pref.

[114] *Cf.* Morgan, *Psychological Teaching of St. Augustine*, p. 31; Carré, *Nominalists and Realists*, p. 5.

[115] "Philosophy," in *The Legacy of Greece* (Oxford: Clarendon Press, 1924), p. 91.

[116] "Plotinus," in *Proceedings of the British Academy*, XV (1929), 4.

Augustine himself says simply that, under God, he owed his discovery of God as a spiritual reality to Plotinus.[117]

Certainly Neo-Platonism introduced him to a higher intellectual standard than that of the Manichees, and helped him to the idea, basic to his epistemology, of knowledge by direct perception.[118] He acquired from the Neo-Platonists the intellectual idiom of his exegesis and sermons. It is in Neo-Platonic terms that he discusses the soul, epistemology, the mystical experience and its culmination.[119] The earlier treatises are particularly Neo-Platonic in idiom, but in time his terminology acquires a more distinctively Christian flavor. *But at every stage, whatever his philosophical idiom,* he is expressing Christian beliefs.[120]

Neo-Platonism lends itself particularly well in certain areas to his purpose. First, it helps him to understand and accept the Christian belief in God as an incorporeal and intelligible Substance, by convincing him of the reality of the invisible, universal, and eternal Platonic Forms. The Forms are Christianized by being conceived as Thoughts existing in the mind of God, and St. Augustine believes that the *ordo universi* revealed in Scripture is identical with the imperfect realization in this world of the Platonic Ideas.[121]

Second, to St. Augustine as to Plotinus the soul is a mediator between Form and Matter, and in sensation uses the body as its instrument to perform a spiritual act.[122]

Third, St. Augustine agrees that evil is nonsubstantial, a privation of good rather than a thing in itself,[123] and at the same time he shares with Neo-Platonists an inconsistent suspicion of matter. Both Plato and Plotinus agree that since God is good His creation cannot be

[117] Carré, *Nominalists and Realists*, p. 2; Garvey, *Saint Augustine, Christian or Neo-Platonist ?*, p. 234; Burnaby, *Amor Dei*, p. 29.

[118] William John Sparrow Simpson, *St. Augustine's Conversion* (London: Society for Promoting Christian Knowledge, 1930), p. 56.

[119] Dom Edward Cuthbert Butler, *Western Mysticism* (2nd ed.; London: Constable, 1951), pp. 31, 87; Morgan, *Psychological Teaching of St. Augustine*, pp. 37, 71; Carré, *Nominalists and Realists*, p. 30.

[120] Garvey, *Saint Augustine, Christian or Neo-Platonist ?*, pp. 230–231.

[121] *Conf.* vii.10.16; *De Div. Quaest.* 46.1; Burleigh, *City of God*, pp. 72–73, 188; Burnaby, *Amor Dei*, p. 193; Bourke, *Augustine's Quest of Wisdom*, p. 67.

[122] See Plotinus *Enn.* 4.7.8.

[123] *Conf.* vii.9.13; *cf.* Plotinus *Enn.* 3.2.5, 7, 10; *De Civ. D.* ix.4; x.24, xii.2; xiv.5. Garvey, *Saint Augustine, Christian or Neo-Platonist ?*, p. 52.

bad, and Plotinus writes against the Gnostic view that the phenomenal world is essentially evil. Similarly St. Augustine insists against the Manichees that nothing can limit or resist the power of God. Jesus showed by his incarnation and ascension that the body is compatible with perfection. Christian asceticism aims not at eliminating the body but at bringing it into a sounder relationship with the soul. But for the Platonists of every school, creation means the imposition of Form upon a substratum more or less recalcitrant, and although the resulting phenomena are not evil, they are less good than as if their substratum were more amenable to the divine stamp. Plotinus sometimes, but not always, distinguishes this substratum from *matter*, which is good in that it has received at least a modicum of form. The material body, for instance, is not evil in itself, but is made of poor stuff, which distracts the soul from higher things. All perturbations arise from the connection of the soul with the body.[124] We shall describe below St. Augustine's adverse view of "worldly goods," and whatever he may say of the essential goodness of the material creation, he certainly recommends detachment and indifference toward it, with a view to our putting ourselves beyond the range of its power to hurt us.

St. Augustine shares belief in the mystical approach to God. Plotinus thinks that the soul, derived from God, yet different from Him, longs for an uninterrupted vision of Him, although according to Apuleius this could come only in lightning flashes. St. Augustine agrees that this vision is the *summum bonum*, and at the same time shares the Neo-Platonic bias against the idea of contact, and describes this experience rather as "vision."[125]

Neo-Platonism throws light on the relationship of God to His creation. He is unchangeable and incorporeal, present in all things although everything is not conscious of His presence.[126] Man must empty himself of irrelevancy, to become aware of the presence of God in himself.[127] St. Augustine, *qua* Christian, could approve the doctrine of a God who is the cause of all existence, the End to which

[124] Plato is praised for admitting that body can be good, and Porphyry for insisting that the gods are incorporeal.

[125] *De Civ. D.* viii.8; ix.17. Simpson, *St. Augustine's Conversion*, p. 61; Edward Ingram Watkin, "The Mysticism of St. Augustine," in D'Arcy and others, *Monument to Saint Augustine*, p. 116.

[126] *De Civ. D.* viii.6. Plotinus *Enn.* 6.9.2.3; 6.8.4.7f.

[127] Simpson, *St. Augustine's Conversion*, p. 55.

all life is directed, the ultimate Reason sought by the understanding, the Object of the Beatific Vision, and the Fountain of blessedness.[128]

Finally, the Neo-Platonists are helpful in describing the immaterial nature and the indissoluble association of the First and Second Persons of the Trinity. Much of St. Augustine's enthusiasm for Neo-Platonism arises from his belief that he can find St. John's Prologue in *Ennead* 5. His study of Plotinus and Porphyry, whether direct or second hand, leads him to think that they have some understanding, at least, of the Father and the Son. He agrees with Plotinus that Wisdom must relate to eternal things, and he identifies the Eternal Light with the Logos.[129]

But where Neo-Platonic thought is inconsistent with Christian premises, St. Augustine stands fast by the latter. First, his God is a personal Entity, Who aids those who call upon Him in prayer, whereas Plotinus' God is above thought, consciousness, will, good, and evil.[130] Second, for St. Augustine the Son is consubstantial and equal to the Father, but in the doctrine of Plotinus, *Nous* is a Second Intelligible Hypostasis following upon and in some sense inferior to the Undifferentiated First.[131] Third, St. Augustine is committed to Jesus the Incarnate Son and Sole Mediator, but the Neo-Platonists regard the idea of a divine incarnation as barbaric.[132] Fourth, for St. Augustine the Holy Ghost is consubstantial with the Father and the Son, and proceeds from Both. Plotinus and Porphyry place the Third Person after, and inferior to, the First and Second, and identify it as the World Soul. St. Augustine begins with some sympathy for the idea of the World Soul, but comes to regard it as "scarcely credible," and says that acceptance of it is "rash."[133] Fifth, St. Augustine disapproves of the Neo-Platonic doctrine of successive emanations; the Son, for him, was begotten, the Holy Ghost proceeds, and all else was created *ex nihilo*.[134] Sixth, St.

[128] *De Civ. D.* viii.1.4–5; viii.6; *De Div. Quaest.* 46.2.

[129] *Contra Acad.* iii.5.11; *De Mag.* 39; *Conf.* vii.9.13; *Quaest. in Hept.* 2, q. 25; *De Civ. D.* x.3, 23; *In Johan. Evang.* 2.4.

[130] *Solil.* i.1.2–6. Inge, *Philosophy of Plotinus*, II, 200; Garvey, *Saint Augustine, Christian or Neo-Platonist?* p. 83.

[131] *De Civ. D.* xi.2. Plotinus *Enn.* 5.2.

[132] *Conf.* vii.21.27; *De Civ. D.* x.23.

[133] *De Civ. D.* x.23, 29; *De Immort. Anim.* 15; *Retract.* 1.5.

[134] *De Ver. Rel.* 35; *Contra Sec. Man.* 4; *De Act. cum Fel. Man.* 2.4.

Augustine rejects the Neo-Platonic doctrine of mediating demons; Christians have only one Mediator.[135] Seventh, St. Augustine thinks that the soul cannot see truth without God's help, whereas Plotinus believes that the soul can raise itself by its own effort to the highest level.[136] Eighth, St. Augustine's emphasis upon authority and faith is contrary to the spirit of Plato and Plotinus, at least.[137] Ninth, St. Augustine rejects the Platonic theory of Reminiscence for one of Divine Illumination.[138] Tenth, St. Augustine cannot accept the Platonic doctrine of metempsychosis; the happiness of heaven can be complete only if it is known to be permanent.[139] Eleventh, St. Augustine will not accept Plotinus' interpretation of the mystical experience as a merging of similar elements, with the soul conceived to be an emanation of the World Soul (itself an emanation at one removed from the First Cause).[140] Twelfth, the Christian *Civitas Dei* is different in character from the Platonic *Politeia*. *Civitas Dei* and *Civitas Terrena* are not to be identified, in quasi-Platonic fashion, with *esse* and *posse*, Form and Imitation, the intelligible and the sensational. Nor did St. Augustine limit the heavenly citizenship to persons of superior intellect.[141] Thirteenth, and finally, St. Augustine's view of history is rectilinear rather than cyclic; the Creation was a unique event in which space, time, and world immediately began. *Nam Christus semel natus est.*[142]

We must remember that not merely Christ crucified, but much else in the Christian creed, was "to the Greeks foolishness." St. Augustine tries to make it seem less foolish by rationalizing it in terms of the best thought of his day. He sets himself the task of making the Faith intelligible, plausible, and intellectually respectable for persons educated like himself in the classical tradition.

[135] *De Civ. D.* viii.12; ix, *passim*; x.1; *Conf.* vii.9.15.

[136] *Contra Acad.* iii.6.13. Plotinus *Enn.* 1.6.9.

[137] Simpson, *St. Augustine's Conversion*, p. 85.

[138] See above, p. 51.

[139] *De Civ. D.* viii.4; *Serm.* 241.8.

[140] Garvey, *Saint Augustine, Christian or Neo-Platonist ?*, p. 156.

[141] Dawson, in D'Arcy and others, *Monument to Saint Augustine*, p. 67; Jean Guitton, *Le Temps et l'Eternité chez Plotin et Saint Augustin* (Paris: Boivin, 1933), pp. 288, 290. *Cf.* Werner Jaeger, *Paedeia. The Ideals of Greek Culture*, trans. from 2nd ed. by Gilbert Highet (Oxford: Blackwell, 1939), II, 77, who lists the undoubted similarities.

[142] *De Civ. D.* viii.7.

Anything useful in pagan philosophy is to be snatched without compunction and pressed into the service of the Faith: it is stolen goods, brought back to the service of its proper Master.[143] There is no feeling here of incurring an embarrassing debt. The practice of pillaging the stores of pagan learning is aptly compared to "spoiling the Egyptians," and St. Augustine comments with satisfaction on the quantity and quality of the loot borne off by Cyprian, Lactantius, Hilary, and "Greeks without number."[144] Christ's authority is primary. Neo-Platonism is *used*, to elucidate the Faith and to put it on a reasonable basis. St. Augustine thinks that he can find support in Neo-Platonism for the characteristic Christian doctrines. Neo-Platonism is the "truest of the philosophies of antiquity," as Maritain says, because it can be an instrument of enlightenment in God's hands.[145] But where it fails to elucidate and agree, it is condemned or ignored.

Such wisdom as can be detected in secular philosophy, and especially in Neo-Platonism, is suspected of being stolen from Judaeo-Christian sources. To support this view, St. Augustine points out that the great pagan philosophers came later than the Hebrew prophets. He thinks it at least possible that Plato may have learned something of Jewish thought from conversations in Egypt, although it is unlikely that he had direct dealings with Jeremiah, or read Jewish scriptures as yet not translated into Greek.[146] Retreating in time, he notes that Pythagoras was contemporary with the return of the Jews from Babylon with most of the prophetic literature already written. Thales was contemporary with the first great prophets, and Orpheus, Linus, and Musaeus were earlier. But Moses, greatest of all prophets, if the Pentateuch is taken as allegorical, preceded even these. Moses himself is said to have been learned in an earlier and undoubtedly secular "wisdom of the Egyptians," but this, such as it was, must have developed after writing had been introduced into Egypt by Io-Isis, daughter of Inachus, king of Argos, who was contemporary with the grandsons

[143] *De Doctr. Christ.* ii.40.60. Garvey, *Saint Augustine, Christian or Neo-Platonist ?*, p. 25.

[144] *Cf. De Doctr. Christ.* ii.40.61.

[145] *Contra Acad.* iii.19.42–43. Jacques Maritain, in D'Arcy and others, *Monument to Saint Augustine*, pp. 157–158.

[146] *De Civ D.* viii.11; *cf. De Doctr. Christ.* ii.28.43.

of Abraham. Not only Abraham, the friend of God, but Noah, and
Enoch, seventh from Adam, were prophets. It is assumed that the
whole Judaeo-Christian revelation was somehow implicit in the
thought of each, and therefore anterior to the best efforts of pagan
thinkers.[147] This implies that for the properly instructed Christian
the study of pagan thought is a work of supererogation.

4. Treatment of the Canonical Scriptures

But St. Augustine's *a priori* approach to the interpretation of
evidence is most clearly revealed in his treatment of the Canonical
Scriptures, which he professes to reverence.[148]

St. Augustine is formally committed to the belief that the
Canonical Scriptures are the revealed Word of God, and are man's
chief source of information relating to the design and details of the
historical process. In themselves they contain all that one need
know for salvation. And nothing which is without value for this
purpose is included, although some detail has value only by building
context for material of greater intrinsic importance. Once accepted,
the Scriptures become the "umpire of faith."[149] But infallible as
they are, they do not reveal their full meaning to every reader.
St. Augustine thinks that one should be able to find, explicit or
implicit, in the Old Testament the Christian interpretation of the
historical process. It follows that one is not really a free agent.
Every portion of the Old Testament must be found to support
Jesus' summary of the law and the prophets, the doctrine of man's
fall and need for repentance, the strengthening of moral feeling, and
the extirpation of lust.[150]

How should one prepare for battle with the sacred texts? In the
first place, by learning Hebrew and Greek, to emancipate oneself
from the numerous translators. St. Jerome finally convinced St.
Augustine that there was merit in bypassing the Septuagint and

---

[147] *De Civ. D.* xviii.27, 39.

[148] *De Doctr. Christ.* ii.8.12–13.

[149] *De Civ. D.* xi.3; xviii.40; xvi.2.3; *De Lib. Arb.* ii.2.5; *Contra Faust. Man.*
xxii. 94. Marrou, *S. Augustin et la Fin de la Culture Antique*, p. 480; Green,
"Augustine on the Teaching of History," p. 327.

[150] *De Doctr. Christ.* iii.10.15f.; ii.7.10; i.36.40.

going directly to a Hebrew original.[151] But St. Augustine seems hardly to have taken his own advice, at least with regard to Hebrew, although he understands the meaning of some Hebrew words, and may even have had a Hebrew word-list. He says that a knowledge of Hebrew can be useful in the interpretation of proper names, a remark which in the absence of more enthusiastic tributes suggests that his ambition in this field burned low.[152] We have already considered the probable limitations of his knowledge of Greek.

Failing a knowledge of the original languages, one should employ as literal a translation as possible, and avoid those which emphasize "the sense" at the expense of the literal meaning.[153] Words and idioms should in any event be carefully checked with experts, by professional researches, and by a comparison of different translations.[154] One wonders how carefully this advice would be followed by those who had already refused his initial advice to master the original languages. The "Italian translation," used in northern Italy before the general acceptance of the Vulgate, is said to be the best. But any and all translations are to be checked against the Greek (but not the Hebrew?), and especially against the Septuagint. The Seventy Translators are said to have worked individually over the whole of the Old Testament, and miraculously to have agreed not only word for word but in the very order of the words. This evidence of inspiration impresses St. Augustine more than does the testimony of contemporary Jews to the superior reliability of St. Jerome's recently published Latin translation.[155]

The Scriptures must be interpreted by competent scholars. The instructor must be able to expound the various meanings, and to understand the use of technical terms. The first object of each instructor should be lucidity. Scriptural writers use all the devices of rhetoric—allegory, enigma, parable, metaphor, catachresis, irony, antiphrasis, and so on.[156] The interpretation offered should be

[151] *De Doctr. Christ.* ii.11.16; *Epist.* 82.34.

[152] *De Doctr. Christ.* ii.16.23; *Conf.* xi.3.5. William Montgomery, *St. Augustine. Aspects of his Life and Thought* (London: Hodder and Stoughton, 1914), p. 190. *De Civ. D.* xvi.11, Hebrew the original language.

[153] *De Doctr. Christ.* ii.13.19.

[154] *De Doctr. Christ.* ii.14.21.

[155] *Epist.* 28.2; 71.5; 82.2; *De Doctr. Christ.* ii.15.22; *cf. De Civ. D.* xviii.42, 43.

[156] *De Doctr. Christ.* iii.29.41; *prol.* 4.

intelligible to all but the very dull, and such difficulties as arise should spring from the intrinsic toughness of the subject, and not from lack of clarity in the exposition.[157] Passages where the Christian sense is hard to bring out should not be chosen for public comment. Cruces should be dealt with in books which will find their proper public, but should not be allowed to unsettle the faith of "babes in Christ."[158]

St. Augustine's approach to exegesis was undoubtedly affected by his own early training. He studied grammar at Madaura, and shows the grammarian's occupational obsession with the trees at the expense of the wood. He has the grammarian's way of reading and commenting exhaustively on each verse, fragment, word. As Marrou says, he treats the Bible as the grammarians treated the Homeric epics, as if they had been written by men of their own times, with contemporary preoccupations.[159]

How does he deal with cruces? Obscurities in the canonical text can lead hasty and careless readers astray. But many of the obscurities were deliberately included for our good, to tease the mind and to subdue intellectual pride. The simple passages give joy and confidence, but the more obscure whet the intellectual appetite and challenge ingenuity. Several tenable interpretations may emerge, and by means of these, further truth and meaning can be dug from, or read into, the passages under consideration.[160]

Tackling cruces is a job for an experienced exegete.[161] When in doubt as to how a passage should be "pronounced or punctuated" to bring out the meaning, he should first apply the meanings already suggested by simpler passages, and then the pronouncements of the Church which seem relevant. If the exegete's expert opinion differs from that of the Church, he is not ordered to concede the point, as one might expect, but is told to resort with trepidation to "reason." One "reasonable" step would be to seek out an explanation

[157] *De Doctr. Christ.* iv.6.9, 8.22.

[158] *De Doctr. Christ.* iv.9.23.

[159] O'Meara, *Young Augustine*, p. 41; Marrou, *S. Augustin et la Fin de la Culture Antique*, p. 480, says that St. Augustine has the characteristic insolent self-confidence of the grammarian. *De Gen. ad Litt.* iii.24.36–37, for example of his technique.

[160] *De Doctr. Christ.* ii.6.7–8; *De Civ. D.* xi.19.

[161] *De Doctr. Christ.* ii.9.14.

consistent with the fairly immediate context. If neither rules nor context help, the exegete can employ any interpretation which comes to mind—*so long as it is in accordance with the orthodox Faith.*[162] Faith is the umpire of Scripture, and not vice versa.

St. Augustine concedes difficulties with regard to the ages of the antediluvians. First, there is a discrepancy between Christian figures, based on the Septuagint, and those of the Hebrew text. The Hebrew account has it that children were begotten a hundred years earlier in their fathers' lives, but compensates by giving the fathers an extra century later, to produce the same total lifespans. But in the sixth generation the figures tally. In the seventh there is the same discrepancy as in the first five. In the eighth the Hebrew account makes Methusaleh twenty years older when he begets Lamach, but "we" give him twenty years later on to make up his lifespan. In the ninth, "our" account gives Lamach twenty-four fewer years than does the Hebrew account. These discrepancies might shake the faith in an infallible Bible, for both texts are held to be inspired. St. Augustine suspects the first transcriber of the Septuagint of failing to see the need of retailing exact figures. He suggests that the transcriber was worried by the lengthy reputed lifespans of the antediluvians, and had come to think ten of their years the equivalent of one of ours. By this reckoning Methusaleh would have died in his ninety-seventh year. The record was judiciously amended, where necessary, to bring men up to an age when they could plausibly have begotten children. No such amendment was necessary in Lamach's case, and St. Augustine can offer no explanation of the discrepancy in figures.[163] Elsewhere he says that he is not unduly worried by small insubstantial contradictions and differences. People will tell stories in different ways and at different lengths, and while this is perhaps to be deplored, stories can be superficially different and still be essentially the same.[164] This is true enough, but small comfort for persons committed to a belief in the divine inspiration of every word in two equally canonical texts.

Second, is it plausible that men so old could have begotten children? For himself he can accept the account as it stands, and is worried only by the well-meaning efforts of persons like the hypo-

[162] *De Doctr. Christ.* iii.2.2, 2.5, 28.39.
[163] *De Civ. D.* xv.10.
[164] *Contra Faust. Man.* xxxiii.8.

thetical amending transcriber mentioned in the previous paragraph to explain the figures away—and with them the literal historicity of Holy Scripture. On the theory of one year for ten, and on the basis of the Hebrew figures, Adam, Seth, and Caanan would have begotten children at thirteen, nine, and seven years respectively.[165] Furthermore the dates given in the account of the Flood prove that the ancient year was of the same length as ours. Reference is made to *the second month, on the seventeenth day of the month,* to *the seventh month, on the seventeenth day of the month,* and to *the tenth month.*[166] St. Augustine insists on the letter of the text. There is no crux here for the man of faith. His only rationalizing concession to men of common sense is to suggest that the patriarchs had probably begotten children earlier, and were continuing, not beginning, the practice.[167] The account must stand, or doubt will be cast on scriptural infallibility.

He feels, too, that some readers may be troubled by the reference in Genesis to Giants. Are these plausible? Vergil and Pliny are offered as pagan "authorities" for the great size of certain ancients; giants are not just figments of *Judaeo-Christian* imagination. More impressively, he cites archeological evidence. Great bones have been found which seem to prove that at one time men existed far larger than any today. In any event, since the inspired authors were so accurate (*ex hypothesi*) in foreseeing the future, we hardly dare impugn their veracity in recording the past.[168]

Another crux relates to the Psalms. St. Augustine attributes them all to David. But some obviously refer to circumstances after David's death, and are actually attributed in the canonical text to later writers. St. Augustine suggests that David *qua* prophet wrote psalms appropriate to later times, and *qua* prophet attributed them to men who would be alive then. What exegesis could be more magisterially *a priori*?[169]

Still another problem arises from the incompatibility of some practices attributed to Old Testament worthies with the moral standards of St. Augustine's Christian age. Some think that only

---

[165] *De Civ. D.* xv.12.
[166] Genesis 7.11; 8.4–5; see *De Civ. D.* xv.4.1.
[167] *De Civ. D.* xv.15.
[168] *De Civ. D.* xv.9; *Epist.* 144.12. *Cf.* Herodotus i.67.
[169] *De Civ. D.* xvii.14.

the customs of their own society are sound, and are too quick to condemn or explain away customs not so much wicked as obsolete.[170] He distinguishes commands of God which have universal and eternal validity from commands *ad hoc*. Men in every age are told that "As ye would that men should do to you, do ye even so to them." Similarly, every man in every age is enjoined to love God and his neighbor. Certain crimes, such as sodomy, which is said to be unnatural, are said to deserve hatred and punishment whenever and wherever committed.[171] These laws can never be contradicted in Scripture. *If they seem to be, the passage must be taken figuratively.* But some social practices, such as polygamy, may be morally acceptable at one time and not at another. Customs tolerable in the patriarchs may be censurable in us. These arguments were directed against the Manichees, who thought that books which seemed to sanction "immoral behavior" on the part of the patriarchs should not be thought inspired.[172]

Various New Testament cruces are also dealt with. First, Matthew and Luke disagree as to Joseph's line of descent. Perhaps Joseph had both a natural and an adoptive father.[173] Second, in Matthew's gospel Jesus attributes a certain prophecy of Zechariah to Jeremiah. St. Augustine faces this ingenuously and for once has no solution. He does not take refuge in the fact that some manuscripts attribute the saying merely to "the prophet." He suggests, quite plausibly, that in these latter cases the transcribers were trying to cover up what they knew to be an error in the original, for he says that those who had checked (did not he ?) say that it is Jeremiah in the Greek.[174] A third difficulty for those who believe in Mary's perpetual virginity lies in the references to Jesus' brothers. St. Augustine suggests that the alleged brothers were really relatives of Jesus' mother, but not her sons. He finds another instance of slipshod terminology in contradictory references to Lot as the nephew, or brother, of Abraham.[175] A fourth crux, for non-Christians, may lie in the account of Jesus' miracles. St. Augustine notes that "miracles" are

[170] *De Doctr. Christ.* iii.10.15.

[171] *Conf.* iii.8.15; *De Doctr. Christ.* iii.14.22.

[172] *Contra Faust. Man.* iv.1, 2; vi.1, 2; x, *passim*; xxxii.1, 8; *De Doctr. Christ.* iii.17.25–26; *Conf.* iii.7.13.

[173] *Contra Faust. Man.* iii.2–3.

[174] *De Cons. Evang.* iii.7.29, on Matt. 27.9.

[175] *In Johan. Evang.* 10.2.

frequent occurrences, and cites twenty "easily credible" instances known to contemporaries. In any event, a supposed miracle is not so much contrary to nature as contrary to what little we presently know of nature; there is no fundamental distinction between natural and supernatural events, since all events happen in accordance with the divine order.[176]

If Scripture is to be put through its paces, one must be able to find various levels of meaning. The Scriptures must be both literally and figuratively true. The fact that a passage has deeper meaning does not detract one iota from its unerring historicity.[177] Every statement of fact must be taken as literally true. But many statements of fact seem to run contrary to Christian hypotheses, and St. Augustine will not, in point of fact, accept them as literally true. He respects the literalism of simple Christians, but not to the point of letting a literal reading of the Old Testament pervert his Christianity.[178] His literalism is qualified.

The Scriptures have several ranges of meaning. St. Augustine would like to think that Genesis, for instance, had been designed to appeal to different levels of percipience.[179] Scripture is *historical* when it sets forth what has been said or done; *aetiological,* when it shows why something was said or done; *analogical,* since the two Testaments consistently support each other (*sic*); and *allegorical,* insofar as certain passages are to be taken figuratively. Jesus and his disciples speak, or write, in all four senses: historically, as when Jesus refers to David's eating of the shew-bread (Matth. 12.3f.); aetiologically, as when he explains why Moses permitted divorce (Matth. 19.8); analogy and allegory tend tó go together, and the latter is used to point the former. Jesus says that "only the sign of the prophet Jonah" shall be given to this generation (Matth. 12.30,40). Here allegory sees Christ's three-day sojourn in Hell, followed by his resurrection, foreshadowed in Jonah's three-day incarceration in the belly of the whale, and analogy can then point to "parallel accounts" in Old and New Testaments.[180]

The Old Testament is fulfilled in the New, and the New

---

[176] *De Civ. D.* xxii.8,   nam etiam nunc fiunt miracula.
[177] *De Civ. D.* xiii.21; xv.27.1; *De Doctr. Christ.* ii.9.14; ii.12.17.
[178] *De Gen. Contra Man.* ii.2.3.
[179] *Conf.* xii.26.36; *De Civ. D.* xv.27.1.
[180] *De Util. Cred.* 5–6.

foreshadowed in the Old.[181] We must beware of taking a figurative expression literally, for "the letter killeth but the Spirit giveth life."[182] Each sentence in the Old Testament has prophetic meaning.[183] It can be taken as a general rule that any passage not conducive to purity and orthodoxy is to be taken figuratively. Personal judgment must play a considerable role. Severity and cruelty may be the just punishment of sin.[184] But seemingly "sinful" acts of God, or of men generally taken to have been holy, must be taken figuratively, for all must support the doctrine of universal and eternal love, and neither malice nor hatred can be attributed to God or to his saints.[185] Furthermore, in this connection, if the exegete misses the literal meaning of a passage, but finds a "deeper meaning" along the *a priori* line, he is not so much awry. His only danger is that if he fails to grasp the writer's immediate meaning correctly, he may become lazy in unraveling apparent inconsistencies in Scriptures *ex hypothesi* infallible,[186] and careless about the historical meaning.

St. Augustine admits that he does not know what Moses had in mind in each passage of the Pentateuch, and wonders if Moses himself, and other inspired writers, realized all the implications which can properly be drawn from their accounts. He concedes that Moses may not consciously have seen as much as he sees in the Pentateuch. But he would like to believe that Moses had at least some idea of the deeper allegorical meaning. We must try to find and honor Moses' immediate meaning; but whether or not we are sure that we have found it, we are justified in selecting and emphasizing any interpretation which seems to us to be true.[187]

The first and foremost task of allegory is to find the Incarnation foreshadowed everywhere in the Old Testament. The whole content of the prophetic books is said to relate to Jesus Christ, explicitly or implicitly, and he is prefigured in all the details of Jewish history.[188] Everything in the Pentateuch refers to him. When Jacob first thrust

[181] *Epist.* 105.32.
[182] *De Doctr. Christ.* iii.5.9.
[183] *De Civ. D.* xvii.1.
[184] *De Doctr. Christ.* iii.10.14, 11.17, 16.24.
[185] *De Doctr. Christ.* iii.10.14, 12.18.
[186] *Conf.* xii.18.27; *De Doctr. Christ.* i.36.40–42.
[187] *Conf.* xii.18.27, 24.33, 30.41–43.
[188] *De Trin.* iv.7.11; cf. *Contra Faust. Man.* xxii.94.

his hand, and then his head, from the womb, he prefigured Christ who first sent patriarchs and prophets before he himself came; and after the Head came his body, the Church.[189]

> Who else is symbolized, when Abraham leaves his home and people to seek wealth and prosperity among strangers, but Christ Who left His native Jewry and is now seen to rule the nations of the world? When Isaac carries the wood for his own sacrifice, whom does he represent but Christ Who bore His own cross? Who is the sacrificial ram, his horns entangled in the bush, but Christ Who was crucified for our salvation?[190]

St. Augustine notes the errors of Philo, an allegorist without the light of Christian faith. Philo claims that Noah's ark is a type of the human body. In St. Augustine's opinion, it is a type of Christ, who came to save us from the floods of worldliness. It is true, however, that since Christ came in a human body, the ark might be thought a type of this, too. In fact, the proportions assigned to the ark are those traditionally attributed to the human body, the length (or height) being six times the breadth and ten times the thickness. Christ may be taken as Man, or at any rate New Man, *par excellence*. Philo's chief blunder lies in his identification of the door of the ark with the lower apertures of the human body. If the veil had been lifted from his eyes, he would have seen that the door represents the riven side of Christ from which the sacraments of the Church flow down. Christ and Church are one flesh, as Groom and Bride, and for that reason the ark may also be taken as a type of the Church. Where Philo and others differ from St. Augustine, they are said to be guilty of "ingenious perversions."[191]

Here are a few miscellaneous instances of allegorical interpretation. St. Augustine is glad to find the doctrine of the Trinity suggested in the first chapter of Genesis: *the Father* creates by *His Word*, and *the Spirit* broods over the waters.[192] The seven days of Genesis correspond to the six ages of toil on earth, to be followed by the eternal Sabbath rest. The first two ages ended with Noah and Abraham respectively. The next three are marked off in Matthew i.

[189] *Contra Faust. Man.* xvi.9; *De Cat. Rud.* 3.5–6.
[190] *Contra Faust. Man.* xii.25.
[191] *De Civ. D.* xv.26.1; *Contra Faust. Man.* xii.39.
[192] Burleigh, *City of God*, p. 113.

The sixth begins with Christianity. These ages are of uneven length, sixteen generations apiece in the first two, fourteen in the next three, while the sixth is still in progress and may be as long as the others together. This corresponds to the life of the individual: the sixth age begins at sixty, and *may* continue for another sixty years.[193] The plagues of Egypt correspond to the Ten Commandments and the ten principal vices. The plague of flies is most ingeniously made relevant to the command, "Honour thy father and thy mother." The fly is the Septuagint *kynómia*, or dog-fly, and dogs, being born blind, cannot even see, let alone reverence, their parents, for a time at least.[194] *Bos* is both "ox" and "preacher" in the passage *bovem triturantem non infrenabis*, a passage taken to support payment of the clergy.[195]

St. Augustine thought that the idea of the Two Cities was derived from, or could be supported by, Scripture. God has freed some men, and put them in a special category, thus creating two communities on earth, *secundum scripturas nostras*. The eternal *Civitas Dei* of "our sacred literature" was imaged in the Jewish state, and especially in Jerusalem, the Holy City.[196] The Jews who received a land of promise are a type of God's Elect, who will receive a heavenly land of promise.[197]

If historical material can be given an allegorical interpretation, how much more easily can the highly allusive and ambiguous prophetic books be made to yield fruit? St. Augustine sees significance in the very fact that the line of great prophets began contemporaneously with the foundation of Rome, in whose empire their message would in time be universally propagated.[198] But some difficulties are acknowledged. Hosea is said to speak so profoundly that it is hard to penetrate to his meaning. But this is only a challenge to pious ingenuity.[199]

St. Augustine has an obsession with numbers. Every number in Scripture has symbolic significance: one is God; two is charity,

[193] *Contra Adeimant.* 16.3; *De Div. Quaest.* 58.2.

[194] *Serm.* 8.

[195] I Cor. 9.19, see *De Doctr. Christ.* ii.10.15.

[196] *De Civ. D.* v.19; e.g., Psalms 46, 48, see *De Div. Quaest.* 11.1; *De Civ. D.* xiv.1; xv.2.

[197] *Epist.* 84.2.

[198] *De Civ. D.* xvii.25, 27.

[199] *De Civ. D.* xviii.28.

residing in Christ's two commandments; three is the Trinity, but may also stand for heart, soul, and mind; four is either universality (the four elements, quarters, winds) or time (the four seasons, parts of the day); five is the Mosaic Law as revealed in the Pentateuch; ten is God's law (the Ten Commandments), or may symbolize His creation of all things; eleven, going beyond law (*transgreditur*), signifies transgression or sin; twelve stands for the disciples; thirty-eight is soul-sickness, being forty ("totality of law") less two ("charity"). As for forty, what intelligent person is not anxious to know why Moses, Elijah, and Our Lord each fasted forty days? Forty in this context signifies universal knowledge: it is the multiple of four (time) and ten (creation), and ten in turn is the sum of three (the Trinity), three (heart, mind, soul), and four (all things made from the four elements).[200]

Christian exegetes were subjected to criticism from sundry lesser breeds, and especially from the Manichees, who asked why a faith of such heavily advertised simplicity needed such fantastic exegesis. Answer was given by quoting, "All things must be fulfilled which were written in the law of Moses, and in the prophets, and in the Psalms, concerning me."[201] St. Paul, too, sanctions this approach. "But all these things happened unto them in a figure. But they were written for our admonition, upon whom the ends of the world have come."[202] The Manichees made much of the idea that Christian exegetes had interpolated into the Old Testament many passages supposedly favorable to Christianity. Even in his Manichaean days St. Augustine had thought this theory overworked. His rejoinder is that the Jews themselves vouch for the authenticity of the verses in question.[203] He tries to discredit Manichaean criticism *ex radice*, by asking whether an enemy of Aristotle should be accepted as a guide to Aristotelianism.[204] Surely, he says, only professed and presumably friendly authorities should be heard. If one grants, for the sake of argument, that Christian theologians present the soundest view of Christianity, the fact

[200] *De Doctr. Christ.* ii.16.25; *De Civ. D.* xv.20.4. Marrou, *S. Augustin et la Fin de la Culture Antique*, p. 432.

[201] *Contra Faust. Man.* xii.4.

[202] I Cor. 10.1–11.

[203] *Contra Faust. Man.* x.3; *De Util. Cred.* 7; *Conf.* v.11.21; *De Fide Rerum Quae non Videntur* 9; *In Johan. Evang.* 35.7.

[204] *De Util. Cred.* 13.

remains that the Old Testament is common ground to Jews, Christians, and Manichees alike, and when experts differ, one of their number can hardly set himself up, with universal acceptance, as judge. St. Augustine says further that many passages which may seem inconsistent or even absurd to ignorant persons can be made by the Christian expert to show good sense and Christian truth. Rather than setting oneself up as a critic, he thinks, or listening to the unenlightened speculations of non-Christian commentators, one should put oneself in the hands of an orthodox teacher—an admission, surely, that an objective approach to the scriptural evidence is not likely to produce the right result.[205]

St. Augustine does not *discuss* the inspiration or veracity of Scripture at any great length, but is content to show that Scripture can be found, or made, to support orthodox doctrine.[206] His grammatical and historical exegesis would be more satisfying if it were less ingenious. Symbols have shifting significance, and all Scripture is consistent with his views![207] When God says that all men will be saved, St. Augustine, committed to the view that most men will be damned, makes free to read this as, *some men from every class.*[208] It is evident that Scripture can be umpire of faith only in a very qualified sense, and that the traditional teaching of the Church takes precedence over a literal reading of the canonical texts. St. Augustine's objective everywhere is not to prove that the Christian interpretation of Scripture is right, but only to show that the Christian faith may have a scriptural warrant, that a Christian interpretation of Scripture is at least plausible.[209] He is not forced against his will to allegorize; he is fascinated by the method, and himself wonders at his own and others' fondness for it.[210] He says that narrative becomes more interesting when its mystical symbolism is noted.[211] In fact, this feeling for allegory was fortunate, for in no other way could Christian thinkers have mustered for their parvenu

[205] *De Mor. Eccl. Cath.* I.I.

[206] *De Cons. Evang.* ii.3.5; *De Doctr. Christ.* ii.6.8.

[207] Simpson, *St. Augustine's Episcopate*, p. 100.

[208] Morgan, *Psychological Teaching of St. Augustine*, p. 65.

[209] *De Doctr. Christ.* ii.28.44; *De Cons. Evang.* ii.3.5; *De Civ. D.* xx.6. Marrou, *S. Augustin et la Fin de la Culture Antique*, p. 465; "Elles sont possibles, et cela suffit pour qu'une voie soit ouverte à la croyance."

[210] *De Doctr. Christ.* ii.12.18.

[211] *De Cat. Rud.* 3.5f.; 13.18.

movement the support of the ancient Jewish scriptures, in an age when great weight was attached to the antiquity of doctrine.[212] His own conversion was advanced by St. Ambrose's allegorical exegesis. He admits that these ingenious explanations often fail with heretics and schismatics, who demand plain statements.[213] But catechumens already committed to Christian premises could be given a strongly allegorical interpretation of the Old Testament to confirm the faith which they already held, by making it seem foreshadowed and supported there.

In his interpretation of the world of experience, St. Augustine is a thorough-going apologist. The Christian faith, as traditionally taught by the Church, must always be taken as if true. Historical evidence, secular sciences, intellectual disciplines, philosophical speculation, and the Canonical Scriptures themselves are used never really to test, but only to illustrate, the plausibility of his *a priori* hypotheses.

[212] *Cf.* Julian the Apostate's reading of Neo-Platonism into the mythology of Cybele.

[213] *Ad Cath. Epist. Contra Donat.* 5; *Conf.* v.14.24; vi.4.6.

CHAPTER FOUR

Intrenched Interpretation of Experience

St. Augustine's *a priori* approach and his short way with dissenters quickly involve him in what most persons would regard as a denial of nature, or at any rate of appearances. In a sense he glories in this. He distinguishes the *Christian* view of life from that of *natural man*. He claims that if Adam had not fallen, we would all share the Christian perspective. He admits that in the world as we see it an intellectual *tour de force*, or a miracle of grace, is needed to bring anyone to adopt the Christian point of view; and that the latter is regarded by most men as an absurd, impractical, disingenuous, or stupid refusal to face facts, however heroic Christians may seem to one another.

Natural man, in each of us, sets himself to master his environment.[1] First, he wants knowledge, and assumes that he can get some, usually by bringing his rational faculty to bear upon sensational evidence. Second, he tends to identify "good" with satisfactions which are mostly but not exclusively material. Third, he wants power, and is willing to fight for it. He may be selfish or altruistic, radical or reactionary, rich or poor. He may be a scientist, a statesman, a humanitarian, an atheist, or a theologian. But in every case, his grand objective, acknowledged or unacknowledged, is to make the best of this world. He is not in sympathy with "God's fools." But his trust in worldly wisdom, wealth, and power dooms him to disillusionment and frustration.

Consider the first great illusion, that he can get knowledge by his own efforts. St. Augustine takes his own professional field, theology, and tries to show how far short of truth natural man falls in this test

[1] E.g., *De Gen. ad Litt.* xi.15.20.

case. Even pagans, he says, recognize a need to rationalize their traditional theology, and admit a difficulty in doing so. He spends much time making fun of divine departmentalization, which in principle at least postulates a god not merely for every separate phenomenon and process, but for the minutest distinguishable part of every process. To cite only two instances of confusion, but on the very highest level, who gives victory, Jupiter or Victoria? And why worship any other deity than Felicitas?[2] St. Augustine sees irreverence in common pagan notions of pantheism, according to which God is the Soul of the world. Does God, in man, trample upon God, as earth? Is He killed in every butchering, and whipped in every schoolboy?[3] St. Augustine notes, with interest, Euhemerus' theory that the gods were once men, whose worship has since been established by lying poets, deceitful demons, and grateful and hopeful survivors.[4] Taking the gods as he found them, Varro classified them as mythical (of the poets), natural (of the philosophers), and civic (of the community). The natural gods of the philosophers *may* be good angels, seen through a glass darkly. But they are classroom phenomena, and have no significance or interest for the man in the street. The mythical and civic gods are confused in the popular mind, and the latter suffer from the impression given by the former of immorality and triviality. They can be dismissed with contempt. "All the arrangements made by men for the making and worshipping of idols are superstitious."[5]

The really damning flaw in the gods of the pagans, as popularly conceived, is that they do not live up to their prospectus. The Romans were happier before they added to their pantheon. Long before Rome was founded, the ancestral gods had shown themselves unable to prevent various circumstances for which they are said to have grieved. They could protect neither Troy nor Priam. But weak as *they* were, Juno could prevent neither them nor their client Aeneas from coming to Italy. After their arrival, they were unable to save their worshipers from innumerable miseries.[6] Various pagan

[2] *De Civ. D.* iv.8, 14, 16, 21; vi.9.   [3] *De Civ. D.* iv.12, 13; vii.5.

[4] *De Civ. D.* iv.9: Varro disapproves of the use of idols in worship; vi.8.1, at enim habent ista physiologicas quasdam, sicunt aiunt, id est naturalium rationum interpretationes; vii.18.

[5] *De Doctr. Christ.* ii.20.30–31; *De Civ. D.* vi.5.1–2.

[6] *De Civ. D.* i.2, 3, 4; iii.11, 12, 17. John H. S. Burleigh, *The City of God* (London: Nisbet, 1949), p. 37.

writers agree that only morality can insure happiness, and many admit that before the birth of Christ the Roman Republic was morally sick. Did the gods abandon Rome because of her profligacy? If so, they had given no warning. And if they had regard for morality, why did they abandon the virtuous Regulus and the treaty-keeping Saguntines, but give Marius seven consulships, and Sulla favorable auspices? It should not be thought that they were able to reward vice and punish virtue, however. The excellent Metellus enjoyed political success, and the vicious Catilina came to a bad end. They are simply ineffectual, and cannot be counted upon to guarantee prosperity to anyone, whatever his way of life.[7] Only habit keeps their worship alive.[8] Natural man who worships, and in some cases creates, such gods can hardly be taken seriously as a connoisseur of coercive wisdom.[9]

The second great illusion lies in a particular application of the first, and involves a misplaced confidence in human judgment. Apparently trusting in Satan's promise, *vos eritis sicut deus, scientes bonum atque malum,* natural man is ready to back his personal judgment of good and evil against that of the Creator of a perfect universe.[10] He identifies as good whatever is pleasant or conducive to pleasure, such as food, clothing, intellectual discovery, music. Wealth is a surplus in any of these departments, and nearly every man would choose to be wealthy.[11] Conversely, it is bad to be hungry, sick, deprived, frustrated, hurt, pillaged, exiled, or killed. The fact that pagan sages condone suicide when such miseries pile up is evidence that their alleged superiority to circumstances is only a pose.[12] This propensity to pass judgment on life seems to be innate. It is sentimental nonsense to speak of "sweet innocent babes." Infants show their true colors in their monumental egocentricity, obsession with creature comforts, lust for power over

[7] *De Civ. D.* i.15.7; ii.4, 14, 23, 24, 26; iii.20; vi.5, 9, 10.

[8] *De Civ. D.* vi.10.3, i.e., the opinion of Seneca.

[9] *De Civ. D.* iv.7; *Assyria* prospered without the support of the Roman gods.

[10] *De Duab. Anim.* 10.12; 11.15; *De Civ. D.* xiii.15; *Conf.* vii.16.22; *cf.* iii.3.5, 6.10, and vi.4.5; *De Nat. et Grat.* 29.33; *De Trin.* iv.10.13; xi.5.8; *De Doctr. Christ.* i.23.22; *Epist.* 101.2.

[11] *De Civ. D.* xv.17; xix.17.1; *Conf.* x.23.33; *De Trin.* xiii. 3.6: a comic actor drew a crowd by promising to tell the secret of every man's heart—which, he said, was to buy cheap and sell dear. *Serm.* 14.5; *Quaest. Evang.* 26.

[12] *De Civ. D.* iii.1; xv.17; xix.4.4; *Conf.* x.23.33.

the ministers of their needs, and mutual rivalries. Their worldliness is limited by impotence, not innocence.[13]

Sexual desire is one of the most powerful of the worldly affections. Speaking from experience, St. Augustine says that nothing so saps both physical and intellectual vigor.[14] In adolescence, he ignored his mother's plea that he remain chaste. He even tried to enhance his credit with his friends by pretending to be more abandoned than he was. When about seventeen, he fell in love, and settled down for about fifteen years in what might be called a common-law marriage. He says that he found then how little happiness is to be had from sexual satisfaction at its most secure.[15] Eventually, at his mother's wish, he decided to make a respectable marriage with an eligible girl of her choice. He says that his mistress was "torn from his side," and that his own heart was "torn and wounded and bleeding." But he felt the need of a *locum tenens* for the period to elapse between this sad scene and his new marriage. He admired continence, but could not practice it. His state of mind was like that of an earlier time when he had prayed, "Grant me chastity and continence, but not yet."[16] His way of life may not have been very scandalous by either ancient or modern standards. But he was depressed and humiliated by the consciousness that he was enchained to a habit which did him more harm than good, if only by promising a happiness which it could not give, and by distracting him from a course of action which, as he already suspected, might bring him peace of mind. The conversion which in the event forestalled his marriage meant, among other things, that he gained the will and the strength to break the sexual habit, and in doing so he freed himself from the anxieties, uncertainties, and shame of being in the grip of something beyond his control, associated in his mind with sex.[17]

Worldly goods, like wisdom, are a snare and a delusion, if we

[13] *Conf.* i.7.11.   [14] *Solil.* i.10.17.

[15] *Conf.* ii.2.2, 3.7, ii.17, sed cum dicitur, Eamus, faciamus; et pudet non esse impudentiam; iii.1.1; vi.11.20.

[16] *Conf.* vi.15.25; vii.17.23; viii.7.17.

[17] *Conf.* viii.11.25. Rebecca West, *St. Augustine* (New York: Appleton, 1933), inveighs against him for not marrying his mistress after his conversion. Hugh Pope, *St. Augustine of Hippo* (London: Sands, 1937), offers the fatuous defense that although he had been faithful to her he had never loved her. "But he *does* tell us that he had fallen in love with Some One Else"—not with Christ, as Pope seems to think, but with the prospect of a more creditable marriage.

pursue them obsessively. It is a sort of slavery to want anything desperately; and worldly advantages, to say nothing of wealth, are often virtually impossible to obtain.[18] Being limited in number, if they are material, there is rivalry for their possession.[19] To have them may help us to do good, but we can do good without them.[20] Worldly success brings *hybris*, offensive to others and dangerous to oneself,[21] as we learn from Attic tragedy and Athenian history. If ever we acquire these things, we cannot keep them long. All are uncertain, dreamlike, and fleeting, and the amount of real pleasure they bring is impredictable. Anxiety and insomnia are a high price to pay for such goods.[22]

Natural man's third great mistake is seen in his regard for power, either in others' hands or preferably in his own. *Libido dominandi* seeks plausibly, but often self-deceptively, to justify itself in terms of the service which power can render. The state, which is taken to be the chief field in which power finds expression, has a five-fold characteristic program: first, to provide and defend the highest possible standard of living at the lowest possible cost in labor and time; second, to provide entertainment, particularly through the theater, which St. Augustine regards as primarily a purveyor of sexual excitement (he suggests that if the theater is to be subsidized, why not prostitution as well?); third, to employ statesmen who show their ability to provide bread and circuses; fourth, to persecute the enemies of these principles; and fifth, to maintain a religion supposedly conducive to the ends desired.[23]

But the quest for power leads to domestic, civic, and international strife, from which someone must always emerge frustrated. The larger the unit, the more unscrupulous its policy. The great states are *de facto* robber bands. Wars between them are assumed by worldly wise men to be inevitable.[24] Rape, abduction, pillage, massacre, and arson always accompany these engagements. During the Punic Wars, for instance, casualties by land and sea were

[18] *De Civ. D.* iv.3.
[19] *De Civ. D.* xv.4.
[20] *Epist.* 130.3.7.
[21] *Ennar in Ps.* 93.12.
[22] *De Doctr. Christ.* iii.12.18; *Conf.* x.31.46; *Ennar in Ps.* 72.19; *Epist.* 130.1.2, 2.3, 2.5; *Serm.* 60.2, 3.
[23] *De Civ. D.* ii.20; xix.17.1.
[24] *Conf.* xi.13.15; *De Civ. D.* xv.5.

appalling, quondam victors were victimized by *peripéteia*, cities were destroyed, districts ruined.[25] The distresses of the Romans even in their palmiest days show the limitations of power as a means to happiness. Within each state some honor may be observed, as between thieves. But in their international dealings, each snatches what it can, and thinks nothing wrong which seems to serve its material interests. In Sallust's opinion, the Romans abandoned Numan pacifism only *to defend* themselves and their allies. St. Augustine thinks that their opinion of what was good for their allies and themselves was conditioned by *ea . . . ipsa libido dominandi.*

Alexander the Great was once given a trenchant answer by a pirate whom he had captured. When the King asked him how he dared terrorize the sea, he insolently replied, "In the same way that you have seized the whole earth. Because I operate with a single ship, I am called a pirate; but you, with a navy, are called a king."[26]

"*Unnatural*," or Christian, man gives up this struggle for wisdom, wealth, and power. Happiness comes from getting what we want;[27] we are well advised to want what we are getting. The Christian sets himself not to conquer environment, but to persuade himself that he likes the world as it is; everything, including rape, murder, and famine, is for the best, for the recipient at least. He may, indeed, pray for relief from unpleasantness—but even if his prayer is not granted, he must not infer that God is ignoring him, or has ceased to love him. If health, prosperity, and all manner of physical, aesthetic, and intellectual satisfactions are good gifts of God—and the Christian is far from denying that they are—so are sickness, poverty, deprivation, and intellectual or aesthetic starvation. Every experience has its justification in a cosmic plan which is benevolent, appearances perhaps to the contrary.[28] St. Augustine might ask us to imagine God as a loving father giving gifts to two children. The one snatches his gift, looks for more, is surly when disappointed, and rebellious when punished. He recognizes his father's love, if at all, only when his father treats him in what he regards as proper fashion.

[25] *De Civ. D.* i.2; iii.26; xv.7; xix.8.

[26] *De Civ. D.* iv.4.

[27] *De Civ. D.* i.11, 14, 16; *Cf. Conf.* ix.12.14; *Epist.* 130. 14.26.

[28] *Conf.* xii.7.7; *De Nat. Bon.* 1, 26; *De Gen. Contra Man.* i.7.11; *De Civ. D.* xii.35.

He has his own views as to what is good and bad for him, and when judged by this standard his father's conduct seems at the least amoral. Consequently he feels no security even in such happiness as his father permits him, and he lives in fear that his father will do him some unpredictable mischief. The other son takes his gift with satisfaction arising chiefly from his belief that the gift is an expression of his father's love; the important thing, for him, is the love expressed through the gift.[29] He is so sure of his father's love that if on some future occasion he failed to receive a gift, or were forced by his father to accept the unpleasant consequences of some piece of folly, he would never lose his sense of being a son in his father's house.

To begin with the obvious, the world about us is marvellously beautiful, and should arouse the enthusiasm of all its inhabitants. Every creature is fearfully and wonderfully made, and man himself the greatest marvel of all, with his complex qualities of mind and body. "How can I tell of the rest of creation, with all its beauty and utility, which the divine goodness has given to man to please his eyes and serve his purposes, condemned though he is, and hurled into these labours and miseries? Shall I speak of the manifold and varied loveliness of earth and sky and sea . . . ?"[30] Our fellow men may be, for some persons, the principal blot on the landscape. But we can hardly claim to have a loving confidence *de rerum natura*, if we let ourselves be exasperated by this most conspicuous landmark on our personal horizon. We can have no "enemies." Folk whose behavior today is unpleasant, although for our good whatever their intention, may tomorrow become easily lovable sharers of our "unnatural" Christian viewpoint.[31]

God made everything good, and everything remains good in itself, although to our jaundiced eye its beauty may be defaced.[32] No dissonances or difficulties can disturb the great design. Fire, frost,

[29] *Epist.* 155.10: earthly goods are like betrothal rings, to be valued, but not for themselves.

[30] *De Civ. D.* xxii.2, 3, 4, 5; *De Fide Spe Car.* 4.12; *De Trin.* xv.4.6; *Conf.* vii.12.18; xiii.34.49.

[31] *De Civ. D.* i.35; xii.21; xv.61; xvi.26; xix.5; *De Mor. Eccl. Cath.* 28.56; *Epist.* 130.10.19; *De Fide Spe Car.* 20.76; *De Op. Monach.* 20; *In Johan. Evang.* 51.12; 65.2; 6.10; *De Doctr. Christ.* i.28.29, 30.31, 35.39; *De Trin.* xiv. 14.18.

[32] *De Gen. ad Litt.* vii.14; *Retract.* ii.24; *De Civ. D.* xi.24; xii.2, Deo . . . essentia nulla contraria est.

and wild beasts can be seen to be excellent in themselves, and in the total scheme of things, and even useful to man if taken in the right way. Thorns, poisonous plants, barren trees, and the like were created for the punishment of our sin; however unpleasant, they are not evil, and they serve a just purpose. Even the ranting of heretics has its use in rousing the faithful to give reason for the faith that is in them.[33] Death is regarded by St. Augustine as the greatest "unpleasantness." It is not imposed simply to test our capacity for cheerful acquiescence, and it would not have come upon us if Adam had not sinned. It is a bitter and deserved punishment. Its "pleasantest" effect lies in its sometimes snatching a man from something even more "unpleasant" than itself. In *the first death*, the soul is driven painfully from the body for a while; in *the second*, it is pent up again in the body, to be abandoned by God to an eternity of hellish torment.[34] Death is not evil for the evil, because they deserve it. For the good it is the gateway to eternal blessedness. Furthermore, martyrs in their deaths often secure not only their own salvation but that of their persecutors, who are likely to be impressed by a faith for which men are willing to die.[35]

Many instances are cited of God's austere kindnesses. All suffering, whether punitive or corrective, is justified in the total scheme.[36] It is never unjust to the sufferer, and never more than he can bear to his advantage, however malevolent the human agent.[37] Sometimes cruel men are given power on a large scale, when nations or mankind as a whole deserve punishment. Those like Job who respond well will receive compensation, if not in this life then in the next.[38] St. Augustine cites his own case. In his adolescence, God was with him, *mercifully vexing him*, to alienate him from immoral obsessions. Later, as the time of his conversion approached, he was

[33] *Conf.* iv.13.20; xii.11.11; xiii.28.43; *De Trin.* xiii.16.20; *De Civ. D.* iii.1; xi.22–23; xix.3; *De Ord.* ii.7.22; *Epist.* 138.2.15; 210.1; *De Lib. Arb.* i.1.1; *De Gen. Contra Man.* i.1.1f.

[34] *Conf.* vi.16.26; *De Doctr. Christ.* i.19.18; *De Fide Spe Car.* 24.93; *De Pecc. Mer. et Remiss.* i.2; *De Trin.* iv.3.5; *De Civ. D.* xiii.2, 12.

[35] *De Civ. D.* i.11; xiii.2, 5; xviii.50; *De Cat. Rud.* 24.44; *Epist.* 185.7.31.

[36] *De Civ. D.* xii.4; xi.22; *In Johan. Evang.* 7.12; 12.14; *Epist.* 111.2; *De Trin.* xiii.16.20.

[37] *De Nat. Bon.* 11; *De Fide Spe Car.* 24.96; *cf.* 25.98.

[38] *De Civ. D.* i.9.3; v.19; vii.30; *cf. Conf.* ix.8.18, re Monica. *De Lib. Arb.* iii.8.23.

favored with "inward stings" of disgust with himself and with his way of life. Monica's prayer, that her son might stay in Africa and so escape the temptations of Italy, was *not directly granted*. But when he had come to Milan, he attended St. Ambrose's preaching to savor the preacher's rhetorical skill, and in time, and contrary to his intention, came under the influence of the matter of the sermons not less than of their form.[39] Persecution for one's own good is perhaps an inevitable accompaniment of discipleship.[40]

God has not spared St. Augustine's generation, and he tries to find good in the atrocities which mark the barbarian invasions. They have brought unity to the Church, showing how God brings good out of apparent evil.[41] Perhaps inconsistently, St. Augustine will let us evade suffering, if no responsibility is shirked. Even a bishop, he says, may flee his post if no specific duty holds him, and if the danger is personal and does not involve his diocese as a whole. One might have thought that a bishop had always a specific obligation binding him to his diocese. He is surely more or less guilty of the sin of private judgment if he seeks to avoid an experience which God would never let befall him unless it could be for his good. The runaway bishop has committed what may be a sin in order to evade something which, as a Christian, he should not think evil in itself.[42] Shortcomings in one's government, inevitable in troubled times, are to be taken not as evil in themselves but as tests of virtue, presumably of patience above all. Hard times and economic disaster smoke out carnal attachments. A Christian tortured to reveal wealth which he does not possess is perhaps being punished for a secret craving for wealth. Or he may be in forced training for a more austere and wholesome life. If he is starved to death, God is perhaps taking him from something even more unpleasant.[43] The neophyte must be given a seriatim demonstration that everything that has happened in history has been for the best.[44]

Rape was a frequent occurrence in the fifth century; a bishop might properly be expected to have something to say on this subject,

[39] *Conf.* ii.2.4; v.8.15, 13.23; vii.8.12.
[40] II Tim. 3.12, see *Ennar. in Ps.* 55.4.
[41] *Epist.* 185.7.31.
[42] *Epist.* 228.3, 7, 10 (A.D. 428–429).
[43] *De Civ. D.* i.10.2–3.   [44] *De Cat. Rud.* 6.10.

for the comfort of his parishioners. St. Augustine asserts that rape can injure its victim only if it causes her to lose her chastity. But chastity is not a state of body, but a state of mind, and cannot be lost in rape unless the victim "assents," by discovering pleasure in the experience. Granting the possibility of this discovery, St. Augustine makes an exception to his general prohibition of lying, and would let a woman lie to protect herself from rape. But no Christian woman should kill herself to avoid assault. She would be committing an undoubted sin with a view to avoiding the merely possible sin involved in "assent." Some women who have committed suicide to avoid rape have been canonized. Perhaps the Church was wrong, St. Augustine thinks; or perhaps they were obeying sudden *ad hoc* revelations which abrogated ordinary rules.[45] Why does God let Christian women be raped? His judgments are admittedly inscrutable. But perhaps they were too proud of their merely physical purity. Or perhaps they were spared a future pride. Perhaps they were being given a demonstration that chastity is not a physical but a psychological phenomenon.[46] St. Augustine is not offering a gratuitous justification for committing rape—the rapist is sinning against himself—but is trying to say something to comfort the many contemporary victims. What else could he say, committed as he was to believing in a wise and loving God, who lets nothing happen to us contrary to His great design, or inconsistent with our own good?

This effort at universal optimism is supplemented by a certain cultivated and not entirely consistent indifference toward what natural man identifies as good.[47] But the goal is never *apatheia* or *ataraxia*.

> Job feels the rod,
> Yet blesses God.

Only stunted personalities are free from emotion. There is nothing wrong with righteous anger, which seeks the correction of an offense; with sadness, which seeks relief by helping others; with

[45] *Epist.* 228.7; *De Mend.* 41; *De Fide Spe Car.* 6.18; *De Doctr. Christ.* i.36.40; *De Civ. D.* i.17, 20, 26.

[46] *De Civ. D.* i.28.1; *cf. De Virg.* 31.

[47] *Conf.* ix.1.1.

ardent desire, to gain men for Christ; with joy, when we succeed in doing this; with fear, lest we or others backslide.[48] But unnatural man's ambition, and emotions, should be primarily concerned with self-conquest.[49] He is indifferent to worldly prosperity in the sense that, while he does not despise it, or any other gift of God, he is aiming at an even higher good.

This is made clear in connection with charity. There is a place for material help: but it is far more important to do something to improve the recipient's outlook on life. The service of the body is called *medicine*, taken to include food, drink, clothing, and shelter, and whatever else that preserves or restores health. Nothing should be given which will harm either donor or beneficiary; but within this limit, we should subscribe to our neighbor's own wishes for himself, and should offer him nothing which we would be disposed to reject for ourselves.[50] If the early Romans could stint themselves for the sake of their state, modern Christians can surely find the means to help compatriots in the *Civitas Dei*.[51] The service of the soul is called *discipline*. The redeemed man's characteristic trait is happy confidence in the universe. He will want his neighbors to share this outlook, not only for their own sake, but for his as well; their adherence will help to confirm him in his faith.[52] The recipient should be advised and instructed in the perils of "nature" and in the happiness and security of "redemption." Personal testimony will have a powerful effect, and St. Augustine suggests that the Elect should press their point with the enthusiasm of theater-goers singing the praises of their favorite performers.[53]

What is the Christian's attitude toward worldly authority? He will accept power for himself, if it is thrust upon him; but he will not seek it. Generally speaking, he sees the secular state, with its rulers pleasant and unpleasant, as something to be endured as patiently as possible. There can be no doubt as to what advice St.

[48] *De Civ. D.* ix.5; xiv.9.4; *In Johan. Evang.* 60.2, 3, 5.

[49] *Epist.* 91.2; *De Civ. D.* xv.6; xix.20, 27; *Conf.* i.1.1; vi.16.26.

[50] *De Serm. Dom. in Mont.* 1.67; *De Ver. Rel.* 46.87, 89.

[51] *Serm.* 36.7; *De Civ. D.* v.18.2.

[52] *In Johan. Evang.* 65; *Conf.* iv.12.18; *De Mor. Eccl. Cath.* 26.51; *De Ver. Rel.* 45–46, 85–86. Étienne Henri Gilson, *L'Introduction à l'Étude de Saint Augustin* (Paris: Vrin, 1929), p. 220.

[53] *Epist.* 48; 185.1.1, 2, 4; *De Mor. Eccl. Cath.* 28.56; *In Johan. Evang.* 57; *De Doctr. Christ.* i.29.30.

Augustine would give Christians of today, who find themselves living under militantly anti-Christian governments. Apparent misgovernment is to be borne with trustful patience. God will not give us a burden greater than we can bear. Our government, like everything else in our experience, is what we deserve, and what is best for us, whatever the unlovely motives and behavior of its operators.[54] One should put up with anything rather than lose one's feeling of charity toward all men. All authorities, pagan or Christian, heretic or orthodox, are to be obeyed, as Christ paid tribute to Caesar, and their commands are to be taken as the commands of Christ, who has given them their authority.[55] St. Augustine often recalls the apostolic ordinance of obedience to the powers of this world, which for Sts. Peter and Paul meant Nero's government.[56] This attitude has many expressions in patristic literature. Theophilus of Antioch says that Christians honor and obey and pray for the king, as the authority set over them by God.[57] Athenagoras of Athens says that Christians who pray for the empire, and who value authority, are the best of subjects.[58] Tertullian says that Christians pray that the Emperor may have a long life, secure authority, a stable dynasty, strong armies, a loyal senate, and an honest people. They do this because they have been commanded to pray for their enemies and for all authorities! Elsewhere he says that Christians must love and revere the Emperor, whom God has raised up. Indeed they do revere him, next to God.[59] But as citizens of an inner kingdom, Christians are subject to laws which take precedence over those of the secular state. When there is conflict, verbal protest and passive resistance are the Christian's weapons.[60] But these clashes are likely to arise only in specifically "religious" issues, where cult practices

[54] *De Civ. D.* iv.33; vii.21; xix.15; *Ennar in Ps.* 124.7. Norman Hepburn Baynes, *The Political Ideas of St. Augustine's "De Civitate Dei"* (Historical Association Pamphlet No. 104 [London: Bell, 1936]), p. 9: our rulers may not be just, but God will not let them do *us* less than justice.

[55] *De Mor. Eccl. Cath.* 30.63; *Epist.* 105.11, hoc iubent imperatores quod iubet et Christus. *Ennar. in Ps.* 124.7; *De Civ. D.* xix.17, 19; *Conf.* iii.8.15. Gilson, *Introduction à l'Étude de Saint Augustin*, p. 231.

[56] *De Civ. D.* iv.33; v.21; *Ennar. in Ps.* 124.7. I Peter 2.13–17; Rom. 13.17.

[57] Prov. 24.21.

[58] *Legat. Pro Christ.* 37 (A.D. 176–179), addressed to M. Aurelius.

[59] *Apol.* 28f.; *Ad Scap.*

[60] *Epist.* 185.2.8; *Conf.* iii.8.15, 9.17; *In Johan. Evang.* 51.10; *De Civ. D.* i.9.1.

are involved. Julian's Christian soldiers obeyed his military orders explicitly, but would have refused to carry out pagan rites. Christians will not make religious issues of language, manners, or political systems, but will conform to the custom of their time and place.[61]

The same principles apply in labor relations. Servants are advised to be loyal to their masters, not just from necessity, but from a carefully cultivated sense of pleasure in their work. The remedy for slavery lies not in legal emancipation but in identification of the slave's will with his master's will.[62] Masters are not let off scot-free. They are asked to be forbearing toward their servants, and "more disposed to advise than to compel." At first glance, these recommendations seem to favor management at the expense of labor. But from the Christian point of view, the slave is in the stronger position. He is given practice in the art of cheerful acquiescence in a will not his own, and is spared the master's constant temptation to self-will.

But however submissive to authority the Christian may be, he will lack enthusiasm for secular organization. As a rule, he will live honestly, peaceably, and harmoniously with his neighbors, all the more law-abiding because for God's sake as an exercise in cheerful acquiescence.[63] But his cardinal virtues are not primarily social: temperance, defined as the giving of oneself wholly to God; fortitude, bearing all things with equanimity for God's sake; justice, serving only God; and prudence, which distinguishes between what helps and what hinders a sound relationship with God.[64] He obeys laws conducive to his own and to his fellow citizens' well-being, but has the attitude of a traveler passing through a strange country. The world, which provides ends for his "natural" neighbors, is for the Christian a sort of moral gymnasium. If he feels that he is becoming too eager to get, or too fearful of losing, worldly goods, he must take himself in hand, and cultivate a contempt for them. His attitude toward the secular government will be loyal but lackadaisical, and

[61] *De Cat. Rud.* 21.37; *Ennar. in Ps.* 124.7; *De Civ. D.* xix.17; *Epist.* 46; 47.3: Christians should not eat meat which has been dedicated in sacrifice to pagan gods.

[62] *De Mor. Eccl. Cath.* 30.63.

[63] *Epist.* 138.2.15; 125.3–4; *De Doctr. Christ.* i.36.40; *De Fide Spe Car.* 6.18; *De Mend.* 3, 4, 41; *Contra Mend.* 1.

[64] *De Mor. Eccl. Cath.* 15.25.

he will have no ambitious drive toward worldly progress.[65] It is the difference between an owner of property with a financial and sentimental stake in his house, and a tenant who expects to move on after a few years; he may not wreck the house, but he will probably not give it much time, energy, or loving forethought.

Not that St. Augustine condemns the state, or social organization, as inherently evil. Food and shelter are good, and may be sought through cooperative effort. The association of rulers and ruled, for the management of earthly and temporal goods needed by both saints and sinners, is certainly not to be described as "organized sin." Its objectives, at worst, are *less good*, and should be regarded as means for the attainment of higher ends.[66] The peace which kings seek is good, as far as it goes. Kings do administer justice of a sort, however inadequate. St. Paul urges obedience to the secular authorities, because they reward virtue and punish vice, if not by intention then as God's unwitting instruments. Clement of Alexandria defines "King" as one who rules in a lawful way—probably in contrast with tyrants, who obtain power through *coups d'état*. St. Ambrose says that justice and beneficence are essential in any community, and might seem to imply that even the secular state has some share in these.[67]

Furthermore, political machinery can on occasion be put to Christian purposes. A Christian *should* accept office if dynastic connections, military pressure, or popular demand seem to be propelling him forward.[68] *Vox populi* (*regnantium, militum*), *vox Dei*. But his secular authority and responsibilities will be a burden to him, if he has a healthy sense of values. First, an official position of this sort is spiritually dangerous, because of the pomp and adulation which it entails. In addition, it is time-consuming; power is held in trust, and the ruler should always be at the citizens' service. Long

[65] *De Civ. D.* xix.17; *De Doctr. Christ.* iii.16.24. Christopher Dawson, "St. Augustine and His Age," in Martin Cyril D'Arcy and others, *A Monument to Saint Augustine* (London: Sheed and Ward, 1930), p. 59; Vernon Joseph Bourke, *Augustine's Quest of Wisdom* (Milwaukee: Bruce, 1945), pp. 236–237.

[66] *De Lib. Arb.* i.5.12; *De Civ. D.* xv.4. John Neville Figgis, *The Political Aspects of S. Augustine's "City of God"* (London: Longmans Green, 1921), pp. 56, 58, 88–89, 103; Burleigh, *City of God*, p. 174; Gilson, *Introduction à l'Étude de Saint Augustin*, p. 233: "La cité terrestre n'est pas l'état."

[67] *De Civ. D.* xix.17, 26. *Cf. Contra Cresc.* iii.47.51; *Epist.* 51.3; 105.5, 6; *Ennar. in Ps.* 101; *Serm.* 2.9.

[68] *De Civ. D.* xix.19.

life, able sons, victory, and security, the conventional blessings of the successful ruler, may distract his attention from more important things, and in any event have been given to many pagan princes as well as to Constantine, and withheld from such authentically pious princes as Gratian and Jovian.[69] The Christian prince is, or should be, primarily concerned with attitudes and beliefs, beginning with his own. He will use what power he has to promote orthodox learning, by supporting the Church, suppressing schism, propagating the Faith, exterminating idols, enacting laws of Christian tenor, enforcing the Judaeo-Christian moral code even when this runs contrary to established local custom, and above all setting a public example of the private virtues. He will be quicker to correct himself than others, slow to punish, apt to forgive, and willing to allow time for self-amendment.[70] In his account of Constantine and Theodosius, St. Augustine offers a "Mirror of Christian Princes." And why is Theodosius praised? He was loyal to his patron Gratian and to the latter's half-brother Valentinian II; he supported the Church, *iustissimis et misericordissimis legibus*; he threw down heathen idols; he did spectacular penance for his impulsive savagery against the Thessalonians.[71] But he is not praised for his contribution to the prosperity and security of the secular state whose chief he was.

One of the chief duties of the Christian ruler is to induce his subjects to think righteous thoughts. St. Augustine has no doubt but that the machinery of the secular state can, and should, be used for this purpose.[72] But is the use of force legitimate? Probably so, for reasons similar to those which might seem to justify a loving parent in whipping his son. But at first St. Augustine seems to have thought not. He was unwilling to invoke the secular arm against a Donatist bishop who had rebaptized an apostatizing deacon, contrary to the law of A.D. 373. He disapproved of the strong measures taken by a Catholic father to recover his daughter from a Donatist convent which she had entered of her own free will. Before his episcopal ordination, he seems to have felt that schismatics, like the poor, are always with us and should be tolerated. He once tried to

[69] *In Johan. Evang.* 6.25; *De Civ. D.* xix.5, 16; *Epist.* 51.2; *De Mor. Eccl. Cath.* 30.63.

[70] *In Civ. D.* v.24; *Epist.* 95.19; 185.5.19; *Conf.* iii.8.16.

[71] *De Civ. D.* v.24, 26.

[72] *Contra Epist. Parm.* i.13–16; *Contra Litt. Petil. Don.* i.2.203.

prevent the execution of some Circumcellions who had murdered a Catholic priest, on the ground that while life remains repentance is possible.[73] But if and when force seemed likely to do good, he came to see no objection to its use, and over the years his opinion of its efficacy rose. He offers several justifications. First, schism is a murder of the soul, and Christ's flock must be protected from spiritual murderers.[74] Second, the schismatic is spiritually sick, and one has a duty to "bind" a delirious man who if left alone might destroy himself.[75] Third, schism is worse than murder or adultery, and offenders should be punished.[76] Fourth, and most important from St. Augustine's point of view, is the command of the Lord of the feast, *compelle intrare*, "Compel them to come in."[77] Fifth, Scripture gives many instances of God's use or permission for the use of force to achieve worthy ends: Daniel's accusers were killed by lions; Elijah put to death the prophets of Baal; Hezekiah forcibly suppressed idolatry; Nebuchadnezzar ordered all men to tremble before the true God; Jesus expelled the money-changers from the temple; Paul was struck blind on the road to Damascus.[78]

St. Augustine's sympathy with the use of force as a persuader was in the first place stimulated by the physical fear inspired in African Catholics by the Circumcellions. These peasant terrorists took, or were given, their name from their habit of prowling around isolated country houses (*circum cellas*); but in towns, too, drunken mobs put law-abiding citizens in fear of their lives. They forcibly demanded that slaves be set free, and called for defiance of authority and repudiation of debt.[79] At first, because of Jesus' comment on those

[73] *Epist.* 23.7; 35.4 (A.D. 396); 133; *Serm.* 252.3–4.

[74] *Epist.* 185.5.20; *Contra Litt. Petil. Don.* ii.8.20, 20.46, 33.54; *Contra Cresc.* iv.21.26; *De Bapt. Contra Don.* iii.1.3; *Epist.* 228.7.

[75] *Epist.* 93.

[76] Prov. 13.24, see *Epist.* 185.6.21.

[77] Luke 14.23, see *Epist.* 93.5. Paul Monceaux, *Histoire Littéraire de l'Afrique* (Paris: Leroux, 1901–1923), VII, 228; "Telle est l'origine du compelle intrare: la coercition pour le salut, la persecution dans l'interêt de persecutés, le Paradis forcé."

[78] *Epist.* 185.3.11, with reference to Psalm 18.37; 185.5.19, 6.22, 6.24.

[79] Violence; see *Epist.* 185. Drunkenness; see *Serm.* 17.2f.; 46.17; 151.4; 225.4; *Epist.* 22.6; 29.5; 93.48–49; *Contra Litt. Petil. Don.* ii.33.78, 39.93, 78.174, 88.195, 101.233; *Contra Cresc.* iv.63.77. Immorality; see *Contra Litt. Petil. Don.* iii.32.37, 34.40, 37.43; ii.26.61. Suicide; see *Epist.* 43.23; 173; 185.3.12; 204.2; *Contra Litt. Petil. Don.* ii.89.197.

who take the sword, they confined themselves to clubs. In time they became sophisticated enough to employ not only swords but slings, axes, stones, javelins, and lime to be thrown in their enemies' eyes.[80] No government, Christian or pagan, which was committed to the maintenance of law and order could tolerate such folk. St. Augustine, like other Catholic clergy, assumes a connection between these social subversives and the Donatist Church. The Circumcellions certainly thought of themselves as Christians, if not indeed as constituting the Church Militant. Sometimes they professed continence and called themselves monks; sometimes they put down "the mighty" from their chariot-seats, replacing them there with their "humble and meek" servants; their slogan cry was "Deo laudes!" There can be no doubt but that the Donatist and the Circumcellion movements appealed to much the same constituency, each being stronger in the more rural and less European districts, and offering outlets for the same feelings of resentment against Italian domination and exploitation. The Donatist bishops disclaimed a connection, and on the official level there probably was none. But St. Augustine has seen Donatist clergy mingling with Circumcellion mobs, and is probably right in thinking that, however critical Donatist bishops may have been of certain practices of the Circumcellions, the schismatists in general were in broad sympathy with the terrorists, when not in fact identical with them.[81] Official action against the Circumcellions was on social, not religious, grounds. If the Donatist Church was persecuted, this was, at one point, because of its supposed guilt by association with criminal elements. This may explain the secular arm's original interest in the Donatists. But in the end they were persecuted as schismatics, and this is clearly shown in the fact that they could put themselves right with the authorities not by undertaking to disassociate themselves from the Circumcellions, but only by abandoning their heresy.

In addition to fining and exiling the Donatist clergy, the government handed over Donatist church property to the Catholics, and St. Augustine thinks it necessary to advise imperial officials *against* killing or physically injuring the unfortunate schismatics. This suggests that in fact, if not in theory, the Donatists were both

[80] *Ennar. in Ps.* 10.5; *Contra Epist. Parm.* i.11.17; ii.88.195, 96.222.
[81] *Contra Litt. Petil. Don.* ii.92.210, 84.184; *Epist.* 43.24; 87.8.

pillaged and physically abused.[82] The Donatists themselves claimed that some of their people had been murdered by agents of the government. But St. Augustine points out that in the best of times Donatists have shown a penchant for suicide, and quotes orthodox witnesses to the effect that certain Donatists have killed themselves in such a way as to throw suspicion on the officials. Whatever the policy of the government—and this was an age of savage enactments —one might expect that troops engaged in rounding up subversives and schismatics would display a certain ruthlessness. There is nothing implausible in the claim of the Donatists that one of their men had been thrown from a great rock, and another dropped down a well. St. Augustine is being either disingenuous or silly when he says that these stories must be false, because such penalties "are not recognized in Roman law."[83] In any event, if he sometimes encourages the execution of penal laws against the Donatists, this may be defended on the ground that he thinks that they are giving at least moral support to gangsters of whom the Catholic community go in fear of their lives.

The second circumstance which persuaded St. Augustine of the merit of forceful secular action was his observation that such action often led to the conversion of many schismatics. Toleration and impunity had brought violence, but disciplinary action had led to reconciliation. Many reconciled former Donatists, he notes, have expressed gratitude. More people are corrected by fear than by love, and St. Paul himself was struck down and blinded before he was instructed in the faith. A rotten conversion is better than none, because it exposes a man to good influences and puts him in the way of considering the claims of orthodoxy. Even if we begin in fear, perfect love will cast out fear in the end. The death of a few men in "self-inflicted flames," a metaphor, one hopes, is a small price to pay for the eternal happiness of the many restored to the Church by "persecution."[84] It must be remembered that violence and restraint are not in themselves evil, from St. Augustine's point of view. God permits no "persecution," nor any circumstance, which is inconsistent with His eternal design, or with the highest good of the

---

[82] *Epist.* 185.3.12; *In Johan. Evang.* 11.15.

[83] *Epist.* 185.3.12; *In Johan. Evang.* 11.15.

[84] *Epist.* 185.2.7, 6.21, 7.29, 8.32; 93.1. Pope, *St. Augustine of Hippo*, p. 342; Gilson, *Introduction à l'Étude de Saint Augustin*, pp. 232–233.

"victim." Intuitive or revealed beliefs do not depend upon conscious ratiocination, and cannot always be communicated by a rational exposition. It may seem that only by forcing our friends to act upon certain assumptions can we bring them, by personal experience of them, to acknowledge their value for happiness.[85]

St. Augustine, despite these sentiments, did not press for forceful persecution—but was ready to profit by it when it occurred.[86] His thesis that persecution is justified if the motives of the agent are charitable is quite consistent with his general principles. Even if a persecutor, with the best intentions, has made what might seem a mistake in judgment, he has not sinned, and his victim remains under the protection of Divine Providence.

Denial of nature, and constant trust in the wisdom of God, did not come easily to St. Augustine, in whom are discernible many traces of "natural man." The doctrine of divine love makes great demands upon his capacity for faith. He seems to think that we love only those who can help us; he cannot see how we can help God, and so attract His love. He supposes that God can put us to *some* use: "Otherwise I am at a loss to discover in what way He can love us." This perplexity is shown in his reluctance to comment upon Biblical passages alluding to the love of God. In his commentary on St. John's Gospel he omits Chapter Three, verse sixteen, and has little to say on I John 4.8–10, "God is love." [87]

His generalized optimism is, of course, a contrived piece of wishful thinking, running contrary to the instinctive feeling of his "natural" self. A true or rather a spontaneous optimist would throw himself upon the friendliness of the universe, savoring every experience, like William James's healthy-minded man, but with a preference for pleasant experiences. But St. Augustine's paper optimism is less concerned with enjoying a world *ex hypothesi* good than with shoring oneself up against the floods of unpleasantness which he expects to wash over one. He tries to maintain that evil has no objective existence and that the universe is friendly, a thesis which, if accepted, should free us from fear.[88] He admits that it is

[85] *Epist.* 93.10; 103.13; *Contra Epist. Parm.* i.9.15; *Contra Gaud.* 1.51; *Serm.* 24.6.

[86] Pope, *St. Augustine of Hippo*, p. 343, note 1.

[87] *De Doctr. Christ.* i.31.34.

[88] *De Civ. D.* xii.1.2; xiv.13; xv.7.1; xix.4.4; *Conf.* i.18.31; x.22.32.

sometimes hard to put a favorable interpretation upon experience. The natural man within him thinks of history as a catalog of miseries punctuated by catastrophes.[89] His Christian self must assume that this viewpoint is wrong, since it brings unhappiness and is an expression of *hybris*.[90] To get right results, we must judge the world of experience not by observation but by the criteria of the Christian faith. The wise man does not judge life, but accepts every experience, on faith, as good. He finds security in this surrender of personal judgment.[91] From the "natural" point of view, this is a deliberate abdication of common sense in favor of wishful thinking.

The "natural," instinctive man in St. Augustine believes that life is predominantly evil, and man generally helpless in the face of it. Worldly pleasures may be gifts of God, but they are gifts hard to come by or to keep. If man lets himself become obsessed with them, he is laying himself open to frustration and disappointment. The general folly of the "natural" approach to life is shown in the unhappiness and perturbations which, in St. Augustine's opinion, are its constant accompaniment.[92] Only a "profound and dreadful ignorance" could throw us into such a maelstrom of cares, disquiet, grief, fear, uncontrollable joys, quarrels, lawsuits, wars, treasons, anger, envy, murder, parricide, cruelty, ferocity, wickedness, luxury, insolence, impudence, shamelessness, fornications, adultery, incest, perversion, sacrilege, heresy, blasphemy, perjury, oppression of the innocent, slander, conspiracy, falsehood, false witnessing, unjust judgment, violence, and plundering.[93]

For all his dislike and distrust of the world, St. Augustine avoids the logical absurdities of the Manichaean Elect, who can have nothing to do with the gathering or preparation of food, and whose very eating is piously assumed to be accomplished in a fit of absent-mindedness. St. Augustine assumes that "life must go on" in a world which, however unpleasant, is the handiwork of God. Contemplation is our highest activity. It would be pleasantest to spend all our time pursuing elusive mystical previews of heavenly felicity,

[89] *De Civ. D.* xiii.14; xv.4; xviii.49.

[90] *De Trin.* xi.5.8; *De Lib. Arb.* ii.9.26–27; *De Civ. D.* xxii.22.1.

[91] *De Trin.* xiv.1.1; *De Civ. D.* ii.1; iv.13; x.28; xv.6; xix.14; *Conf.* vi.3.3; x.42.67–68; *In Johan. Evang.* 55.7; 4.13.

[92] *De Nat. Bon.* 7; *De Civ. D.* xiv.10.

[93] *De Civ. D.* xxii.22.1.

and without something of this we should lose sight of our objective and be overwhelmed by the daily round. Sacrifice and intellectual humility are prerequisites to these fleeting intimations of future happiness. The sacrifice required is sacrifice of our independent judgment of good and evil, and the identification of our wills with God's will expressing itself in the circumstances which constitute our experience.[94] But we have only an occasional and feeble capacity for contemplation. We have other obligations, less exhilarating but perhaps easier to fulfill. For each Jacob among us, Leah symbolizes the ordinary hard work, and Rachel the joyful expectations. We oscillate between *otium* and *negotium,* and must share in each, although our circumstances at various times may be more conducive to one or to the other. St. Augustine established a monastery at Thagaste, along Italian lines, where pre-ordinands might strengthen themselves with unusually generous draughts of contemplative *otium.* The inmates led a communal life, and were introduced to learning and Christian scholarship. A monk was expected to pay for his own happiness by instructing others. But even here, physical labor was part of the program. A monk too prayerful to work was thought to be too prayerful to eat.

St. Augustine is perhaps inconsistent on the subject of violence. The redeemed man is not supposed to repay unpleasantness with unpleasantness. He should try to improve unpleasant incidents by showing an example of cheerful patience and by trying to convert his would-be persecutor to better ways of thinking. He must not kill even in self-defense, and certainly not to secure worldly good which he professes to despise, or at most to regard with good-humored indifference. Killing is permissible only when it is specifically enjoined by the divine law, or by *ad hoc* authorization, as in the case of Samson and the Philistines.[95] But what is specifically forbidden to the individual seems to be permitted to the group. St. Augustine is affected by the conflict between the Christian ideal of joyful acquiescence in the face of God's instruments Nero, Attila, or even, one presumes, Mao Tse-tung, and "natural man's" inclination to have what he holds. A government, he concedes, is justified in keeping order by means of physical punishments, including executions, and may defend itself and its territories against rebellion and

[94] *De Civ. D.* x.6, 15; xix.19.
[95] *Epist.* 46; 47.5; 138.2.11; *De Lib. Arb.* i.5.12; *De Civ. D.* i.21.

external aggression.[96] But one would have thought, from what he says elsewhere, that Christians even when members of an organized group should practice to be content with the circumstances, however unpleasant, in which they find themselves—circumstances consistent with God's plan for them—and should not commit the *certain* crime of murder simply to avoid *possible* conquest, loss of material advantages or freedom, or death itself, circumstances which, however distasteful, could never come upon them unless God could turn this to their best advantage. St. Augustine concedes that war is the product of an evil will, but suggests that the will to make war may, on occasion, be the lesser of two evils. But surely one can try to avoid any evil choice, however painful the immediate result seems likely to be. St. Augustine says further that when a decision has been taken to make war, the goal must be *peace*, a doctrine as hard to understand in its ancient as in its modern expression. In a letter to the imperial officer Darius, congratulating him on his truce with the Vandals, St. Augustine praises the efforts of the troops, who were, he says, "fighting for peace," that is to say, to maintain the Roman hold upon certain pieces of terrestrial real estate with the natural resources pertaining thereto. That the military profession is an honorable one is said to be shown in the fact that John the Baptist did not advise soldiers to throw over their jobs, but rather to be satisfied with their pay and to avoid violence not in the line of duty.[97] This toleration of the idea that Christians should lend themselves *collectively* to practices which *as individuals* they would shun and abhor, and for reasons which in private life they would despise, is a humiliating concession either to the "natural man" in each of us, or to the strength of personality of allegedly Christian rulers anxious to enlist the aid of the Christian community in the defense of the secular state where their real treasure is laid up, for all their formal, and perhaps up to a point sincere, adherence to Christianity.

St. Augustine is willing to treat *as certain* various Christian propositions which, as he admits, cannot be proven, may perhaps be revealed by God to a few people, and by most must simply be accepted on faith. He will not let experience dislodge these prop-

[96] *De Lib. Arb.* i.4.9; *Epist.* 189.5, 6.
[97] *Epist.* 138.2.15; 189.4, 6; 229.2. Figgis, *Political Aspects of S. Augustine's "City of God,"* p. 65.

ositions. If necessary, the evidence of the senses and reason will be subjectively interpreted, ignored, or denied. This high-handed approach to what normal persons regard as facts leads him on to a denial of nature, as normal persons see it. He is ready to deny the appearances, and to put upon life a subjective interpretation based upon Christian premises which he holds on a deliberately unquestioning faith. Furthermore, he is prepared to use force, if necessary, to make others accept, or seem to accept, this interpretation of life, which he himself can accept only on faith.

It is "unnatural" to look for the good side of the bubonic plague, or for evidence of God's love for all concerned as shown in the death of a promising child. But these perversities obviously challenge some men in a satisfying way. Primitive Buddhism can be reduced to the equally perverse proposition that everything is not for the best but for the worst, and that the way to conquer unhappiness is to extirpate desire. In either case, one is asked to pay a high price, in terms of common sense and rational judgment, for peace of mind, the Buddhist by giving up all normal pleasure, the Christian by trying to deny that pain is really a matter for sorrow. In each case, there is an abdication of private judgment, an agreement to accept certain propositions unexamined.

CHAPTER FIVE

A Divine Comedy

I. PROLOGUE

In a world of uncertainties, St. Augustine is ready to live by faith; he will take his chances with unproven propositions. The propositions which he will accept are for the most part supported by appearances which have not as yet been contradicted; if future appearances run contrary, or if he finds himself holding hypotheses which are logically incompatible with one another, then he will change his tentative views. At the moment, appearances suggest that the sun will rise tomorrow, that milk is good food for most babies, and that the volume of a gas varies inversely with the pressure upon it. He is also willing to assume that the Christian view of life is sound, although appearances here may give some difficulty. It is *not obvious* to everyone that Alpine avalanches and the bubonic plague illustrate a loving Providence. St. Augustine agrees that the Christian viewpoint is "unnatural," and this means, among other things, that it runs counter to what most men regard as the appearances.

The skeptic, in his tentative way, may indeed try to interpret his experiences in accordance with Christian assumptions. But if he does so, this is not because they are more plausible in light of appearances, but simply because they are more inspiriting than their opposites and are not demonstrably false. But he is willing to admit that experience may bring him to change his mind. He may come to see the absurdity of the consistently optimistic point of view. St. Augustine diverges from the skeptic, and from his own normal skepticism, by putting his Christian faith, as distinct from the host of other propositions which he accepts on faith, in an intrenched position. He apparently does this not because he can prove it true, or because it has been revealed to him personally, in detail, but because of the peace of mind which unquestioning acceptance seems to bring. For the sake of this psychological benefit, the Christian creed is *not* to be critically examined; experience is to be interpreted as invariably supporting it; it is to be taken *as if true*, even by those who can accept it only on faith.

St. Augustine is willing to believe that every event in the world of our experience has its predestined place in a wise and loving providential scheme. Historical material, whatever its source, must be found to contribute in all its detail to a "true myth," in which the ways of God are justified, and in which even the stubborn fact of human unhappiness is somehow reconciled with belief in a God both omnipotent and loving. To this end, the universal process is presented as a Divine Comedy, which begins well, passes through a dramatically difficult phase, and then moves to a serene conclusion. The comedy, if "divine," is certainly not "human." In the *dénouement*, most of the human actors will be found to have been expendable stage properties, consigned in the end to the dustbin of eternal damnation, but without prejudice, St. Augustine assumes, to one's belief in an essentially "happy ending." Every event in the drama is foreseen by its Divine Author. A man reciting a poem can be said to have present in his mind, from the beginning to the end of the recitation, the past which he has already recited, the present which he is momentarily reciting, and the future which he has yet to recite. In the same way, past, present, and future are eternally present in the mind of God.[1]

The Comedy will be played only once. Ancient philosophers who were inclined to think the world eternal and without a beginning were embarrassed by the shortness of recorded history. Rather than postulate, in modern fashion, a late development of the human race, and a very late flowering of culture, they speculatively populated the long reaches of eternity with recurring historical cycles. But for St. Augustine the historical process is rectilinear. The earth is about 6,000 years old, and the Incarnation an event unique in time. "For once Christ died for us, and rising from the dead He dieth no more."[2]

[1] *Conf.* xi.7.8.

[2] *De Civ. D.*, e.g., xii.13, 14, 17. John H. S. Burleigh, *The City of God* (London: Nisbet, 1949), pp. 118, 205; Henri Irénée Marrou, *L'Ambivalence du Temps de l'Histoire chez Saint Augustin* (Paris: Vrin, 1950), pp. 17, 32.

2. ACT ONE

In the First Act, God creates a perfect universe and peoples it with actors who, whatever their *thoughts*, can *do* only what is consistent with the plot.

God first makes heaven and earth. This heaven is the first of three: the intellectual heaven, the firmament, and the atmosphere which surrounds the earth. The intellectual heaven is the House of God, a living creature, incorporeal and eternal, created like everything else *ex nihilo*. As an intellectual being, it contemplates the God who dwells in it. Its will is identical with His. In this last regard, it serves as a model for all intellectual creatures, including man. God is the object of its entire affection. It hopes for nothing better than it now enjoys.[3]

The earth created simultaneously with the intellectual heaven is to be understood as matter, unseen and undifferentiated, but with a modicum of form to distinguish it from *nihil*. The statement, "Darkness was upon the face of the deep," suggests its utter obscurity.[4] All things made of it have something of the mutability and corruption which might be expected in objects but two removes from *nihil*.[5] This may seem to attribute to "nothingness" a malignant character, and Harnack and others see here an echo of the Manichaean *naturale principium mali*. Julian of Eclanum suggests ironically that St. Augustine's *nihil* is the virtual equivalent of the Manichaean Prince of Darkness: it has great influence from the fact that it never existed, and its power was greatest after it had lost its name—by assuming form and acquiring identity. But whatever else it is, it is passive, like the Platonic substratum, which makes imperfection possible without being itself positively evil.[6]

Invisible angels were created with free will, perhaps at the moment when God said, "Let there be light." St. Augustine describes them

[3] *Conf.* xii.11.12, 15.19–20.

[4] *Conf.* xii.3.3.

[5] *De Lib. Arb.* iii.15.42.

[6] *Op. Imperf. Contra Jul.* 5.32–33. William Montgomery, *St. Augustine. Aspects of his Life and Thought* (London: Hodder and Stoughton, 1914), p. 164; James Morgan, *The Psychological Teaching of St. Augustine* (London: Elliot Stock, 1932), p. 77.

as real and substantial, though immaterial, and they play important parts in the unfolding drama. But they can also be thought of as magnified types of Christian and "natural" man.

Next God created the visible heaven and earth, and nature began to assume its predestined forms. All beasts of the water, the field, and the air came into existence, *in esse* or *in posse*.[7] In its turn, the soul of man was created by God, inferior in function but equal in nature to the angelic creation.[8] It is not a fragment of the divine substance, imprisoned in matter, as the Manichees believe, but like everything, apart from the Creator himself, is created *ex nihilo*. Certainly it is not coeternal with God, and the idea of a prior existence for the sins of which the soul is now suffering—which would see our world as a sort of hell—is specifically rejected, for all its plausibility.[9] The body, like the soul, is created by God, and is therefore good in itself. Together with the soul, to which it is tied for all eternity, except for a relatively brief separation between death and Judgment, it constitutes the human personality, made in the image of God, but not more so than the angels.

The universe thus created is perfect. All things work together for good, and a wise Providence guides a harmonious universal process to a blissful predestined end. Every creature has a part to play, and has the capacity to play that part to perfection. Unhappiness would seem impossible in such a world. But however strong one's will to accept this optimistic proposition, it is perfectly obvious that most men are unhappy a great deal of the time. Unless this paradox, of unhappy denizens in a perfect universe, can be explained in plausible fashion, we are likely to lose our faith in a loving God. How can a wise and loving God allow pain and unhappiness in a "perfect" universe completely subject to his divine will?

According to St. Augustine, God could not have willed that any of his creatures should be unhappy; if we find ourselves unhappy, it must in some way be our own fault. When God created angels and men, He gave them the gift of free will, to make them more like Himself. Free will is recognized by us in the same direct way, and at the same time, as self-existence.[10] There is no external cause for an

[7] *De Gen. Contra Man.* i.7.11; *Conf.* xii.1.2, 12.15–16.

[8] *De Lib. Arb.* iii.2.32.

[9] *Epist.* 155.1; 143.7; 156.9; 166.2; *De Anim. et eius Orig.* i.4.4, 14.22, 15.25; ii.3.5; *De Civ. D.* viii.5; x.31; xii.17, 26; *De Gen. ad Litt.* vii.3–4; x.6, 10.

[10] *De Civ. D.* v.4.

act of free will; and in some instances, at least, our wills are completely free.[11] If we are unhappy, our unhappiness must spring from mistakes made by us in this area where we have an entirely free hand.

Pride is the first sin. Some angels, and then man, presume upon their likeness to God, and *will* not submit their wills to his. They wish for what seems *to them* good. Adam is attracted by the fallen angel's false promise, *vos eritis sicut deus, scientes bonum et malum,* and as God's supposed equal he feels free to pass judgment upon God's handiwork. He is free to will this, but he lacks the capacity to carry it out successfully, and makes drastic errors in judgment. He confuses secondary goods with primary goods, and means with ends; in pursuing the good he misses the better, and brings down upon himself disappointments and frustrations. Above all, he discovers, or thinks that he discovers, *malum* in a divinely ordered world in which every experience which presents itself is *optimum* in its time and place. Fear of this imaginary evil, whether of specific things or events, or of deprivations or frustrations, is the source of his unhappiness. But the only real evil is within him, in his proud wish to judge things too deep for him, in his unwillingness to identify his will with God's, and in the tragic misunderstandings to which this leads. This unhappy confusion, arising from an abuse of free will, constitutes "The Fall."

Each of us seems to fall in the same way; few of us are very satisfied with God's world. The Biblical account suggests that we have in some way inherited Adam's wish to judge for himself. But how is this spiritual disease transmitted? *Creationists,* like St. Jerome, St. Thomas Aquinas, and later Catholic theologians, declare that a soul is created for each new body.[12] St. Augustine says that he wishes that he could accept this theory. But if the soul of each newborn baby is a separate creation, then the propensity to sin must be transmitted through the body alone, and this would imply that it is a physical rather than a spiritual taint.[13] The *traducian* view is that souls are transmitted in some way, whether through generation or some other means, from a primitively tainted source. Lacking a

[11] *De Civ. D.* xii.6.

[12] Hieron. *Opera* 3.493. Morgan, *Psychological Teaching of St. Augustine,* p. 143; Vernon Joseph Bourke, *Augustine's Quest of Wisdom* (Milwaukee: Bruce, 1945), p. 236.

[13] *Epist.* 166.6.

scriptural lead, St. Augustine displays suspense of judgment: *nunc autem nescio nec me pudet ut istum fateri nescire quod nescio.*[14] And in the *Retractationes* he says, "I did not know then, and I do not know now." The problem is to understand how sin can appear from the very beginning in every descendent of Adam, at precisely the same time as his physiological characteristics, and yet be recognized as involving an abuse of *his own free will* in every individual sinner. He rejects as too crudely corporeal Tertullian's idea that the soul is transmitted in the act of physical generation: that would seem to put the soul's propensity to sin on the same basis as the body's propensity to assume a certain shape.[15] He even suggests a pool of souls, in some mysterious way tainted with a propensity to Adam's sin, and finding their way by some natural process into new-born bodies.[16] But this still involves an inheritance—one does not *will* to be born with this propensity to sin, and it is somehow derived from Adam. All that is gained is a formal disassociation of physical from intellectual propensities. But elsewhere St. Augustine seems not merely to countenance the idea of an inheritance direct from father to son,[17] but even to suggest that men who will not submit to God are punished by finding that their own sexual organs are beyond control, and that every man derives his sinful and unsubmissive nature from the unsubmissive character of the organs which begot him.[18] Before Adam sinned, he had power to choose to submit, or not to submit, joyfully to the will of God. Before Adam sinned, the nature which he was to hand down to posterity had not been fixed beyond the possibility of change. But his sinful choice affected the nature which he would transmit; and now, by whatever means, all men inherit from him a propensity to sin, and in that sense were condemned in his condemnation.

In Adam's fall
We sinned all.

Our propensity to sin is humanly ungovernable. Our wills are free, but only in the sense that we can make one evil choice rather than

---

[14] *De Anim. et eius Orig.* i.15.24; *Op. Imperf. Contra Jul.* ii.68.

[15] *De Gen. ad Litt.* x.14.24, 24.40.

[16] *De Gen. ad Litt.* vii.35–36. At one time, St. Augustine wondered if there might not be one universal soul for all mankind; later he came out strongly for the individuality of each soul; see *De Quant. Anim.* 32.69.

[17] *Epist.* 166.4; 190.1; 202.6; *De Lib. Arb.* iii.20.55.

[18] *De Nupt. et Concup.* i.6.7.

another.[19] And yet no one is condemned for Adam's sin, St. Augustine insists, or for sins as yet uncommitted. One is punished for the sins *which one has chosen to commit*—and we have noted St. Augustine's belief that infants rebel against God's universe with their first yell—and by making this sinful choice rather than that we destroy any claim to mercy on the grounds of inherited propensity.[20] We have free will, but it is far from completely free, and unlike Adam before the Fall we are *not* free to choose the good.

But is human free will compatible with divine omnipotence? How can we believe, at one and the same time, first, that Adam freely chose to disobey God, and that we are continually making free evil choices, and second, that every event in the historical process has its place in the eternally fixed design of a wise and loving God? St. Augustine's Christian faith obliges him to accept both Divine Providence and man's personal responsibility for his own unhappiness. He tries to reduce the scope of the dilemma by suggesting that in some important respects the human will is not, in fact, free. He seeks to resolve the paradox altogether, by distinguishing free will from the actual accomplishment of what is willed.

We have already noted his belief that fallen man cannot even will the good, let alone accomplish it. In addition to this limitation, the will may be subject to the intrusion of an external Agent, and in such a case its freedom is illusory. God can assume direct control, diverting the apparently spontaneous direction of the human will at His pleasure.[21] There are instances of divine illumination, in which the soul sees and is convinced by a coercive personal revelation of truth.[22] The will is neither completely free nor completely enslaved. God gives us a certain freedom of choice, but reserves the right sometimes to dictate our choice, as by salvation by grace.

There remains the problem of how *any* measure of free will can be reconciled with the idea of Divine Providence. A distinction is made between an inner, subjective world of the mind, and an outer

[19] *De Spirit. et Litt.* 2.3; *De Civ. D.* xiii.14; *De Anim. et eius Orig.* iv.11.16; *In Johan. Evang.* 44.1; *De Civ. D.* xiii.3.

[20] *Contra Duas Epist. Pelag.* iv.4.6; *In Johan. Evang.* 1.15; *De Fide Spe Car.* 13.46.

[21] *De Civ. D.* v.9.2; *De Fide Spe Car.* 25.98, quis porro tam impie desipiat, ut dicat Deum malas nominum voluntates quas voluerit, quando voluerit, ubi voluerit in bonum non posse convertere? 28.105; *Ennar. in Ps.* 93.11.

[22] *De Gest. Pelag.* 7.

world consisting of the experiences which happen to us. The outer world develops in accordance with an inexorable predetermined pattern; but we are generally free to adopt what attitude we will toward the inevitable. We can accept it confidently and happily, or we can kick against the pricks. We can wish certain things to happen, or to be done by us; but the extent to which we can actually obtain or carry out our wishes will depend upon the power of accomplishment granted us by God.[23] I am free to wish to jump over the moon, to become Emperor of China, or to found a successful new religion. My will is free. But I shall accomplish just as much, and no more, of my will than is compatible with the Divine Plan.[24] God is continually watching the operation of the human will, judging, helping, and giving or withholding power of accomplishment. If Tom has a malicious wish to injure Dick, and is able to break his back, we can be sure that the "injury" is for Dick's good. Tom has committed a sin, because of his evil intention; but Dick takes no harm, for God lets nothing happen to him incompatible with His wise and loving plan. Dick's only danger lies in the possibility that he may not trust God's providence, but make a presumptuous and false judgment, taking Tom's act at its face value as an injury to himself. The outer world of experiences and events is completely predetermined, and we can *do* nothing, either to ourselves or others, which does not conform to the Master Plan. But men's thoughts are generally free, and it is in this subjective world, and only here, where God does not generally intervene, that we encounter evil.

All men are born with a propensity to sin, and no man of his own accord can so much as will the good. But it is God's will that a few men should be restored to loving confidence in His plan. This handful are retrieved not because they choose, or deserve, this, but by a miracle of grace. The lightning may strike unlikely targets, and the fortunate ones can only be astonished at their good fortune. No man has obvious qualifications, or any claim, to divine favor.[25] Abel, the *second-born*, was the first chosen member of the *Civitas Dei*

[23] *De Civ. D.* v.10.1.

[24] *De Lib. Arb.* iii.2.4, 2.5, 3.7, 3.8; *Epist.* 143.6; *De Trin.* xiii.11.16; *De Civ. D.* v.11; xxii.1.2; *De Fide Spe Car.* 26.100; *De Nat. Bon.* 37; *Contra Epist. Man. Fund.* 41.47; *De Nat. et Grat.* 24.27; *In Johan. Evang.* 7.7; *Conf.* vii.13.19.

[25] *De Civ. D.* xii.21; xv.1.2; xxi.12. Bernard Roland-Gosselin, "St. Augustine's System of Morals," in Martin Cyril D'Arcy and others, *A Monument to Saint Augustine* (London: Sheed and Ward, 1930), p. 242.

on earth. Jacob, the *younger* twin, was elected in the womb, with no personal merit to commend him.[26] No man can so much as want to be saved, until the thought is put into his mind by God, through no choice of his own.[27] Man cannot be saved by his own good works. He cannot even do good, until God has given him the will and the power of accomplishment. Even when he has the will, some works, which might seem good in themselves, are beyond his power to do. God is the only source of will, power, and perseverance, either in faith or in good works. When the elect pray, "Lead us not into temptation," they are acknowledging their need of a continuing miracle of grace.[28]

How does God effect the miracle of salvation? Does He tempt the will, or does He coerce it? St. Augustine's view seems to have stiffened over the years, under Pelagian prodding, and he comes increasingly to emphasize the role of the external Agent at the expense of the subject's free will.[29] Thus in A.D. 397 he says that God moves us to delight in Him, and helps us to attain salvation by inspiring us with a desire to come to Him. It is not clear in the context whether he thinks of God as enticing or as tampering with the will. As yet he feels no need to clarify the issue.[30] In A.D. 412 he writes that God helps us, but we must respond to His help. This would suggest that God's direct intervention is limited, and that we are left to choose whether or not to seize the opportunity which He offers us.[31] In another essay of the same year, he states more specifically that God summons us, but lets us choose our response to His summons. There are three factors in salvation: the intervention of the Holy Spirit, the teachings of Scripture and Church—

[26] *De Civ. D.* xv.1.2; xvi.35.

[27] *Contra Duas Epist. Pelag.* i.2.5–7; *Ennar. in Ps.* 93.11. *Cf.* Rom. 1.17.

[28] *De Fide Spe Car.* 9.30; *De Dono Persev.* 5.9; *De Corrept. et Grat.* 12.37; *De Grat. Christ.* i.14.15; *De Grat. et Lib. Arb.* 14.28; 15.31.

[29] The Pelagians held that each man is born with Adam's original capacity for good. Each man has what endowment he needs to work out his salvation. The only obstacle is remediable ignorance. Grace is not a supranatural infusion, but appears in our original endowment, in the instruction which we receive, and in the forgiveness of our sins. The Pelagians held that St. Augustine's doctrine of the continuing need for divine intervention disparaged human nature as created by God. William John Sparrow Simpson, *St. Augustine's Episcopate. A Brief Introduction to his Writings as a Christian* (London: Society for Promoting Christian Knowledge, 1944), p. 77; Montgomery, *St. Augustine*, p. 170.

[30] *Conf.* i.1.1; xiii.1.1.   [31] *De Pecc. Mer. et Remiss.* ii.6.

and an exercise of free will.[32] In A.D. 415 he says that the fact that God commands implies that something is left for man to do, and suggests the possibility of disobedience. But the command to pray would seem to imply that without God's continuing help we could not, of ourselves, carry out the other commands. We are not entirely free, then, to respond as we might ourselves wish to the divine challenge.[33]

But in A.D. 418 he goes much further in emphasizing divine grace at the expense of human free will, and says that God actually binds men's wills to yield to His summons.[34] In A.D. 420 this is made still clearer. "And moreover, who will be so foolish and blasphemous as to say that God cannot change the evil wills of men, whichever, whenever, and wheresoever He chooses, and direct them to what is good?"[35] Men are not merely given a summons; they are given the will to respond.[36] In A.D. 426–427 we are told that a man may be given both the will to accede to the divine summons and the power to do so. Virtually nothing is left to truly voluntary effort.[37] Finally, we read that God not merely works upon the souls of His Elect, to draw them to Himself, but interferes freely with all wills, good and bad alike. "Man's good intentions, which God may convert from bad ones, and even man's worldly intentions, are so much at God's disposal that He can divert them in any direction He pleases."[38]

St. Augustine cannot commit himself to *total* determinism, because his Christian faith requires some scope for free will. But one thing that a man *cannot* do is to save himself by an effort of free will.[39] He thinks the Pelagian view "mere intellectualism," because it ignores the great gulf between knowing what is good and being willing and able to do it. Free will, and a considerable knowledge of Christian teaching, had not been enough to bring *him* to righteousness.[40] He does not agree with St. Jerome that, while man needs

---

[32] *De Spirit. et Litt.* 34.60; 3.5.   [33] *De Perf. Iust. Hom.* 10.21.
[34] *De Grat. Christ.* i.14.15, 24.25.   [35] *De Fide Spe Car.* 25.98.
[36] *Contra Duas Epist. Pelag.* i.19.37   [37] *De Grat. et Lib. Arb.* 15.31.
[38] *De Grat. et Lib. Arb.* 20.41.

[39] *De Anim. et eius Orig.* iv.11.16; *De Praedest. Sanct.* 10.19; *De Civ. D.* xviii.47.

[40] *Conf.* ix.1.1. Roland-Gosselin, in D'Arcy and others, *Monument to Saint Augustine,* p. 231; Simpson, *St. Augustine's Episcopate,* p. 82; Bourke, *Augustine's Quest of Wisdom,* pp. 175–176.

help to do good, he can at least decide for himself whether he will try to do good. Sinful men cannot reconcile themselves to God and slough off the burden of their past. Man is not master of his first thoughts. God must help, to enable man to will and do what is right.[41] For if man ever had power to do good on his own initiative, he has certainly not got it now.[42]

God, who is prescient of the whole historical process, must know from the beginning who will receive His free and undeserved grace. He may call and confirm His elect through the agency of human evangelists.[43] It is His wish that all who will should be saved. But only those whom God has elected will have the necessary will to be saved.[44] Grace is *an irresistible persuasion*, a delighting and attracting of the mind, the interposition of a stronger motive, with God's sweetness driving out the love of lesser goods.[45]

Predestination can sound harsh and repellent. Burnaby says that St. Augustine's attempted justification of original sin and eternal damnation is "not acceptable."[46] The Council of Orange, speaking in A.D. 529 for the Catholic Church, differs from him, declaring that all baptized persons can choose to accept Christ's aid in working out their salvation.[47] St. Augustine might reply that he is acknowledging, not creating, grim facts and grim premises. It is apparently God's will that some men should be feeble-minded and others physically crippled or in constant pain. And if acceptance of Christ, in this life, is a *sine qua non* of salvation, then it is perfectly clear that only a handful have been elected to salvation. The vast majority of men are either beyond the geographical or temporal range of Christian teaching, or seem impervious to it. But sometimes he seems harsher than his premises absolutely require. The text that God "would have all men to be saved" is said to mean not "all men" but only some from every race. He passes over the "all" in

[41] *Quaest. in Exod.* 133; *De Spirit. et Litt., passim; De Beat. Vit.* 4.35.

[42] *De Lib. Arb.* iii.18.52.

[43] *De Corrept. et Grat.* 7.9; 9.25; *Conf.* x.20.29; *De Dono Persev.* 14.35.

[44] *De Spirit. et Litt.* 58. (Sister) Mary Patricia Garvey, *Saint Augustine, Christian or Neo-Platonist?* (Milwaukee: Marquette University Press, 1939), p. 179.

[45] *Expos. in Galat.* (5.22f.) 49.

[46] John Burnaby, *Amor Dei* (London: Hodder and Stoughton, 1938), p. 192. *De Fide Spe Car.* 25.99; *De Praedest. Sanct.* 8.14.

[47] Simpson, *St. Augustine's Episcopate*, pp. 91, 95.

Romans 8.32, "He Who spared not His only Son, but freely gave Him for us all, will He not also give us all things ?" Whatever else this means, he will not have it mean that Christ has saved *all* men, including those who have never heard of Him. Most men, he says, are condemned because God is just, and it is just that they should suffer the natural effects of their sin, even if this is committed because of an inherited propensity. A few are saved, because God is merciful; but only a few, because forgiveness of sin and error must never be taken for granted.

St. Augustine is a Christian teleologist. He believes that the plot of the Divine Comedy has existed from eternity in the mind of God, who has created performers, ourselves among them, who can and must carry out that plot in every external detail. In dubious kindness, God permits us a more or less free inner life, foreseeing that we will use our freedom to criticize and misunderstand the play; and our misunderstanding involves us in unhappiness. Misunderstanding and unhappiness seem to be inevitable, unless God in His mercy intervenes. Every external circumstance, and the ultimate fate of every actor or stage property, is predetermined. Subjective rebellion, in the performers, has not the slightest power to alter the smallest detail. The drama moves inexorably forward.

3. ACT TWO

The Second Act comprises man's life on earth, not just as the secular historian might see it, but from the Fall to the Last Judgment. St. Augustine is not primarily interested in our progressive conquest of nature, in the development of social organization from the family to the universal society, or in the growth of scientific knowledge and metaphysical speculation. His concern is with man's relationship to God, and with the gradual realization of God's will. God is even now marking out His elect, and training them for heaven. What are the visible criteria of election, or are there any such ? What is the subsequent relationship of these fortunate people to God, the angels, and one another ? To their unsaved and perhaps hostile neighbors ?

At first glance, the historical process may seem a battlefield for the forces of good and evil. But the struggle, if there is one, is not so much in the field as on a stage; the Christian man is not so much testing as displaying his strength against the natural man within and without. The result is never in any doubt. All we performers are in the hands of the Divine Director, playing the parts written for us. The misfortunes of this or that actor are dramatic seasoning; they help, by contrast, to bring out the serene loveliness of the comedy as a whole. Behind the seeming chaos of the moment is a perfect order which will later be obvious to those of us fortunate enough to be favored with the confidences of the Divine Author. Behind apparent indifference, not to say cruelty, is love, revealed in the giving of these confidences, but perhaps never recognized by those unfortunate players who do not share God's enthusiasm for the plot, and in consequence are consigned by Him to hell-fire.

The two sorts of performers, the saved and the unsaved, are identified collectively as the mystic Jerusalem, or *Civitas Dei*, and the mystic Babylon, or *Civitas Terrena*. Jerusalem, the "city" of God's elect, longs for eternal peace, and its name signifies "vision of peace." It is being built up and perfected in the Church. But the Church Visible contains many who, in point of fact, may not have been called to eternal felicity, and it does not contain some few who have been called. Babylon, the "city" of those whose concern is with the apparent good and evil of this world, signifies "confusion." It stands for conquest of nature, acquisition of power for worldly and not necessarily ignoble ends, and accumulation of knowledge. If we may regard the *Civitas Terrena* as a sort of Platonic Idea, a society seeking to conquer life by self-help, then it has been partially realized in innumerable states and lesser social units. But neither Jerusalem nor Babylon is to be identified out of hand with any particular social entity existing on earth. The actual Jerusalem, in the days of the Hebrew kingdoms, was the capital of a society devoted for the most part to worldly ends, and we have seen that the Church today is not conterminous with the *Civitas Dei*. Conversely, the most worldly state imaginable is likely to contain some citizens of the *Civitas Dei*, cooperating up to a point with their non-Christian neighbors, and sometimes able to make the machinery of their secular state serve spiritual purposes.

The mystic Jerusalem and the mystic Babylon are symbols of two points of view, of a distinction of wills, loves, and objectives. The "cities" are entangled and intermingled. As St. Augustine says, one's body may be in Babylon, one's heart in Jerusalem. The conflict may exist both among individuals and within one individual. While our life on earth lasts, we may pass from one camp to the other, and only God knows in which we shall end. We can discover the city of our present choice by asking ourselves whether or not we trust God's love in *every* circumstance.[48]

Angels differ from us in being immaterial. But they are fellow citizens with us in the mystic Jerusalem and the mystic Babylon. The good angels were either predestined to election, or election was the reward of their fidelity when Satan rebelled and fell, foreshadowing Adam's later fall.[49] In any event, they know now that they will always be blessed. They identify their wills with God's, and their lives are in consequence serene and happy. They are God's messengers to men. The gods of the philosophers are probably good angels, dimly seen, and doubtless horrified at the honor done them. They wish for us the happiness which they enjoy, and communion with them will be one of the delights of Heaven.[50]

If the angels were created when God said, "Let there be light," perhaps they fell when He is said to have separated the light from the darkness. The fallen angels are magnified types of natural man. They share his mental perturbations, are exasperated by injuries, grateful for services, gifts, honors, and worship, and provoked when these are not forthcoming. They are self-centered and jealous, malicious, and frustrated by unfulfilled desires. They do as much of their evil will as God allows, compatible with His universal design. Like man, they are the victims of their own pride and error. They are "old in iniquity and incorrigible in punishment." Evil deeds attributed by pagans to "the gods" are really the work of these angels, identified by St. Augustine with the demons described by Apuleius; and magicians can sometimes compel them to enter

[48] *Ennar. in Ps.* 184.4. Burleigh, *City of God*, p. 165; A. Lauras and Henri Rondet, "Le Thème des Deux Cités dans l'Oeuvre de Saint Augustin," in Rondet, Lauras, and others, *Études Augustiniennes* (Paris: Aubier, 1953), pp. 119, 137.

[49] *De Civ. D.* xi.34; xii.1–2; *cf. De Fide Spe Car.* 15.59; *De Trin.* xiv.12.16; xv.4.6; *De Anim. et eius Orig.* iv.21.35; *Epist.* 9.3; 95.8; *De Fide et Symb.* 10.24.

[50] *De Civ. D.* x.1, 8; xi.33; xix.9.

inanimate bodies or statues.[51] Their divinity is of course fraudulent, but God lets them effect miracles and oracular responses, though never to the point where they can accomplish anything contrary to His great design.[52]

The idea that good and evil are perpetually at odds in the world of our experience is far older than Augustinianism. It is implied in Plato's doctrine of the evil world-spirit. It is traditional in Christianity. Christ himself speaks of Satan's kingdom, and St. John suggests the antithesis between Light and Darkness, and St. Paul the contrast between the Old Adam and the New Man. In the *Pseudo-Clementines* the kingdom of this world is said to be opposed to the kingdom of the other world, and the idea is obvious in the writings of Origen, Lactantius, and St. Ambrose. It is, of course, highlighted in Manichaean dualism, drawn from Persian sources, and St. Augustine's dualism has been attributed to the Manichees. But, as Marrou says, if the two-City antithesis is peculiarly Manichaean, then St. Paul is a Manichee. Probably the Manichees, perhaps the Neo-Platonists, and certainly Tychonius helped to make this traditional Christian point of view vivid for St. Augustine, and his expression of it follows Tychonius' closely.[53] His originality lies in the thorough-going way in which he relates all experience to this antithesis; world history, for him, is the growth, social expression, and interaction of the Christian and the "natural" points of view. Every visible event, the stuff of history as the secular historian sees it, is interesting and significant only insofar as it can be shown to express, punish, or reward good or evil judgments, contributing to God's divine plan for the developing of the *Civitas Dei* and the *Civitas Terrena*.

[51] *De Civ. D.* viii.23; ix.3; x.10.

[52] *De Civ. D.* ix.3; xxi.24.2; ix.8; viii.16, 24; x.12; xi.11, 33; *Ennar. in Ps.* (2nd *in Ps.* 68.3).

[53] Reginald Haynes Barrow, *Introduction to St. Augustine, The City of God* (London: Faber, 1950), p. 273; Norman Hepburn Baynes, *The Political Ideas of St. Augustine's "De Civitate Dei"* (Historical Association Pamphlet No. 104 [London: Bell, 1936]), p. 5; Henri Irénée Marrou, *S. Augustin et la Fin de la Culture Antique* (Paris: Boccard, 1938), pp. 39–40; Morgan, *Psychological Teaching of St. Augustine*, p. 36: for Tychonius; Christopher Dawson, "St. Augustine and His Age," in D'Arcy and others, *Monument to Saint Augustine*, p. 59; Lauras and Rondet, in Rondet, Lauras, and others, *Études Augustiniennes*, p. 153; *cf.* V. Stegeman, *Augustins Gottestaat* (Tübingen: Mohr, 1928), p. 32; John Joseph O'Meara, *The Young Augustine* (New York: Longmans, 1954), p. 287.

St. Augustine imposes pattern upon world history by dividing the Second Act of the Divine Comedy into six scenes. Development is neither cyclical nor spiral, but rectilinear, and the division into "scenes" is based upon certain obvious divisions in Old Testament history, and not, in the case of the earlier scenes at least, upon any very dramatic differences in tone or tempo. The six scenes (and the term is not St. Augustine's) are, first, from Adam to Noah; second, from Noah to Abraham; third, from Abraham to David; fourth, from David to the Babylonian Captivity; fifth, from the Captivity to the birth of Christ; and sixth, from the birth of Christ to the Last Judgment. St. Augustine notes a parallel to the six days of Creation.[54] He also suggests a parallel between the development of world history and the growth of an individual man. In infancy the physical predominates, as symbolized by the giants in Genesis. In the early manhood of the race, Kings and Prophets appear. Christ comes in the time of old age, a period of life not to be thought less truly vigorous because the emphasis is shifting from the outer to the inner life.[55] But it is in terms of the six scenes that he marshals his evidence from Scriptural and secular sources.

Antediluvian history, recorded only in Genesis, constitutes the First Scene. Cain (*Civitas Terrena*) shows by building a city that he is ready to invest his capital in this world. Abel (*Civitas Dei*) is described as a sojourner only. Who inhabit Cain's city? The Old Testament does not pretend to list each descendant of Adam, and early men enjoy a remarkable extension of the period of fertility.[56] In this time before the Flood, the elect with the exception of Abel are chosen from the line of Seth. The very names are significant. Abel means "grief," and Seth, "resurrection," the two foreshadowing Christ's death and resurrection. Enoch corresponds to the Latin *vir*, male, as distinguished from *homo*, which may be either male or female; this name is said to suggest the marriageless state beyond the resurrection. In Genesis 4.26 it is said of Enoch that he "hoped to call upon the name of the Lord God." In this, he is the highest

---

[54] There was a very old notion that the history of the world is divided into epochs of 1,000 years. William MacAllen Green, "Augustine on the Teaching of History," in *University of California Publications in Classical Philology*, XII, 18 (1944), 322–323.

[55] *De Ver. Rel.* 27.1; *Retract.* i.2.6; *De Gen. Contra Man.* i.23.40.

[56] *Ennar. in Ps.* 61.4; *De Civ. D.* xv.1.2; xv.8.

type of natural man, unable to help himself, but hoping to be given grace to call upon God for help.[57] The ark prefigures the hierarchical Church, future refuge from the floods of secularism.[58] It will be noted that St. Augustine's interest is in the symbolic significance of things. The period from Abel to the Flood may be considered to witness the infancy of the *Civitas Dei.*[59]

According to the Septuagint and Vulgate versions, 1,072 years elapse between the Flood and Abraham, constituting the Second Scene of the Second Act of the Divine Comedy. Ham, himself the type of the hot, impatient race of heretics, re-establishes the *Civitas Terrena,* and seventy-two nations are said to have appeared on earth during this period. St. Augustine thinks it unlikely that the postdiluvian *Civitas Terrena* was drawn exclusively from Ham's descendants. Nimrod may spring from the race of Shem or of Japheth. In any event, it is the *Civitas Terrena* which engrosses the divine attention at Babel.[60] The *Civitas Dei,* now in its childhood, must be understood to have representatives during this age. If none are mentioned, this is because their record would make no appreciable addition to our knowledge of the Divine Plan.[61]

The period from Abraham to David, the Third Scene, sees the adolescence of the *Civitas Dei.* Various deeds of the patriarchs are discussed for their allegorical significance. Moses takes rank as a major prophet, in virtue of his alleged authorship of the allegedly prophetic Pentateuch. In the time of the Judges, God permits the Israelites to win or to lose battles, according to whether His justice or His mercy prevails.[62]

This epoch sees the rise of three great secular kingdoms, "Assyria," Egypt, and "Sicyon." The first, by far the greatest, anticipates in its quasi-universal character the Roman Empire, and St. Augustine sees significance in the fact that Rome does not begin

[57] *De Civ. D.* xv.8, 17, 18, 21.

[58] *De Civ. D.* xv.26.1.

[59] *De Civ. D.* xvi.43.3.

[60] *De Civ. D.* xvi.2.1, 10.3.   [61] *De Civ. D.* xvi.2.3, 43.3.

[62] *De Civ. D.* xvi.43.3; xvi.20: Abraham's division of the land between Lot and himself perhaps established the precedent whereby the stronger divides and the weaker chooses; 16.25: Hagar was taken not to gratify lust, but to secure an heir; 16.26: Abraham's circumcision of his servants suggests a universal brotherhood not restricted to lineal descendants; 16.34: his marriage to Keturah shows that God has no objection to second marriages.

its great development until after Assyria has fallen. St. Augustine is no more aware than his contemporaries of the civilization of Sumer and Akkad, and shows no interest in the independent development of Assyria Proper, Babylonia, and Elam after the fall of that society. To the best of his knowledge, the civilization of Mesopotamia is a single social experiment. Various states in fact independent for longer or shorter periods are apparently to be regarded as temporarily autonomous provinces of an enduring Empire "Assyria" centered upon "Babylon." Nineveh, one gathers, is essentially a provincial town. The "Assyrian" state is founded by Bel, and lasts for over 1,200 years. In the reign of its second king, Ninus, Abraham is born in Ur of the Chaldees. Ninus, who greatly strengthened the kingdom, is followed by his widow Semiramis, eventually put to death by her son for seeking incestuous relations with him. In the reign of the seventh Assyrian ruler, Abraham leaves Ur to seek fulfillment of the divine promises. This state is said to have less trouble than Rome in founding an empire because the world has not yet recovered from the Flood, and military science is still primitive. As a result all Asia, except India, is incorporated into this empire, as is Egypt.[63] The history of "Assyria" is brought into chronological relationship with Old Testament history. "Assyrian" military prowess and peaceful achievement are denigrated. St. Augustine's account of what he regards as the second greatest social manifestation of the *Civitas Terrena* is of this sort, neither detailed nor deep.

St. Augustine's remarks on Egypt are largely confined to depreciation of the so-called wisdom of the Egyptians, which is said to consist chiefly of astronomy and other such trivialities. He suggests that Egyptian wisdom, such as it is, postdates Abraham, in whose thought all Judaeo-Christian wisdom is implicit. Atlas, Isis, and Hermes Trismegistus are cited as historical characters.[64]

The account of "Sicyon," following Varro, is expanded to deal with Greece in general. St. Augustine's chief, perhaps only, concern is to point out the theological absurdities of the Greeks. Colonization and commerce, tyrants, the merits and defects of Athenian democracy, and so forth, have no bearing on this theme and are therefore ignored. Here, as with "Assyria" and Egypt, he seems to prefer dealing with mythological and quasi-historical figures. Inachus

[63] *De Civ. D.* iv.6, 6; xviii.2, 22; xvi.17.
[64] *De Civ. D.* xviii.39; *Conf.* v.4.7.

built Argos in the time of Abraham's grandchildren, and this is taken to imply the prior origin of the Judaeo-Christian traditional prophetic wisdom. Phoroneus, the second king, is deified after his death by his brother, probably because of his building chapels to the gods throughout his territories and his teaching his people to measure time by months and years. Those who admire "these novelties" either think him a god or resolve that he be honored as a god as a posthumous reward for his good services to society. Phoroneus' sister brings the art of writing to Egypt, and is worshiped there as Isis. Later, Apis, king of Argos, crosses to Egypt, where on his death he is deified and worshiped as Serapis. Argus, his son, is a culture hero of the agricultural persuasion, and is honored with temple and sacrifices for his introduction of formal agriculture into Greece. He is abetted in this by a contemporary commoner, Homogyrus, first to yoke oxen to the plow, and himself deified after being struck by lightning. Mercury and Hermes, too, are culture heroes. "But whenever they were born, serious historians who have recorded these ancient accounts agree that both were men, and were given divine honors because of their contribution to the improvement of the standard of living." [65] Minerva-Athene is in the same category. This attribution of great and distinctive cultural innovations puts us at once in a world like that of the idealized emperors of Chinese prehistory, or of Thucydides' King Minos. St. Augustine notes in passing that the rites of Dionysos, celebrated by the Greeks of the archaic age, are later outlawed by the Romans, not themselves squeamish by Christian standards. Coeval with the Hebrew prophets are such worthies as Triptolemus, the Minotaur, the Centaurs, Cerberus, Jason, the Gorgons, and Oedipus. Orpheus, Musaeus, and Linus have inklings of the one true God, but this monotheistic seed is lost in the jungle of polytheism. [66] The ascendancy later passes from Argos to Mycenae, and we find ourselves among the heroes of the Trojan War, of whom at least Diomedes is deified. St. Augustine notes Varro's account of Circe's transformation of Odysseus' companions into animals, as well as the failure of various gods to save their favorites from disaster. Demons are permitted by the one true God to accomplish only what is compatible with His own design. [67]

[65] *De Civ. D.* xviii.3, 5, 6, 8.   [66] *De Civ. D.* xviii.8, 9, 13, 14.
[67] *De Civ. D.* xviii.16, 17, 18.

During the Fourth Scene, from King David to the Captivity, the Jewish State is a sort of image of the *Civitas Dei*, but by no means identical with it. The very appellation "Holy City," applied to Jerusalem, should have suggested to men's minds the truly holy City. The Jews are never so much God's pampered favorites as His object-lesson for humanity. The kingdom of Solomon fulfills the carnal promises made by God to Abraham, and St. Augustine infers that the more spiritual promises, too, will be kept.[68] The division of the kingdom is foreordained, and Rehoboam and Jeroboam are merely God's instruments. Various kings of Judah and all the kings of Israel are described in Scripture as more or less wicked. But the high incidence of wickedness among the kings does not prevent a lively representation of the *Civitas Dei* in the goodly fellowship of the prophets.[69]

"Assyria" and Greece continue to perpetrate follies during this age. Codrus is deified in Athens because of his self-sacrifice in battle. The Seven Sages are mildly commended; but praise given to pagans is always qualified by the insinuation that anything good in their thought is stolen from an earlier Judaeo-Christian source.[70] Pagan historians are mentioned, to point out that their disagreements detract from their creditability. St. Augustine follows Sallust in suspecting that Athenian writers have overrated Athenian achievement.[71]

The chief event in the Fifth Scene, from the Babylonian Captivity to the birth of Jesus is the rise of Rome. St. Augustine is not entirely immune to patriotic enthusiasm for the Roman past. "O admirable Roman race, the progeny of your Scaevolas and Scipios, of Regulus and Fabricius."[72] He quotes Cato's explanation of Roman greatness: hard work, honest government, freedom in deliberation, and moral austerity.[73] The Romans of this age have a passion for praise and honor, for the good opinion of their fellow men. It pleases God to give them honor, and through them to scourge the offenses of other nations, allowing authority as a sort of consolation prize to men who, while they may and indeed do lack the highest wisdom,

[68] *De Civ. D.* xv.2; xvi.3.2; xvii.2.
[69] *De Civ. D.* xvi.43.3; xvii.1, 21, 22, 23; xviii.1.
[70] *De Civ. D.* xviii.19, 37.
[71] *De Civ. D.* xviii.2.2; xviii.40. Sallust *Coniur. Cat.* 8.
[72] *De Civ. D.* ii.29.1.   [73] *De Civ. D.* v.12.5.

are at least ready to sink private ends for the public good: men who crave public approval rather than wealth. This relative selflessness makes the Roman Republic, with all its faults, a more admirable state than the eastern monarchies. The so-called natural virtues are real, but unstable, fragile, and incomplete, not being grounded in the love of God. But if love of good fame does not make the Romans of the early republic *sancti*, it at least keeps them *minus turpes*, and they receive the reward of their second-class virtues.[74]

But this relatively commendable earthly society has its contemptible side. The deification of Aeneas is an absurdity. The murder of Remus, the rape of the Sabine women, and the deification of Romulus are not pretty incidents. The Romans show their own instinctive lack of confidence in their gods when they appeal not to them but to the fifth-century Athenians for help in drafting a legal code. The restless *libido dominandi* of the race is shown in the parricidal war with Alba Longa. The unhappy deaths of so many Roman kings should argue against the notion that the monarchical period was a golden age.[75]

The republic itself is inaugurated with the unjust banishment of Collatinus and the murder of the "virtuous" Brutus.[76] In St. Augustine's opinion, the republic is better administered in earlier than in later times; but there is enough injustice in the earliest period to give rise to the secession(s) of the Plebs.[77] These brave and powerful people pay a high price in danger, labor, and destruction for the empire which they slowly acquire. For all her victories, the republic is in constant difficulty, down to the end of the Punic Wars. The calamities of the period are recalled with gusto. Regulus, who is beaten by the Carthaginians, is praised for his unavailing virtue, and full justice is done to Hannibal's victories. St. Augustine suggests that in the end the victors come off about as poorly as the vanquished, and one may suspect here a trace of provincial patriotism.[78]

[74] *Epist.* 22, 23: he admits that he enjoys praise, and is uneasy about the spiritual dangers of episcopacy—for the bishop.

[75] *De Civ. D.* ii.16–17; iii.13–15; xv.5; xviii.19; xxii.6.1.

[76] *De Civ. D.* iii.16.

[77] *De Civ. D.* ii.18, 21.

[78] *De Civ. D.* iii.17–20; xviii.22; *cf. Epist.* 17.2 (A.D. 390), chiding Maximus for reluctance to write in Punic.

The weakness of the *Civitas Terrena,* in what might have seemed its finest hour, appears in its poor reaction to prosperity, and in its lack of understanding of what would contribute to its peace. Sallust says that the period immediately subsequent to the Second Punic War is the most satisfactory in Roman history; but even then Scipio is unjustly exiled, and luxury begins its corrosive inroads on *priscae mores.* St. Augustine expresses no opinion on the Gracchi, but calls attention to the wars which break out after a temple has been erected to Concord on the spot where Gaius Gracchus was done to death. He reminds us of the massacres and devastations which accompany the Social, Servile, and Civil Wars of the first century B.C. No foreign fury could equal the venom shown by citizen against citizen in the most successful state in history. We have already noted his tacit condemnation of both Marius and Sulla, although he gives no explicit reasons for this.[79] His purpose is not only to show the miseries of secular society at its best, but to remind his readers that times are bad even before Christianity comes to interfere with the worship of the gods. The history of the Roman Republic shows the ineffectiveness of human wisdom, wealth, and power as means of securing happiness.

Cicero is cited for the republican ideal, and is given sympathetic treatment. According to him, a people is a multitude united in a common agreement as to law, and in community interest. But if true law must have a basis in justice, then the Romans can never have constituted a *populus*; for there can be no justice where God's due is given, as it was in Rome, to demons.[80] But St. Augustine has a certain kindness for Rome, God's secular sergeant-major, and will not deny that it is a state of some sort, even though it falls into discord and lacks the ultimate justice. He is ready to accept, as a *populus,* or state, a multitude bound together in the pursuit of a common objective. But a state is no better than its *raison d'être,* and in this case the objective is worldly and falls short of the good of the God-lover.[81] He fastens eagerly upon the admission of Cicero and other pagans that the republic decays for moral rather than for military reasons. There is an inherent rottenness in terrene states which brings them down with no need for special divine interventions. Pursuit of the three great terrene ends, knowledge, material

[79] *De Civ. D.* ii.23.1; iii.21, 26.   [80] *De Civ. D.* ii.21.2; xix.24.
[81] *De Civ. D.* xix.24.

goods, and power, must bring each terrene society in turn to disappointment and dissolution.

Pagan sages admit that wise men may become involved in wars, and in wartime neither pagan religion nor pagan philosophy can prevent the perpetration of atrocities. St. Augustine was spared full knowledge of the kind of warfare possible between so-called Christian powers. Sallust witnesses for him to the rape, abduction, massacre, and arson which normally accompany pagan warfare. He makes frequent reference to the distresses which afflicted victors and vanquished alike during the period of the Punic Wars. The horrors of the Roman civil wars of the first century B.C. are said to exceed the horrors of the great Gallic and even of the recent Gothic invasions.[82] Good men cannot rejoice in victory, for it is wickedness on someone's part which leads to fighting; and good men, however pleased by the spectacle of God bringing good out of the evil designs of men, must be saddened by their enemies' self-torturing wickedness.[83]

The Sixth Scene begins with the Incarnation, the central event in world history. It is foreshadowed in all that precedes it, and it dominates all that follows. For it is through the Incarnate Christ that God rescues His elect in every age from the eternal alienation from Himself which is the natural implication of their sin. Jesus comes when, with Herod's accession, the Jews for the first time have no prince of their own race.[84]

A skeptic prepared to see value in a carefully cultivated optimistic outlook may find that the doctrine of the Incarnation, instead of dramatizing God's love in a convincing manner, puts an additional and seemingly unnecessary strain upon his already hard-pressed credulity. But the historical *Christian* faith accepts Jesus Christ as the one avenue to salvation.[85] It is not enough to have faith in the friendliness of the universe; one must also believe in the divinity, resurrection, ascension, and redeeming grace of a felon condemned and executed in the reign of Tiberius. The theology is preached on the same authority as the comforting point of view. To abandon the theology while trying to retain the approach to experience which

[82] *De Civ. D.* i.2; iii.18.1; iii.26; xv.7; xix.7, 8.
[83] *De Civ. D.* iii.10; iv.15.
[84] *De Civ. D.* xviii.45.3.
[85] *De Civ. D.* xviii.46: no sympathy with Docetism; *De Ver. Rel.* 8.14.

arose from it would be to reduce the faith either to a vague senti-
mentality or to a cool philosophical proposition, with the divine
sanction removed which confirms the faith of most believers.[86]

"No man cometh to the Father but by me."[87] But how does
Christ save men? He is held to be both man and God. As God, the
Son is one with the Father. If we could imagine the sun without
its brightness, or "the beauty of holiness" as something distinct
from holiness, we could conceive of the Son apart from the Father.
Father and Son are eternally one, as the brightness of fire is coeval
with the fire whose brightness it is. The Father, like the fire, may
be described as prior *qua* cause, but in no sense as prior in time.
The Holy Ghost is similarly of one substance with the Father, and
no operation of any Person of the Trinity can be understood as
undertaken apart from the operation of the other Persons.[88] Jesus'
humanity is derived from His mother. But since His conception by
her was passionless, He is spared the sinful propensity of Adam
which is transmitted in ordinary generation.[89] God and man are
united in one Person. He *must* be man, and yet more than man, to
play his role. As man, He has a human soul and a human body. As
God, the human soul and body are to the godhead in Him as the
human body, in man, is to the human soul. As the soul and body in
an ordinary man form not two persons but one, so in His case the
godhead together with the humanity form not two persons but
One.[90] But *why* must a Christian accept, on faith, this very difficult
proposition?

It is assumed that when Adam falls he becomes Satan's slave in a
fairly literal sense, and death is the most spectacular badge of his
subjection. If the elect are to be removed from Satan's possession,
he is entitled in equity to some compensation for his loss. Accord-
ingly, he is permitted to assert a mastery over Jesus, even to the
point of killing Him as if He were an ordinary man and not the
incarnate Son of God. But Jesus is untouched by original sin, and
His life is not properly forfeit. Satan suffers no injury, then, if in
compensation for his illicit triumph he is made to disgorge some of

[86] John Neville Figgis, *The Political Aspects of S. Augustine's "City of God"*
(London: Longmans Green, 1921), pp. 34–35; Burleigh, *City of God*, p. 153.
[87] *Cf. De Civ. D.* x.32.2.
[88] *De Symb. ad Catech.* 8; *In Johan. Evang.* 19.15; 20.3, 13; 40.4.
[89] *De Trin.* xiii.18.23. *Cf.* pp. 151–153.   [90] *In Johan. Evang.* 19.15.

his human victims. When Jesus "elects" a soul for redemption, that soul is said to be reconciled to God. This soul must still give its old master the satisfaction of seeing it torn painfully, if temporarily, from the body. But when once it has submitted to this *first death* it is quit of responsibility to him; when rejoined to its body it will be spared the *second death*, to eternal damnation, and will rise with Christ to a new life of freedom.[91] In His death, Jesus not only ransoms His elect from Satan but gives all men a striking illustration of divine love. He could free us from Satan's power without subjecting Himself to death, but He chooses to show us that He loves us enough to die for us.

Jesus must be both man and God to effect the salvation of His elect in this way. Only *man* could die, and so put the devil under obligation. Only *God* could rise from the dead, raising His humanity by means of His undying godhead, and thus conferring upon some men, at least, a new capacity for a new birth free this time from the evil propensities of Adam's race.[92] This new faculty or capacity is not conferred upon all men, St. Augustine believes, but only upon those whom He elects to be members of his risen Body. Membership in the Body of Christ is not conceived metaphorically. Christ is said to suffer in the afflictions of His earthly members, and the relationship is strengthened by man's participation in the Eucharist. It is only as members in this as yet only partially risen Body that the elect gain the faculty to rise in glory. The Fatherhood of God is seen primarily in His relationship with the Son; *our* sonship is by grace through adoption into the mystical Body of Christ. The elect can be recognized by their love for Jesus, by their belief in His resurrection, and by their behavior in accordance with His teachings. They hope in faith for a physical resurrection on the grounds that, as He is the Head, so they are the members of His mystical Body, and must rise with their Head.[93]

In this age, from the Incarnation to the Last Judgment, the unity of all Christians comes from their common participation in the Eucharist which the Church offers up.[94] The Church is Christ's earthly agent of grace, and the chief habitat of the earthly *Civitas*

[91] *De Trin.* xiii.10.13, 14.18; *De Cat. Rud.* 4.8; *In Johan. Evang.* 22.13.
[92] *De Trin.* iv.2.4.
[93] *De Trin.* iv.7.11; v.16.17; *Serm.* 137.1-2; *De Civ. D.* ix.15, 17; xiii.23.3.
[94] *De Civ. D.* xxi.25.

Dei.[95] The validity of her sacraments does not depend upon the personal integrity of the celebrant, but upon his being validly commissioned by the Church. The recipient should look beyond the human agent to the divine Source.[96] The Church has the keys of heaven, and God will ratify her absolution of those "that do truly and earnestly repent."[97] The Church's work is a necessary link in a process begun, guided, and completed by God, and her sacraments have their place in a predestined process. God must call the sinner and prepare him inwardly if the Church's action is to have significance.[98]

But St. Augustine refuses *to identify* the corporation of the elect with the visible Church. It is true that he sometimes says that the Church *is* the City of God, and that the two names are interchangeable.[99] But more often the *Civitas Dei* is presented as both larger and smaller than the Church of our observation, which is at most the *Civitas Dei* in a state of pilgrimage, accompanied by many unauthorized camp-followers and fellow-travelers, and with some bona fide stragglers detached by circumstances from the main body. The Church Visible is like a net let down into the ocean of life; it has caught good fish and bad, and the catch will eventually be sorted.[100] Many persons join the Church for temporal advantage, and earnest seekers may be put off by the pseudo-Christians who infest her congregations.[101] The stragglers are of two sorts. First, before the Incarnation some men are elected to salvation, and have a prophetic faith in the coming of Christ. They should be regarded as members of Christ's body born before the Head. Among Israelites, Moses, Joshua, Samuel, David, and the Prophets, and among Gentiles Noah, Job, Abraham (*sic*), and perhaps even the Sibyl who

[95] *De Fide Spe Car.* 15.56; *Ennar. in Ps.* 98.4; *De Civ. D.* xx.9.

[96] Simpson, *St. Augustine's Episcopate*, p. 38; Figgis, *Political Aspects of S. Augustine's "City of God,"* p. 71; Geoffrey Grimshaw Willis, *St. Augustine and the Donatist Controversy* (London: Society for Promoting Christian Knowledge, 1950), p. 117.

[97] *De Fide Spe Car.* 17.65; *cf. Ennar. in Ps.* 5.17; *De Doctr. Christ.* i.18.17.

[98] *De Doctr. Christ.* iv.16.33; *In Johan. Evang.* 4.1; *De Civ. D.* xv.6.

[99] *De Civ. D.* xv.26; xx.9.

[100] *Epist.* 208.2–3; *De Gest. Pelag.* 64. Burleigh, *City of God*, pp. 178ff.; Baynes, *Political Ideas of St. Augustine's "De Civitate Dei,"* p. 14; Étienne Henri Gilson, *L'Introduction à l'Étude de Saint Augustin* (Paris: Vrin, 1929), pp. 233–234.

[101] *De Cat. Rud.* 7.11; *In Johan. Evang.* 25.10.

foretold Christ's coming belonged to an *invisible* Church of which Abel was once the only human member. Second, even in this age martyrs and unbaptized men who confess Christ in the hour of their death are saved, presumably, if their faith is orthodox and their failure to take the sacrament involuntary; but in the end St. Augustine wonders if he has not conceded too much, and notes that there is no documentary proof that the Dying Thief, the great type of all who scrape through without proper qualifications, had *not* been baptized upon some prior occasion! [102] The visible hierarchical Church is the normal instrument of God's grace and, largely but not completely corresponding with it, is an invisible Church consisting of his elect, angelic and human, chosen by him in every age. This invisible *communio praedestinatorum*, which contains pre-Christians, perhaps even some ostensible pagans, but which does not contain all members of the Church Visible, is the true *Civitas Dei*. [103]

The first visible step toward salvation is submission to baptism, which washes away all sins and brings a "new birth" marking, for the elect, the end of their alienation from God. Baptism, if it is possible to receive it, is the first prerequisite of salvation. Infants who die unbaptized cannot go to Heaven. Catechumens, however seemingly pious, carry their full load of sin until they have been baptized. [104] For infants who have not come to the age of reason, baptism in itself insures a felicitous resurrection. [105] Jesus Himself was baptized, to warn us against a pride which might otherwise refuse this homely rite. [106] The sacrament can be received outside the Church. Schismatic baptisms are valid. [107] But the authority of the Church is safeguarded. If one is baptized by a schismatic, the effect of the baptism is dammed back by the obstacle of the recipient's presumed adherence to schism. Should he later come into communion with the orthodox Church, the sacrament immediately

[102] *De Civ. D.* viii.24; xx.9; xiii.7; *De Perf. Just. Hom.* 19.42; *Ennar. in Ps.* 128.2; *De Bapt.* iv.21.29; *Retract.* i.18, 26, 55; ii.18.55.

[103] Figgis, *Political Aspects of St. Augustine's "City of God,"* p. 68; Burleigh, *City of God*, p. 181.

[104] *De Symb. ad Catech.* 15, 16; *De Anim. et eius Orig.* i.19.34; *In Johan. Evang.* 13.7.

[105] *De Civ. D.* xxi.16.   [106] *In Johan. Evang.* 4.13.

[107] *In Johan. Evang.* 6.16; *De Bapt.* i.1.2; *De Symb. ad Catech.* 16; *Contra Litt. Petil. Don.* ii.2.5.

becomes effective and need not be repeated. Baptism washes one free from all sin, but one does not stay clean. Subsequent sins can be healed by alms-giving in the right spirit, by penance and prayer. But these remedies are of no use unless one has been baptized.[108]

Does St. Augustine acknowledge the disciplinary and doctrinal supremacy of the Roman See? Let us consider the disciplinary question first. Peter is called the first of Apostles, and Rome *the Catholic See*.[109] Commenting on Matthew 16.18ff., "Thou art Peter," he notes that *Petrus* comes from *petra*, and not vice versa; Christ is the rock, and Peter is the Church founded upon the rock.[110] In a work, now lost, against the Donatists, he would seem to have identified Peter with the rock itself; but at the last, in the *Retractationes*, he merely mentions this view and goes on to discuss at length the representational theory before he leaves the question to the judgment of the reader. The representational theory would have it that the keys are not received by a single man but by the "unity of the Church," and that Peter is no more than the representative of the Church, and not merely of the Apostles but of the entire Christian people.[111] During St. Augustine's episcopate, the African bishops consulted the Pope on occasion, and received directives from him, but how seriously his rulings were taken, and whether he was acting in a papal or patriarchal capacity, it is impossible to say.[112] St. Augustine may not specifically deny the disciplinary supremacy of Rome, but it is perhaps fair to say that his expressed views do not seem to imply a belief in Roman disciplinary supremacy.

As for doctine, *Letter* 177 is addressed to Pope Innocent on behalf of the Council of African bishops, asking for his condemnation of Pelagianism: "We want only your written approval of our decision, which is founded, though less definitively, upon the same authority as yours . . ." Innocent confirms their judgment and approves their

[108] *De Fide Spe Car.* 19.71; 20.75; *De Symb. ad Catech.* 15.
[109] *In Johan. Evang.* 56.1; 66.2; *Contra Duas Epist. Pelag.* ii.3.5.
[110] *Serm.* 76.1.
[111] *Retract.* i.21; *Serm.* 295.2; *De Agone Christ.* 32; *Epist.* 53.1–2.
[112] Giovanni Domenico Mansi, *Sacrorum Conciliorum Nova et Amplissima Collectio*, IV, 401–440. *Epist.* 219 seems to concede a real authority to Pope Celestine; but Fussala lies within the Western Patriarchate, and it is impossible to say whether this authority is papal or patriarchal.

consulting him, which he says accords with an ancient rule recognizing Peter's successor as occupying a special position among bishops.[113] His successor, Pope Zosimus, without approving what passes for Pelagianism, voices confidence in the personal orthodoxy of Pelagius. The African bishops find this position dangerously vague, reaffirm their adherence to the more clear-cut ruling of Innocent, and appeal for a ruling to the secular authorities. Zosimus, while insisting on the prerogatives of his see, sees fit to declare that he, too, stands by the ruling of Pope Innocent. These incidents suggest that the African bishops want the approval of the Pope, or Patriarch (?), but it is noteworthy that in each case they want his backing for a position which they have already adopted.

It might seem from St. Augustine's reference to Rome as the Catholic See that he regards her faith as peculiarly pure, perhaps even as a touchstone of orthodoxy. But he does not specifically assert that the bishop of Rome is *ex officio* and *proprio motu* the infallible interpreter of orthodoxy. What he does say may imply the contrary. Thus it is an article of faith that the Canonical Scriptures are the revealed Word of God. St. Augustine says that we must accept as canonical the books so described by the Catholic *Churches*, or by a majority of these. If a minority which includes the apostolic foundations differ from the majority, then "equal weight" is to be attached to the minority view. The apostolic foundations are conceded to be more authoritative than the others, but not to the point where their collective authority clearly overrides the opinion of a larger number of less illustrious sees. The strength of Rome appears to lie in her membership in the apostolic group. Her faith is pure, but so presumably is that of Antioch and Alexandria; and the agreement of all is the guarantee of each. Furthermore, one must prefer the established ruling of the universal Church to the authority of any single bishop or provincial council.[114] There is one Church, *and one episcopate*, and one is in communion with this Church and episcopate when one is in communion with St. Peter's Chair—and, he adds, with the Seven Churches of the Book of the Revelation.[115] The term "catholic" as applied to the Roman See need imply nothing more than primacy of honor and contemporary purity in faith.

[113] *Epist.* 181, 182, 183.
[114] *De Doctr. Christ.* ii.8.12.
[115] *Epist.* 53.1–2; *Ps. Contra Part. Don.* 229; *Contra Cres.* ii.37.46; iv.25.32.

If St. Augustine makes no clear-cut pronouncement either for or against Roman supremacy in any of his many works, this suggests that he is not aware of it as a lively issue.[116]

In the period after the Incarnation, the Roman state first opposes and later supports the Christian Church. At no stage is it to be identified absolutely with either *Civitas Terrena* or *Civitas Dei*. Even in its pagan phase it is an instrument for accomplishing God's will, whatever the intention and character of its rulers. In its Christian phase, it continues to pursue secondary goals, although its individual citizens, as members of the Body of Christ, may in addition be pursuing primary goals. In his general indifference toward the working of political machinery, St. Augustine indicates a preference for Augustus and Vespasian over Nero and Domitian, but he knows that God uses each set to fulfil His purposes.[117] He approves Caracalla's extension of the Roman citizenship to all free subjects, and as a bishop perhaps rather than as an economist, he approves the principle of the public welfare program in metropolitan Italy, wishing only that it could have been extended to the entire empire.[118]

We have noted his praise of Constantine and Theodosius, and his belief that Christian rulers can, and should, use their political power to further the cause of their religion. But his references to the so-called Christian Empire are surprisingly meager. Certainly he never confuses it with the *Civitas Dei*. Perhaps he would have given it more consideration if he had realized that the state would be nominally Christian from that time forward. He does not appreciate the full significance of the new relationship between Church and State, and does not explore the possibility of a *res publica christiana* as that term would be conceived in a later age. Apart from the perhaps temporary phenomenon of Christian emperors, he sees nothing very cheering in the contemporary scene, and thinks

[116] Giovanni Papini, *St. Augustine* (Paris: Plon, 1930), pp. 200–201: "Augustine always recognized and defended the doctrinal and disciplinary supremacy of the Roman bishop." Siricius, who issued decrees claiming for himself the right to decide what the whole Church should accept or reject, is said to be a pope after St. Augustine's own heart.

[117] *De Civ. D.* iv.27; v.21; xviii.43.3. St. Augustine is not taken in by Augustus's claim to have restored the Roman Republic.

[118] *De Civ. D.* v.17.

spiritual development on an individual basis the only sort of progress for which one can legitimately hope.[119]

St. Augustine need not enter a defense against the relatively modern view that Christianity helped to destroy the empire by turning men's thoughts toward another world, and was "logically false, morally diseased and politically corrupt."[120] The charge with which he is concerned is simply that Christianity, by interfering with the worship of the ancestral gods, who have brought prosperity and victory in past ages, is responsible for the troubles which accompany the barbarian invasions. *Pluvia defit, causa Christiani.*[121] Against this view, propagated by men who in his opinion know better, he cites the evidence of Sallust and Cicero, that Roman society was degenerate before the birth of Christ, let alone the triumph of the Church. He calls attention to the horrors of pre-Christian warfare, and cites Apuleius for pre-Christian earthquakes, floods, tidal waves, storms, volcanic eruptions, and the like.[122] He suggests further that *every* terrestrial state is bound to fall, because of its own weaknesses.[123] He perhaps overlooks the possibility that with more experience of multiracial and multicultural societies men will become more competent than the Romans in working them. For him, progress is conceived in terms of the growth of the invisible and interior *Civitas Dei.* The material ends sought by the state are secondary goods, and Christians are ready to use the machinery of the state to secure these. There is nothing wrong with the state as such. But the Christian, with his hopes of Heaven, has other objectives closer to his heart. He is not *against* the state, and may even be attached to it as one is to an old chair, but it is never very important to him.[124] It is much more important to the *Civitas Terrena*, because the goods which it pursues are the primary objective of the *cives terreni.*

[119] Dawson, in D'Arcy and others, *Monument to Saint Augustine*, p. 10; Burleigh, *City of God*, pp. 170, 203.

[120] Ernest Renan, *Marc-Aurele* (5th ed.; Paris: Colmann Lévy, 1885), p. 589.

[121] *De Civ. D.* i.30; ii.3; *cf. Ennar. in Ps.* 80.1.

[122] *De Civ. D.* ii.18; iii.31; iv.1, 2.

[123] He suggests that great size is a liability; see *De Civ. D.* ii.2, 21; xviii.45.3. Figgis, *Political Aspects of S. Augustine's "City of God,"* p. 24; Marrou, *Ambivalence du Temps de l'Histoire chez Saint Augustin*, p. 34.

[124] *De Civ. D.* xxii.24. Dawson, in D'Arcy and others, *Monument to Saint Augustine*, p. 46; Papini, *St. Augustine*, pp. 268–269.

How will *Civitas Dei* and *Civitas Terrena* fare during what remains of this last scene on earth ? The pagan rumor that the Church would last for only 364 years has been disproved.[125] Most Christians hope, he says, for an earthly and visible Kingdom of Christ, as the culmination of human history. St. Augustine himself attaches a mystical and present sense to the Millennium.[126] Since Christ's coming, Satan has been bound. This present age sees the reign of the saints foretold in the Revelation of St. John. This is the time of the harvesting of the elect.[127] Almost certainly St. Augustine thinks that this sixth scene will last for a thousand years. He has no hope of an earthly state much better, from a Christian point of view, than the one he sees before him,[128] much less of a progressive realization of the Kingdom of God on earth. The Second Act of the Divine Comedy will see no end of the tension between those whose efforts to get "natural" happiness in this world are doomed to frustration, and the few elect who refuse to see evil in God's creation, and look for confirmation of this intellectual *tour de force* only in the perfect serenity of a life beyond the grave. Toward the end, Elijah will come (the Jews believe), the Devil will be unleashed for a while, the *Civitas Terrena* will enjoy a last, feverish, short-lived triumph, and the *Civitas Dei* endure a furious but short-lived persecution.[129] The Second Act of the Divine Comedy will close with the coming of Christ in judgment.[130]

4. ACT THREE

Act Three brings the *dénouement*. The fugue is resolved, objective evil explained away, serenity restored.[131] Justice is done in the Second Act; now it is seen to have been done. St. Augustine believes

[125] *De Civ. D.* xviii.54.

[126] *De Civ. D.* xx.7, 30.

[127] *De Civ. D.* ii.9. Marrou, *Ambivalence du Temps de l'Histoire chez Saint Augustin*, p. 21.

[128] Nicolai Aleksandrovich Berdyaev, *The Meaning of History* (trans. George Reavey; London: Bles, 1936), pp. 198, 58.

[129] *De Civ. D.* xx.8.3; Rev. 20.1. See *De Civ. D.* xx.7.1; xx.30.

[130] *Contra Faust. Man.* xii.8; *In Johan. Evang.* 9.6.

[131] Burnaby, *Amor Dei*, p. 10; Figgis, *Political Aspects of S. Augustine's "City of God,"* pp. 9, 42, 70, 76; Green, "Augustine and the Teaching of History," p. 235.

in faith in a future life, commencing with the resurrection of the body and its reunion with the soul. In this future life, the elect will see that all is for the best when earthly life seems pointless and cruel; they may believe this now, but then they will know it. They will also enjoy in perfection the happiness promised them, which follows upon reconciliation with God, but of which they catch only fleeting glimpses here for all their godliness.[132] In this future life the worldly, who seem to go unpunished, and whose serenity for all its shallowness may sometimes puzzle Christians and put them to shame, will be consigned to eternal damnation.[133] Each party will have, in the highest degree, the relationship with God which they seem to seek on earth. The elect will find their wills identical with His in a perfect world. The reprobate will be completely "independent," cut off from Him in a world which will seem to them totally evil.

Christians expect a bodily resurrection, and various arguments are offered in support of this proposition, which can be accepted only on faith. First, man is the only *reasonable* earthly creature; this suggests a unique status which may involve immortality. Second, the soul thinks the eternal thoughts of God; truth could not survive if its habitat died, and since truth is immortal so must the soul be. One might think that the blessed angels and God himself provided habitat enough, and that if divine truth existed before the creation of individual souls it could survive their extinction.[134] Third, the soul craves happiness; happiness to be complete must be, and be recognized to be, eternal, and God will not let this craving which he has implanted be frustrated.[135] Gilson notes that St. Augustine, like Descartes, was sure of the immortality of the soul.[136] But St. Augustine himself says elsewhere that belief in immortality rests ultimately upon faith, and that even wise men offer no proof.[137]

If we can believe, in faith, that Jesus rose from the dead, it should be easier to believe, in faith, that we too will live again. The arguments, as we might expect, prove nothing, but show that the

[132] *De Civ. D.* I *praef.*; xi.4; xiii.20; xxi.5: pagans, too, accept "unreasonable" propositions. *Epist.* 143.7.
[133] Burnaby, *Amor Dei*, p. 183.
[134] *De Immort. Anim.* 11.18.
[135] *De Trin.* xiii.8.13; *De Civ. D.* x.1.
[136] *De Civ. D.* xi.27; *De Trin.* xiii.8.11.
[137] *De Trin.* xiii.9.12. *Cf. Conf.* vi.4.6–8, 11.18: is certain, but cannot prove.

belief is at least plausible. First, one cannot fail to be impressed by the Apostles' conviction that Jesus rose from the dead. Second, Resurrection and Ascension are "incredible"; it is "incredible" that so many persons, educated and uneducated, should accept these "incredibles"; it is "incredible" that the world should have been persuaded by a few men of low birth and no education. If the second and third "incredibles" are true, and they obviously are, then why not the first?[138] Third, the miracles attributed to Jesus suggest that he is the sort of being who might well be expected to rise from the dead and ascend into Heaven; and the miracles since performed in his name add plausibility to the claim that he is divine and can raise the dead.[139] Fourth, in St. Augustine's opinion, Hebrew rites, altars, and priesthood all foretell, and so tend to confirm faith in, the resurrection of Jesus.[140] Fifth, he tells of a physician convinced by two dreams that the dead survive. In the first, a young man took him along the wall of a city, and from the other side he could hear singing which his guide attributed to the elect. In the second dream, the young man returned and asked him questions about what he had seen and heard in the first.[141]

Certain technical problems are disposed of summarily. Since Plato concedes that the gods have immortal bodies, no pagan can insist that immortal bodies are a patent absurdity.[142] The material of the body is not destroyed in death, but will return to the soul to which it was first joined. This will be no harder to accomplish than the original act of creation.[143] This body restored to the soul will have the stature and physical condition which it would have had ideally at the age of thirty.[144] Can earthly bodies rise to Heaven? If birds can fly, and men build metal vessels which float on water, God can be trusted to solve this problem in levitation.

Where is the soul between death and Judgment? Separated from the body, it awaits the Last Day in such tranquillity or pain as its behavior on earth has warranted.[145] The future damned suffer with

[138] *De Civ. D.* xxii.5.
[139] *De Civ. D.* xxii.8, 9.
[140] *De Civ. D.* vii.32.
[141] *Epist.* 159.3–4.
[142] *De Civ. D.* xiii.17; xxii.26.
[143] *De Fide Spe Car.* 23.88; *De Cat. Rud.* 25.46.
[144] *De Civ. D.* xxii.14; *De Ver. Rel.* 12.25; *De Mus.* vi.5.3; *Retract.* i.11.
[145] *De Fide Spe Car.* 29.109.

Dives in a preliminary hell, from which they can observe the better fortune of the elect in Abraham's bosom.[146] But even these must expiate their earthly sins, in purgatorial fires, for longer or shorter terms. Souls in Purgatory can profit by masses or alms offered on their behalf by the loving, but only to the extent that their behavior on earth has won them the right to receive such help. But no man is left to burn for lack of friends or money. The Church, the common Mother, extends her charity to all the baptized dead.[147] St. Augustine does not actually affirm that her efforts do for the poor and friendless all that in other instances God permits loving friends to accomplish. The dead have some knowledge of the living, drawn either from fresh arrivals or from divine revelation. The fact that Monica does not return to him suggests to him that normally the dead have no direct communication with the living. But he believes that martyrs are sometimes permitted to visit and help friends still on earth.[148]

What is the nature of eternal punishment? Some kindly souls would like to think that the torment of the dead is *only* psychological, like that of a man with no liking for music who finds himself locked up in a music hall. But St. Augustine is a literalist. The soul may be in anguish because of its absence from God, but the body is burning in real fire. How can bodies burn in hell and not be destroyed? St. Augustine gives instances of things like asbestos which are not destroyed by fire, and thinks that God could easily give our bodies the quality of incombustibility.[149] We need not concern ourselves with how immaterial devils will be punished in material fire. God will find a way. Pain *may* be proportionate to guilt—an unusual concession, this, to human notions of equity.[150]

Who will go to Hell? Nearly everyone—and their torment will be no more and no less permanent than the felicity of the elect. Scripture uses the same terms to describe the duration of each.[151] We must not ask if sins committed in this short life *deserve* eternal punishment. God's will is *ex hypothesi* just.[152] Some sentimentalists think

[146] *Ennar. in Ps.* 6.6.
[147] *De Fide Spe Car.* 18.69; 29.110; *De Civ. D.* xxi.13.
[148] *De Cura pro Mort.* 18–19.
[149] *De Civ. D.* xiii.22; xxi.4; xxii.12; *Epist.* 95.7.
[150] *In Johan. Evang.* 89.4. But *cf. De Civ. D.* xxi.9, 16.
[151] *De Civ. D.* xiii.23.3.
[152] *De Civ. D.* xxi.11, 12.

that God who spared Nineveh, to the annoyance of Jonah, will yield to the prayers of His saints and save everyone.

> Behind a frowning Providence
> He hides a smiling face.

But the Church does not admit this hope. She prays neither for devils nor for the dead who have died impenitent. God will make good his threats as well as his promises. One must be grafted onto the Body of Christ in this earthly life or not at all. Sentimentalists of less sweeping benevolence hope for the salvation of certain borderline cases. What of heretics who "in good faith" have taken heretical sacraments? Unluckily for them, St. Paul has listed heresy among the sins incompatible with membership in the *Civitas Dei*. St. Augustine makes no concession to "invincible ignorance."[153] What of Catholics who have taken the sacraments, but later die in heresy? A renegade Catholic is guiltier than a born heretic. Will every orthodox Catholic, who believes what the Church believes, be saved regardless of his sins? Not if he dies in any of the sins, such as fornication, described by St. Paul as mortal. But it is true that, *if they sincerely repent*, the Church can forgive the sins of its members at any time, and this absolution will free them from Hell, though not from Purgatory.[154]

St. Augustine claims no detailed knowledge of Heaven. No one can hope to describe a state so completely, or almost completely, without precedent in human experience. But it can be assumed that the familiar anxieties of earthly life will disappear.[155] Also, the felicity of Heaven, sometimes glimpsed in the mystical experience, will be permanent, for happiness, to be complete, must be recognized to be permanent. The elect will enjoy perfect peace and fellowship with God, and know that their happiness will never end.[156] This happiness will consist, in the first place, of complete understanding of the Universal Scheme fulfilled first on earth and then in Heaven. The elect will not only see *how* every experience has its place in God's Providence, but *why* every circumstance is in the fullest sense for the best. Christian faith will be replaced by knowledge. On

---

[153] *De Civ. D.* xxi.18, 19, 24, 25. But *cf*. Gal. 5.19–21; *In Johan. Evang.* 45.5.
[154] *De Civ. D.* xxi.20, 21, 22, 25, 27.
[155] *De Fide Spe Car.* 15.58; 29.111; *De Civ. D.* xxii.29, 30.
[156] *In Johan. Evang.* 124.5; *Conf.* i.1.1; *De Civ. D.* x.30; xix.10.

earth men struggle to believe in God's wisdom and love; disbelief will be impossible in Heaven. The elect will find peace, contemplating the tranquillity of order, where everything is in its proper place, including the soul itself, which is now in a position to realize its highest potentialities. Soul and body will have everything needed for their happiness; there will be no sense of lack. The body will be completely at the service of the soul, willing only what the soul wills, and the soul will want nothing contrary to the will of God, and therefore nothing which it cannot have or do.[157] A tranquil memory of past troubles, now understood as blessings in disguise, will remain to season bliss.[158]

The second element in heavenly happiness will be a continuous and permanent enjoyment of the experience granted to a few now in the mystic trance. The elect will "see" what they now believe in faith, perhaps by recognizing at a glance God's controlling presence everywhere, as we now sense from the movements of a body the presence of a living soul. But the souls of the elect will not be converted to pantheism. "The universe was created by God, and is not His body," but is, rather, a medium for the expression of His will and purpose. He rules it as the soul might wish to rule its body. The souls of the elect will be fully conscious of His ruling presence in themselves and in every part of creation. Either their eyes will acquire a new faculty for *seeing* abstractions, which St. Augustine thinks unlikely, or they will see God *in the spirit*, in much the same way that the illuminated understanding now "sees" the laws of mathematics. God will be as obvious to the elect as the truth of the proposition *two plus two equal four* is now to mathematicians.[159] God will rest in his elect as now he works in them, and their sole employment will be to glorify, love, and praise him with no sense of satiety.[160] St. Augustine concedes that this last will require a change in human nature.

[157] *De Civ. D.* xiii.23.3; xxii.21, 30.
[158] *De Quant. Anim.* 76; *De Fide Spe Car.* 28.105; *De Civ. D.* xix.13; xxii.24.5; xxii.30.2; *De Doctr. Christ.* i.19.18.
[159] *De Trin.* i.8.17, 10.20, 13.31; xii.14.22; *De Civ. D.* x.32.3; xxii.29.
[160] *Conf.* xiii.37.52; *De Civ. D.* xxii.30.1.

CHAPTER SIX

A Philosophy of History

Philosophy explores the nature of reality and truth, and draws certain conclusions, however tentatively. The philosophy *of history* shows how such conclusions are applied in the particular field of historical studies. It is concerned with the way in which the historian determines what he will accept in historical evidence. But it is not directly concerned with the application of general principles to specific historical instances. The philosophy of history should not be confused with the interpretation of specific episodes or even of the historical process as a whole. But if philosophy and interpretation are distinct in essence, in practice they are as indissolubly joined as Aristotelian Form and Matter. Every practicing historian works in accordance with certain usually implicit epistemological principles, and has a philosophy of history, whether or not he recognizes it. And acknowledged philosophers of history are irresistibly tempted to display in works of historical interpretation the principles which they explicitly accept. Each is to some extent the victim of his specialization, and if the practicing historian is likely to be weak in theory, the philosopher of history is likely to be weak in fact.

A man's philosophy of history will be determined by his answers, explicit or implicit, to two very general questions philosophical rather than peculiarly historical. First, does he believe in an objective reality, or does he feel himself imprisoned in subjectivity? Second, if he believes in an objective reality, what does he think are his avenues of communication with it? What weight does he attach to the evidence of sensation, reason, direct awareness, divine revelation? What distinction does he make between knowledge and opinion? His answers to these questions will condition his thinking in every particular field, the historical included.

St. Augustine accepts the existence of a world more comprehensive than the self of which he thinks that he is directly aware. Granted an objective reality, how much of it is to be taken as "historical"? Some practicing historians would restrict the classification to conscious and purposeful actions and the thoughts which find expression in them. Others would extend it to include the record of one, some, or all "historical civilizations," of the human race, of all living things, of all things organic and inorganic. Most limit the field, in practice, to the record of states and societies and of men who play a prominent part in these. St. Augustine treats all reality as historical, and with justification. It will soon appear that all conscious experience (and we can hardly be aware of any other kind) has a historical dimension, involving as it does a sense of continuity, of succession, and of relative pastness. One is continually formulating, confirming, or applying generalizations based upon what must inevitably be "the past," however immediate. Only by relating the impression of the moment to a context drawn from time past or future are we saved from the imbecility of a perpetual present. If all experience is in some sense historical, then the various delimitations of the field, in so-called historical studies, must be regarded as arbitrary and conventional.

What information has St. Augustine regarding the all-inclusive world of history? Some few things he thinks that he *knows*. But for the most part he *believes*, with something less than complete assurance. Where he does not know, faith is the basis of his belief.

Knowledge, for St. Augustine, consists of propositions concerning which he can entertain no shadow of a doubt. He knows that he exists, that he has free will, that he has a material body and an immaterial soul, that he has contact through sensation with an external reality. He knows these things *because he is directly aware of them*. These propositions may not seem as self-evident to us as they did to St. Augustine. But this supposed knowledge gave him assurance that there was an external reality worth studying, and that he was not totally without means of exploring it. He also knows that God exists. *This much at least was revealed to him*, whether in the mystical experiences which he describes, or even earlier in a sense of certainty, thought to be God-given, that what he had heard and read in mundane quarters about the existence of God was undoubtedly true. We have no assurance that he *knew* anything further, and he assumes that most people, himself perhaps included, must accept other propositions, sacred and secular, upon some other basis than certainty.

We may be said to believe a proposition, implicitly or explicitly, when we are observed to act on the assumption that it is true. If we are absolutely sure of it, we may prefer to say that we *know*. We will be said *to believe* a proposition when, though less than certain of its truth, we are willing, for reasons which seem good to us, to take a chance with it. In this sense, St. Augustine believes much of what parents and teachers have told him, and much of what he sees and hears. He believes in the generalizations which he makes upon his observations. He believes in most of the pronouncements of geographers, physicists, antiquaries, and biologists. He believes in the Platonic theory of Forms. He believes in what the Christian Church alleges to be revealed truth. It would be safe to say that ninety-five per cent of his thoughts are concerned with belief rather than with knowledge.

Beliefs are founded upon sensation and reason. Sensation gives us sights, sounds, tastes, smells, and touch. Through sensation we hear parents, teachers, and other conveyors of information. Reading is a sort of visual sensation. In one way or another, sensation brings us personal impressions, other men's impressions, other men's ideas on all sorts of subjects, whether derived from reason or—as they may claim—from divine revelation. St. Augustine distrusts sensation. The information which it conveys *may* be distorted, and there is no criterion within sensation itself for distinguishing the true from the false. Reason is obliged to do its work with this uncertain material. It can distinguish inconsistencies in the sensory evidence, but could not discover truth in a situation where the sensory evidence, though false, was self-consistent and in agreement with other propositions which one was disposed to accept. Furthermore its generalizations can be shown to apply only in specific instances; there is no assurance that they have eternal and universal validity. There is no certainty in sensation, or in the ideas based upon it, or conveyed through it.

Where we lack knowledge, we must believe on *faith*. Our belief, whether in our fathers' identity, Boyle's Law, or the resurrection of the dead, will be strong or weak in proportion to the strength of our faith, or confidence, in it. Our faith in a proposition is strong to the extent that it agrees with our observation (John is loved by his mother), is consistent with other inferences accepted by us (Titus captured Jerusalem in A.D. 70), or is suggested "on good authority" (a physician tells us that we have diphtheria). Our faith in authority is not really different in kind; our observation of the physician suggests that he is usually right. Faith may be said to depend upon *coherence* in the body of our beliefs: the agreement of all is taken to be the guarantee of each.

Religious beliefs seem to come chiefly from sensation; we hear, or read, rather than infer. They may be supported by reason, but for the most part they are accepted on the authority of the Church. The authority of the Church is great because so many people in every age seem to have accepted it, and because of the assurance with which some of its representatives have claimed to be the beneficiaries of divine revelation. But propositions accepted on any authority, however high, are not *known*; they can only be believed in faith. St. Augustine believes that there is a God who made all things visible and invisible; whose wise and loving providence foresees and guides the universal process to a predestined end; who brings good out of all apparent evil; who sent his only begotten Son into the world to save his elect from the consequences of their sin and folly; "Who spake by the Prophets"; whose Word is revealed in the Canonical Scriptures. All beliefs are more or less uncertain, and such beliefs as these are especially so, because they depend so much upon the authority of those who preach them, and can be defended directly only by a partisan interpretation of ambiguous evidence.

St. Augustine maintains a skeptical approach to most beliefs. He is ready to modify or reject them if experience runs counter to them. His attitude is soundly scientific in the modern sense. A person of skeptical temperament prepared to take a chance with Boyle's Law, democracy, and vitamin pills may accept religious propositions in the same spirit. If their basis seems somewhat uncertain, his faith in them will be somewhat weak. If they give subjective satisfaction, and can be reconciled without too much difficulty to the world of his experience, he continues to hold them. If it becomes impossible for him to believe that the world around him is the work of a wise and loving God, he gives up that belief, with no profound surprise at his discovery that like many other notions which he has entertained it does not stand up to experience.

This approach to religion may not commend itself to religious enthusiasts. It has the effect of reducing theology to an uncommonly tentative branch of science. But if religious propositions do seem to stand up to experience, the resulting belief can lead to a steady increase in faith, and to a piety none the worse for being rational.

But St. Augustine deliberately lays aside his normal skepticism when it comes to his religious beliefs. Although he admits that these must be held for the most part on nothing stronger than faith, *he chooses to intrench them.* He agrees to treat them not as opinions but as knowledge. He refuses to submit them to the testing of experience, with the modification and possible rejection which such a testing might bring. The first defense which can be offered for this intellectual aberration is that those few who *know* the truths of religion, or who can act as if they did, seem to be the happier for it. The second defense is that if these propositions cannot be proven true, it is equally impossible to prove them false. Hearty acceptance, where this is possible, brings even greater satisfaction than hearty acceptance of Boyle's Law or the Quantum Theory, and belief is likely to grow stronger if one *can* refuse to admit any evidence that could prevail against it. Intrenched beliefs are on more or less safe ground when they relate to matters beyond the range of human observation or inference. The reality of a Divine Creator, of a pre-destined End, and of personal survival after death are topics in point. They are almost equally safe when they admit the observed fact, but insist upon an interpretation based upon an idea beyond human power to disprove. The proposition that every circumstance in our experience has its place in a Divine Plan, and is an expression of Divine Love, is such a point of view. A determined searcher can usually find blessings, however recondite, in what "natural man" would take for catastrophes. But intrenched beliefs can come to grief when they attempt to lay down the law in the fields of observation or of inference upon observation. The beliefs that the Canonical Scriptures give an accurate account of human history, that the Old Testament everywhere foreshadows the New, that non-Christians are characteristically miserable, and that wealth, wisdom, and power make no significant contribution to real happiness are instances of propositions which can be, and are, challenged very readily indeed in the light of experience. But St. Augustine intrenches all his *Christian* beliefs, in whichever category they fall.

If anyone *knows* that all so-called Christian truths are indeed true, we have no quarrel with him. If anyone is ready to try to accept them on faith, he can be given credit for intellectual honesty. But to intrench beliefs which one admits have no stronger basis than faith is to execute an intellectual abdication. One abandons the criteria of credibility applied in the case of other beliefs, that they should agree with appearances and be consistent with one's other beliefs. One deliberately, if frankly, gives up, as far as these beliefs are concerned, the skepticism appropriate to persons who know that they must live by faith and not by knowledge. This abdication puts the science concerned, whether theology, agriculture, geology, or historical studies—and it can happen to any—in a false and risky position in a world where other beliefs are held subject to modification in the light of experience and reason: false, because those who profess them are likely to seem hypocrites, pretending to a knowledge which they do not possess, although this does them less than justice; risky, because beliefs which seem to be defended disingenuously may be dismissed out of hand, and not given the consideration which they perhaps deserve.

St. Augustine draws the whole world of experience into the field of historical studies: the parochial and the national, the public and the private, the political, the scientific, the philosophical, and the literary, past and future, time and eternity. Every item in the world of our experience is foreseen by God, but St. Augustine does draw a wavering distinction between a world of external events, which follows the Divine Plan in exact detail, and an inner world of thought, where God *may* intervene, but where there is at least some measure of human freedom. *Christian beliefs, held on faith, are intrenched guides to the significance of the historical process, thus broadly conceived.* They are intrenched in the sense of being treated *as if* they were above question. Most persons, he admits, think them utterly implausible. But for those who are able to accept them wholeheartedly, they bring a sense of order behind apparent chaos, love behind apparent indifference, purpose behind apparent aimlessness.

Some of St. Augustine's Christian beliefs involve him in difficulties. He believes that the Canonical Scriptures never err, but cannot explain Jesus' attribution of a verse of Zechariah to Jeremiah, in St. Matthew's Gospel. He believes that the Old Testament, including the Pentateuch, everywhere foreshadows the Christian message, but can show this only by a display of allegorizing likely to alienate anyone not already strongly committed to his point of view. He believes that where secular thought differs from Scripture, Scripture is always right; and this ties him to the proposition that the earth came into existence no more than a few thousand years ago. He believes that all truth is Christian. When pagan philosophers disagree, they are necessarily wrong; when they agree, he suspects that the ultimate source of their wisdom is the Judaeo-Christian tradition. The neutral reader may find his arguments disingenuous, and infer that all his beliefs are as wrong-headed as these seem to be.

But St. Augustine's most important historical belief is that the historical process is teleological. This is not too dangerous a theme for intrenched belief, because it transcends the range of observation and inference. We were not present at the beginning of things, and have not yet seen their culmination. We cannot apply prophetic generalizations to a process by definition unique: who could predict the oak from his observation of a single acorn? Our attempts to explain the causation of particular instances is unsatisfactory, partly because we oversimplify the context, and partly because the "laws" which we apply in our exposition can never be shown to be universal or eternal. If we cannot explain the causes of a particular circumstance, we can hardly prove—or disprove—a general theory of causation.

There is no incentive, in St. Augustine's thought, to free inquiry. Historical studies can only be apologetical, giving more or less superfluous support to an intrenched theory formulated and accepted before they are begun. The historical fact is less important than the lesson, and the lesson which the fact must teach is known before the fact itself has been discovered. St. Augustine holds no brief for factual inaccuracy. He assumes that the facts will support his view. He is especially anxious to discover the exact and literal meaning of scriptural evidence, which he holds to be infallibly true. But it follows from this last that if secular evidence is to be taken as accurate, it must agree exactly with Scripture. Where it does not, it must be either denied or "interpreted." Furthermore, it is unfortunately true that mistaken facts can be forced into line about as easily as true ones, given an ingenious and determined apologist. St. Augustine admits that, if one is in difficulty, the great end can perhaps be served almost as well if one draws the right moral from the wrong facts.

St. Augustine sees God's wise and loving Providence revealed in every circumstance in the historical process. Those who lack an undeviating trust in God, and put their trust in humanity, are doomed to find that an open-minded and "natural" response to experience will land them in misery, both in this life and the next. Only an intrenched Christian optimism can ensure serenity. St. Augustine freely concedes that for the vast majority of men his point of view seems, and indeed is, unnatural and perverse.

The term "Divine Comedy" has been used to describe his picture of the universal process. This should not be taken to imply a belief that he deliberately sets himself to devise a pretty fable to illustrate his opinions *de rerum natura*. Every element in his account is drawn from Christianity *as he sees it*. Not every Christian, or group of Christians, has seen Christianity in quite St. Augustine's terms. Most Christians think that he went too far in the direction of predestination. Many think that in condemning all pagans and heretics to eternal damnation he did less than justice to the divine love. Few would think that he has given an adequate explanation of the nature and transmission of original sin. But from his own point of view, he is never inventing, but at most interpreting, Christian data. He is not imagining, but disclosing, the grand outline of God's eternal plan.

St. Augustine's "Divine Comedy" provides a framework for the entire historical record interpreted in the light of his Christian beliefs. There are no obviously loose ends. Creation, mankind's past and future history on earth, the Last Judgment, Heaven and Hell, are all accounted for. The text is written before the play is played. The production holds no surprises for the Divine Play-wright. St. Augustine does not discover the plot in the course of a "free inquiry." He has its outline in mind before he comes to the details in which it is embodied. His aim in historical studies is not *to discover* the pattern of events, but to show how history must conform to the pattern which he is already prepared to accept *as if* true. He is operating on a radically different principle from that which motivates the open-minded historian. To share in his "truth," the secular historian must not just accept his premises as if true—as working hypotheses to be tested; he must treat them as beyond question, as beyond the power of experience to overthrow. But no historian with any scientific pretensions will agree to intrench beliefs which he admits that he can hold only on faith, but which control his interpretation of history. In the end, the most that the skeptic can say for the "Divine Comedy" is that if many of the beliefs which it embodies are not very plausible, they at least cannot be proven false.

St. Augustine's account will seem "true" to those who *know* that his Christian propositions are true, or who are prepared to accept them *as if* true. Others, including Christians of more skeptical temperament, may prefer to subject it to a literary criticism, and ask whether or not it gives effective expression to *his* beliefs. Is it a good play? Is it convincing? The general effect is good. There is moral exhilaration in his idea of the world as a battleground where two points of view struggle for men's souls. There is something exciting in his vision of the universal process, in his belief that *every* circumstance has its place in one grand scheme, the outline of which he is prepared to reveal. But here, as with other universal histories, the picture seems less satisfactory when one gets down to details. Leaving aside the question of factual accuracy, there are at least five unresolved paradoxes which spoil the effectiveness of the drama. In the first place, if God is omnipotent, how can man have free will? He offers the ancient solution that while external events may be fixed, man can choose his inner reaction to those events. Few are likely to find this distinction convincing, in an age when the relationship between behavior and thought, and the possibilities of thought control, have been so widely explored both in theory and practice. Most persons would probably agree that if any circumstances are determined, either by God or by the operation of mechanical cause and effect, it will be hard to show what circumstances are not. Second, if God is all-wise, why did He create us able to flout His will and alienate ourselves from Him to His apparent displeasure? Third, if natural man sins because of an irresistible propensity to sin, it is hard to believe, as St. Augustine professes to believe, in human responsibility. Fourth, he overstates the horrors of the non-Christian life, and does less than justice to the pleasures and serenity obtainable by virtuous, and efficient, non-Christians. Actual observations of Christians and non-Christians may suggest that Christianity does indeed offer an unnatural and perverse interpretation of life.

A fifth paradox shows a wise and all-loving God consigning the greater part of the human race not merely to absence from Himself but to an eternity of hell-fire. Some few persons can rise to the intellectual challenge of these and other paradoxes. But St. Augustine admits that they are exceptions to the rule. For others, the "Divine Comedy," in St. Augustine's edition, will seem to end on a sour note, for all the bliss of the saints in Heaven. Many Christians may think St. Augustine's text corrupt, and some have attempted new editions supposedly more faithful to the divine original. Perhaps this is what anyone does who tries to think for himself.

But can St. Augustine be said to have a *philosophy of history*? If so, he must have a theory of truth and of reality, and this must find application in his approach to historical studies. It has already been suggested that every historian has a philosophy of history, willy nilly, explicit or implicit. St. Augustine's is explicit. He believes in an external objective reality. He believes that we can learn something about this through direct awareness, divine revelation, sensation, and reason. He thinks that nearly all our beliefs rest upon faith, which is something less than knowledge. Most such beliefs should be held in a tentative, skeptical way, and should be strengthened, modified, or abandoned in the light of our experience. But he is ready to intrench beliefs which can be certified as Christian. He may accept them only on faith, but he is ready to treat them as if they were sacrosanct. These general beliefs determine what he will accept in historical evidence. His intrenched Christian beliefs give him what he regards as the pattern and framework of the universal process. What he can gather from other sources is held to be thoroughly uncertain, and is used, or distorted, or interpreted in such a way as to flesh out and conform to his *a priori* universal scheme.

St. Augustine has a philosophy of history. But it is not one which appeals to us. When he intrenches his Christian beliefs, he is deliberately closing his mind on issues of basic importance. He abandons, as far as these beliefs are concerned, the ordinary criteria of credibility. It is not as if he thinks that he *knows* that his Christian propositions are true. That would be an involuntary closing of the mind. But in his case there is a deliberate abandonment of the search for truth, a willingness to settle for mere opinion, and not merely that but a frank willingness to treat opinion as if it were incontrovertible truth, if there is such a thing. He refuses to lay himself open to possible new enlightenment on these issues. He may be considered prudent by some, pious by others; his faith may even be justified by experience; but it goes against the grain to call his attitude "philosophical." Nor is it in the best interests of religion.

His philosophy of history is fatal to historical studies as pursued by men of open mind. It leads to a flouting of the ordinary canons of probability. It leads, *de facto* though not *de jure*, to carelessness with detail. It leads to what must seem to persons not committed to his intrenched views a disingenuous treatment of evidence. It cuts off the propositions and reconstructions which it canonizes from normal modification in the light of new evidence and insights. It prevents consideration of other and contradictory hypotheses which might not only fit the appearances better but give greater subjective satisfactions to those who accepted them. It petrifies a particular stage of historical thought, and keeps historical studies from performing the proper function of every human science. This function is not to lay down eternal and universal truth, but to offer mankind a variety of fallible propositions, tentatively held, and subject to change, which draw upon *past* experience to enlarge our sense of *possibilities* in present and future.

Select Bibliography

I. Works of St. Augustine

References in the notes are to the *Patrologia Latina* of the Abbé J. P. Migne, not the best edition, but the one most generally available.

Ad Catholicos Epistola Contra Donatistas
Confessiones
Contra Academicos
Contra Adeimantium
Contra Cresconium Grammaticum Donatistam
Contra Duas Epistolas Pelagianorum
Contra Epistolam Manichaei quam vocant Fundamentum
Contra Epistolam Parmeniani
Contra Faustum Manichaeum
Contra Fortunatum Manichaeum
Contra Gaudentium
Contra Julianum Pelagianum
Contra Litteras Petiliani Donatistae
Contra Mendacium
De Actis cum Felice Manichaeo
De Agone Christi
De Anima et Eius Origine
De Baptismo contra Donatistas
De Beata Vita
De Bono Coniugali
De Bono Viduitatis
De Catechizandis Rudibus
De Civitate Dei contra Paganos
De Consensu Evangelistarum
De Continentia

De Correctione Donatistarum, *see* Epistola 185
De Correptione et Gratia
De Cura pro Mortuis
De Diversis Quaestionibus
De Diversis Quaestionibus ad Simplicianum
De Doctrina Christiana
De Dono Perseverantiae
De Duabus Animabus contra Manichaeos
De Fide et Symbolo
De Fide Rerum quae non Videntur
De Fide Spe Caritate
De Genesi ad Litteram
De Genesi contra Manichaeos
De Gestis Pelagi
De Gratia et Libero Arbitrio
De Gratia et de Peccato Originali
De Mendacio
De Moribus Ecclesiae Catholicae
De Moribus Manichaeorum
De Musica
De Natura Boni contra Manichaeos
De Natura et Gratia
De Nuptiis et Concupiscentia
De Opere Monachorum
De Ordine
De Patientia
De Peccatorum Meritis et Remissione
De Perfectione Justitiae Hominis
De Praedestinatione Sanctorum
De Sermone Domini in Monte
De Spiritu et Littera
De Symbolo ad Catechumenos
De Trinitate
De Utilitate Credendi
De Virginitate
Enchiridion, *see* De Fide Spe Caritate
Ennarationes in Psalmos
Epistolae
Expositio in Galatios

In Epistolam Johannis ad Parthos
In Johannis Evangelium
Opus Imperfectum contra Julianum
Psalmus contra Partem Donati
Quaestiones Evangeliorum
Quaestiones in Exodum
Quaestiones in Heptateuchum
Sermones
Soliloquia

II. Modern Works

ALEXANDER, SAMUEL. "The Historicity of Things." In Raymond Klibansky and Herbert James Paton (eds.), *Philosophy and History. Essays presented to E. Cassirer* (Oxford: Clarendon Press, 1936), pp. 11–25.

ALFARIC, PROSPER. *L'Évolution Intellectuelle de Saint Augustin.* Paris: Nourry, 1918.

ANGUS, SAMUEL. *The Sources of the First Ten Books of Augustine's "De Civitate Dei."* Princeton: Princeton University Press, 1906.

ARQUILLIÈRE, HENRI XAVIER. *L'Augustinisme Politique.* Paris: Vrin, 1934.

AYER, ALFRED JULES. *The Foundations of Empirical Knowledge.* London: Macmillan, 1955.

BARROW, REGINALD HAYNES. *Introduction to St. Augustine, The City of God.* London: Faber, 1950.

BATTENHOUSE, ROY WESLEY. *A Companion to the Study of St. Augustine.* Oxford: Oxford University Press, 1955.

BAYNES, NORMAN HEPBURN. *The Political Ideas of St. Augustine's "De Civitate Dei."* Historical Association Pamphlet No. 104. London: Bell, 1936.

BERDYAEV, NICOLAI ALEKSANDROVITCH. *The Meaning of History.* Trans. by George Reavey. London: Bles, 1936.

BERLIN, SIR ISAIAH. *Historical Inevitability.* London: Oxford University Press, 1954.

BONAFEDE, G. *Scepsis Agostiniana.* Palermo, 1950.

BLONDEL, MAURICE. "The Latent Resources in St. Augustine's Thought." In Martin Cyril D'Arcy and others, *A Monument to Saint Augustine* (London: Sheed and Ward, 1930), pp. 317–353.

BOURKE, VERNON JOSEPH. *Augustine's Quest of Wisdom*. Milwaukee: Bruce, 1945.

BOYER, CHARLES. *Christianisme et Néoplatonisme dans la Formation de S. Augustin*. New ed. Rome: Libri Catholici, 1953.

———. *Essais sur la Doctrine de Saint Augustin*. Paris: Beauchesne, 1932.

———. *L'Idée de Vérité dans la Philosophie de Saint Augustin*. Paris: Beauchesne, 1921.

BURLEIGH, JOHN H. S. *The City of God*. London: Nisbet, 1949.

BURNABY, JOHN. *Amor Dei*. London: Hodder and Stoughton, 1938.

BUTLER, DOM EDWARD CUTHBERT. *Western Mysticism*. 2nd ed. London: Constable, 1951.

CALOGERO, GUISEPPE. "On the So-Called Identity of History and Philosophy." In Raymond Klibansky and Herbert James Paton (eds.), *Philosophy and History. Essays presented to E. Cassirer* (Oxford: Clarendon Press, 1936), pp. 35–52.

CARRÉ, MEYRICK HEATH. *Nominalists and Realists*. London and New York: Oxford University Press, 1946.

CASE, SHIRLEY JACKSON. *The Christian Philosophy of History*. Chicago: Chicago University Press, 1943.

CAYRÉ, FULBERT. *Initiation à la Philosophie de Saint Augustin*. Paris: Desclée de Brouwer, 1956.

CHAIX-RUY, JULES. *Saint Augustin. Temps de Histoire*. Paris: Desclée de Brouwer, 1956.

CLARK, SIR GEORGE NORMAN. *Historical Scholarship and Historical Thought*. London: Cambridge University Press, 1944.

COCHRANE, CHARLES NORRIS. *Christianity and Classical Culture*. Oxford, New York, and Toronto: Oxford University Press, 1939.

COHEN, MORRIS RAPHAEL, AND ERNEST NAGEL. *Introduction to Logic and Scientific Method*. 2nd ed. Madison: Harcourt Brace, 1949.

COLLINGWOOD, ROBIN GEORGE. *An Autobiography*. London and New York: Oxford University Press, 1939.

———. *The Idea of History*. Oxford: Clarendon Press, 1946.

————. *The Philosophy of History.* Historical Association Leaflet No. 79. London: Bell, 1930.

COMBÈS, GUSTAVE. *La Doctrine Politique de Saint Augustin.* Paris: Plon, 1927.

————. *S. Augustin et la Culture Classique.* Paris: Plon, 1927.

CONZE, EDWARD. *The Scientific Method of Thinking. An Introduction to Dialectical Materialism.* London: Chapman and Hall, 1936.

CROCE, BENEDETTO. *History as the Story of Liberty.* Trans. by Sylvia Sprigge. London: Allen and Unwin, 1941.

————. *Logic as the Science of the Pure Concept.* Trans. by Douglas Ainslie. London: Macmillan, 1917.

————. *My Philosophy.* Trans. by E. F. Carritt. London: Allen and Unwin, 1949.

————. *Theory and History of Historiography.* Trans. by Douglas Ainslie. London and Sydney: Harrap, 1921.

D'ARCY, MARTIN CYRIL. "The Philosophy of Saint Augustine." In Martin Cyril D'Arcy and others, *A Monument to Saint Augustine* (London: Sheed and Ward, 1930), pp. 153–196.

D'ARCY, MARTIN CYRIL AND OTHERS. *A Monument to Saint Augustine.* London: Sheed and Ward, 1930.

DAWSON, CHRISTOPHER. "St. Augustine and His Age." In Martin Cyril D'Arcy and others, *A Monument to Saint Augustine* (London: Sheed and Ward, 1930), pp. 11–77.

DEANE, HERBERT ANDREW. *The Political and Social Ideas of St. Augustine.* New York and London: Columbia University Press, 1963.

DIESNER, HANS JOACHIM. *Studien zur Gesellschafts-lehre und Sozialen Haltung Augustins.* Halle: Niemeyer, 1954.

EIBL, HANS. *Augustinus. Vom Götterreich zum Gottesstaat.* Freiburg im Breslau: Walter, 1931.

EINSTEIN, LEWIS DAVID. *Historical Change.* Cambridge: Cambridge University Press, 1946.

FABRE, LUCIEN. *Saint Augustin.* Paris: Hatchette, 1951.

FIELD, GUY CROMWELL. *Some Problems of the Philosophy of History.* London: Humphrey Milford, 1938.

FIGGIS, JOHN NEVILLE. *The Political Aspects of S. Augustine's "City of God."* London: Longmans Green, 1921.

FRIBERG, HANS DANIEL. *Love and Justice in Political Theory. A Study of Augustine's Definition of the Commonwealth.* Chicago: University of Chicago Press, 1944.

GARDINER, PATRICK L. *The Nature of Historical Explanation.* London: Oxford University Press, 1952.

GARVEY, (SISTER) MARY PATRICIA. *Saint Augustine, Christian or Neo-Platonist?* Milwaukee: Marquette University Press, 1939.

GEHL, PIETER. *Debates with Historians.* London: Batsford, 1955.

GENTILE, GIOVANNI. "The Transcending of Time in History." In Raymond Klibansky and Herbert James Paton (eds.), *Philosophy and History. Essays presented to E. Cassirer* (Oxford: Clarendon Press, 1936), pp. 91–105.

GILSON, ÉTIENNE HENRI. *The Christian Philosophy of Saint Augustine.* New York: Random House, 1960.

———. "The Future of Augustinian Metaphysics." In Martin Cyril D'Arcy and others, *A Monument to Saint Augustine* (London: Sheed and Ward, 1930), pp. 287–315.

———. *L'Introduction à l'Étude de Saint Augustin.* Paris: Vrin, 1929.

GREEN, WILLIAM MACALLEN. "Augustine on the Teaching of History." In *University of California Publications in Classical Philology*, XII, 18 (1944), 315–332. Berkeley and Los Angeles: University of California Press, 1944.

GUITTON, JEAN. *Le Temps et l'Eternité chez Plotin et Saint Augustin.* Paris: Boivin, 1933.

GUNDOLF, F. "Historiography." In Raymond Klibansky and Herbert James Paton (eds.), *Philosophy and History. Essays presented to E. Cassirer* (Oxford: Clarendon Press, 1936), pp. 277–282.

HEINSIUS, DANIEL. *The Value of History.* Trans. by G. W. Robinson from the edition of 1613. Cambridge, Mass.: privately printed, 1943.

HEISENBERG, WERNER. *Physics and Philosophy. The Revolution in Modern Science.* New York: Harper, 1959.

HICK, JOHN. *Faith and Knowledge. A Modern Introduction to the Problem of Religious Knowledge.* Ithaca, N.Y.: Cornell University Press, 1957.

HODGES, HERBERT ARTHUR. *Wilhelm Dilthey. An Introduction.* London: K. Paul, Trench, Trubner, 1944.

KLIBANSKY, RAYMOND, AND HERBERT JAMES PATON (eds.). *Philosophy and History. Essays presented to E. Cassirer.* Oxford: Clarendon Press, 1936.

KLUBACK, WILLIAM. *Wilhelm Dilthey's Philosophy of History.* New York: Columbia University Press, 1956.

McDOUGAL, ELEANOR. *St. Augustine.* London: Student Christian Movement, 1930.

MACINTOSH, DOUGLAS CLYDE. *The Problem of Religious Knowledge.* New York: Harper, 1940.

MAIER, F. G. *Augustin und das Antike Rom.* Stuttgart: Kohlhammer, 1955.

MANDELBAUM, MAURICE H. *The Problem of Historical Knowledge. An Answer to Relativism.* New York: Liveright, 1938.

———. "Can There Be a Philosophy of History?" *American Scholar*, Vol. IX, No. 1 (1940).

MARITAIN, JACQUES. *On the Philosophy of History.* London: Bles, 1959.

———. "St. Augustine and St. Thomas Aquinas." In Martin Cyril D'Arcy and others, *A Monument to Saint Augustine* (London: Sheed and Ward, 1930), pp. 197–223.

MARROU, HENRI IRÉNÉE. *L'Ambivalence du Temps de l'Histoire chez Saint Augustin.* Paris: Vrin, 1950.

———. *S. Augustin et la Fin de la Culture Antique.* Paris: Boccard, 1938.

MARTINDALE, CYRIL CHARLIE, S. J. "A Sketch of the Life and Character of St. Augustine." In Martin Cyril D'Arcy and others, *A Monument to Saint Augustine* (London: Sheed and Ward, 1930), pp. 79–101.

MASCALL, ERIC LIONEL. *Christian Theology and Natural Science. Some Questions in Their Relations.* London: Longmans, 1956.

MONTGOMERY, WILLIAM. *St. Augustine. Aspects of his Life and Thought.* London: Hodder and Stoughton, 1914.

MORGAN, JAMES. *The Psychological Teaching of St. Augustine.* London: Elliot Stock, 1932.

NIEBUHR, REINHOLD. *Faith and History. A Comparison of Christian and Modern Views of History.* London: Nisbet, 1949.

OAKESHOTT, MICHAEL JOSEPH. *Experience and Its Modes.* Cambridge: Cambridge University Press, 1933.

O'MEARA, JOHN JOSEPH. *The Young Augustine.* New York: Longmans, 1954.

ORTEGA Y GASSET, JOSÉ. "History as a System." In Raymond Klibansky and Herbert James Paton (eds.), *Philosophy and History. Essays presented to E. Cassirer* (Oxford: Clarendon Press, 1936), pp. 283–322.

PAPINI, GIOVANNI. *St. Augustine.* Paris: Plon, 1930.

PLEKHANOV, GEORGII VALENTINOVICH. *In Defence of Materialism. The Development of the Monist View of History.* Trans. by A. Rothstein. London: Lawrence and Wishart, 1947.

———. *The Materialist Conception of History.* London: Lawrence and Wishart, 1940.

———. *The Role of the Individual in Society.* A reissue. London: Lawrence and Wishart, 1950.

POPE, HUGH. *St. Augustine of Hippo.* London: Sands, 1937.

POPPER, KARL RAIMUND. *The Poverty of Historicism.* London: Routledge and Kegan Paul, 1957.

PRZYWARA, ERICH. "St. Augustine and the Modern World." In Martin Cyril D'Arcy and others, *A Monument to Saint Augustine* (London: Sheed and Ward, 1930), pp. 249–286.

REEVES, JOHN-BAPTIST, O. P. "St. Augustine and Humanism." In Martin Cyril D'Arcy and others, *A Monument to Saint Augustine* (London: Sheed and Ward, 1930), pp. 121–151.

RENIER, GUSTAAF JOHANNES. *History. Its Purpose and Method.* London: Allen and Unwin, 1950.

RICKABY, JOSEPH JOHN, S. J. *St. Augustine's City of God.* London: Burns, Oates, and Washbourne, 1925.

ROLAND-GOSSELIN, BERNARD. "St. Augustine's System of Morals." In Martin Cyril D'Arcy and others, *A Monument to Saint Augustine* (London: Sheed and Ward, 1930), pp. 225–248.

RONDET, HENRI, LAURAS, A., AND OTHERS. *Études Augustiniennes.* Paris: Aubier, 1953.

RUSSELL, BERTRAND RUSSELL, 3RD EARL. *The Analysis of Mind.* London: Allen and Unwin, 1921.

———. *Mysticism and Logic, and Other Essays.* New York: Longmans Green, 1918.

RUST, ERIC CHARLES. *The Christian Understanding of History.* London and Redhill: Lutterworth, 1947.

SALVEMINI, GAETANO. *Historian and Scientist. An Essay on the Nature of History and the Social Sciences.* Cambridge, Mass.: Harvard University Press, 1939.

SIMPSON, WILLIAM JOHN SPARROW. *St. Augustine's Conversion.* London: Society for Promoting Christian Knowledge, 1930.

———. *St. Augustine's Episcopate. A Brief Introduction to His Writings as a Christian.* London: Society for Promoting Christian Knowledge, 1944.

SPYKMAN, NICHOLAS JOHANNES. *The Social Theory of George Simmel.* Chicago: Chicago University Press, 1925.

STEBBING, LIZZIE SUSAN. *Logical Positivism and Analysis.* London: Humphrey Milford, 1933.

———. "Some Ambiguities in Discussions Concerning Time." In Raymond Klibansky and Herbert James Paton (eds.), *Philosophy and History. Essays presented to E. Cassirer* (Oxford: Clarendon Press, 1936), pp. 107–123.

STEGEMAN, V. *Augustins Gottestaat.* Tübingen: Mohr, 1928.

Theory and Practice in Historical Study: A Report of the Committee on Historiography. New York: Social Science Research Council, 1946.

TREVELYAN, GEORGE MACAULAY. *History and the Reader.* London: Cambridge University Press, 1945.

TRUDEL, J.-P. *Saint Augustin, Humaniste.* Trois-Rivières, Que.: Bien Public, 1954.

VAN DER MEER, F. *Augustine the Bishop. The Life and Work of a Father of the Church.* Trans. B. Battershaw and G. R. Lamb. London, New York: Sheed and Ward, 1961.

VICO, GIOVANNI BATTISTA. *The New Science.* Trans. by T. G. Bergin and M. H. Fisch from 3rd ed. 1744. Ithaca, N.Y.: Cornell University Press, 1948.

WALSH, WILLIAM HENRY. *An Introduction to the Philosophy of History.* London and New York: Hutchinson's University Library, 1951.

WATKIN, EDWARD INGRAM. "The Mysticism of St. Augustine." In Martin Cyril D'Arcy and others, *A Monument to Saint Augustine* (London: Sheed and Ward, 1930), pp. 103–119.

WEST, REBECCA. *St. Augustine.* New York: Appleton, 1933.

WILLIAMS, CHARLES HAROLD. *The Modern Historian*. London and
New York: Nelson, 1938

WILLIS, GEOFFREY GRIMSHAW. *St. Augustine and the Donatist
Controversy*. London: Society for Promoting Christian
Knowledge, 1950.

WIND, EDGAR. "Some Points of Contact Between History and
Natural Science." In Raymond Klibansky and Herbert James
Paton (eds.), *Philosophy and History. Essays presented to E.
Cassirer* (Oxford: Clarendon Press, 1936), pp. 255–264.

Index